COOK
HEALTHY
& QUICK

Contents

Introduction

Eating healthily is easiest when it's convenient. So in *Cook Healthy and Quick* we have collected together recipes that are speedy to prepare and that will help you make good choices. We have grouped them around mealtimes—a protein-filled breakfast, say, or a plant-based main meal. Then we have done a detailed nutritional analysis for you: not just the calories per serving, but also the amount of carbohydrates, fats, salt, and fiber that you will be consuming.

We hope that this will help you to make healthy choices throughout your day, and keep within recommended daily intakes. For an adult consuming 2,000 calories, these are as follows: no more than 90g sugars; 70g fats, with only 20g saturated fats; and about 1 teaspoon (6g) salt. You should also try to eat 18g fiber per day. Alongside this analysis we have added color bands so that you can identify the key benefits of a recipe at a glance.

Remember, none of this is complicated—or restrictive. Eating well does not have to mean dialing down on your enjoyment. Some days, what you want is a brownie. So go ahead, have one. Just make it yourself, with our recipe that uses fruit to reduce the sugar content.

True, reducing the sugar does not mean that a brownie can be for every day. Nor can cheesecake or ice cream. But whether you want a snack or you're planning dinner for friends, here are recipes that are full of flavor and mindful of healthy principles. Take a look at the nutritional analysis, and make your choice.

If you have specific dietary needs, there are also recipes here that do not use dairy products or that avoid gluten. And many more can easily be adapted to be dairy-free and gluten-free. The color bands will help you to identify these quickly.

Additionally, we offer easy Variations—simple ideas for you to create new dishes by substituting just one or two ingredients. We also highlight on each recipe the time it will take, first to prepare and then to cook. Many recipes need no cooking and can be both prepared and cooked within 30 minutes. Only the time required for marinating, say, or freezing is excluded from our calculations.

So when your time is short, flip through these pages. With more than 300 recipes to choose from, you won't find it hard to *Cook Healthy and Quick*.

Cheap and healthy

It's easy to assume that eating healthily is a costly business.
These recipes prove that anyone with a well-stocked pantry
can eat well on a budget.

20 minutes

1 Pad Thai page 162
PREP 5 MINS   **COOK** 15 MINS

2 Mint frittata page 24
PREP 5 MINS   **COOK** 10–15 MINS

25 minutes

30 minutes

35 minutes

Low-fat but filling

Sometimes a low-fat meal can be unsatisfying. These recipes are all low in saturated fat, but they're full of flavor and they won't leave you hungry.

15-20 minutes

1 Avocado, cilantro, and lime tabbouleh page 86
PREP 15 MINS, PLUS SOAKING AND CHILLING

2 Swordfish in salmoriglio page 210
PREP 10 MINS, PLUS MARINATING
COOK 8 MINS

3 Spicy Asian chicken salad page 106
PREP 10 MINS   **COOK** 7–10 MINS

25 minutes

4 Chicken salad with radicchio and asparagus page 102
PREP 5–10 MINS   **COOK** 10–15 MINS

5 Roasted chickpeas with spinach page 178
PREP 5 MINS   **COOK** 15–20 MINS

6 Keralan fish curry page 230
PREP 10 MINS   **COOK** 15 MINS

7 Spicy turkey burgers page 124
PREP 15 MINS, PLUS CHILLING   **COOK** 10 MINS

30-35 minutes

8 Mixed root tempura page 196
PREP 10 MINS   **COOK** 20 MINS

9 Cured mackerel sashimi with salad page 254
PREP 30 MINS

10 Beef and edamame stir-fry page 268
PREP 10 MINS   **COOK** 25 MINS

Fish in a flash

Fish and seafood are low in fat and a good source of protein, so they are a healthy choice at any time of day. They can be quick to prepare, too: these dishes are ready within 20 minutes.

5-10 minutes

1 Nori maki page 257
PREP 5 MINS

2 Shrimp, sweet chili, and
Greek yogurt wraps page 120
PREP 10 MINS

3 Pilpil shrimp page 244
PREP 5 MINS **COOK** 1–2 MINS

15-20 minutes

4 Crayfish panini with herbed
mayonnaise page 123
PREP 15 MINS

5 Crispy cornmeal fish sticks
with easy tartar sauce page 317
PREP 10 MINS, PLUS CHILLING **COOK** 5 MINS

6 Baked fish with an herby crust
page 221
PREP 5 MINS **COOK** 10 MINS

7 Blackened salmon page 236
PREP 5 MINS, PLUS RESTING **COOK** 10 MINS

8 Shrimp kebabs page 318
PREP 10 MINS, PLUS MARINATING
COOK 6 MINS

9 Cajun-spiced salmon page 238
PREP 10 MINS **COOK** 10 MINS

10 Red snapper in rakı sauce
page 218
PREP 5 MINS **COOK** 12 MINS

11 Pan-fried shrimp in garlic
butter page 247
PREP 5 MINS **COOK** 10 MINS

Spice up the salad

A salad can be so much more than lettuce. Make it from whatever you like—seeds, nuts, grains, or fruits. Take inspiration from these recipes, which are all ready in 35 minutes or less.

10-15 minutes

1 Jeweled couscous in a jiffy
page 88
PREP 12 MINS, PLUS COOLING

2 Fattoush   page 100
PREP 15 MINS

3 Mixed bean and goat cheese
salad   page 98
PREP 10 MINS

20–30 minutes

35 minutes

Easy vegetarian

A vegetarian meal is often naturally high in fiber, which is good for digestion, keeps your heart healthy, and keeps you feeling full for longer.

15-20 minutes

1 Gazpacho page 80
PREP 15 MINS, PLUS CHILLING

2 Black-eyed pea, spinach,
and tomato curry page 183
PREP 5 MINS   **COOK** 15 MINS

3 Spaghetti with garlic, oil,
and red chile page 198
PREP 10 MINS   **COOK** 10 MINS

4 Fava bean tortilla page 30
PREP 5 MINS   **COOK** 10–15 MINS

25-30 minutes

5 Veggie burgers page 310
PREP 15 MINS, PLUS CHILLING
COOK 12–15 MINS

6 Roasted asparagus with aïoli
sauce page 288
PREP 10 MINS   **COOK** 20 MINS

7 Mexican quinoa salad page 90
PREP 10–15 MINS, PLUS COOLING
COOK 20 MINS

35+ minutes

8 Millet cashew stir-fry with chile
and lime sauce page 272
PREP 20 MINS   **COOK** 20 MINS

9 Buckwheat pancakes with cherry
almond sauce page 52
PREP 10 MINS, PLUS SOAKING   **COOK** 30 MINS

10 Avocado and lime cheesecake
page 384
PREP 30 MINS, PLUS CHILLING   **COOK** 20 MINS

Fabulous with five

Eating well can often mean eating simply. There are ideas here for breakfasts, main meals, snacks, and desserts and none contain more than five ingredients.

10 minutes

15-20 minutes

25-35 minutes

Quick and easy desserts

You might have to factor in time for chilling or freezing,
but none of these recipes will take more than 30 minutes
to prepare.

5-10 minutes

1 Quick banana ice cream page 376
PREP 5 MINS, PLUS FREEZING

2 Summer fruit fool page 366
PREP 10 MINS, PLUS CHILLING

3 Espresso granita page 380
PREP 5 MINS, PLUS COOLING AND FREEZING
COOK 5 MINS

4 Mango, orange, and passion
fruit fool page 373
PREP 10 MINS, PLUS CHILLING

15 minutes

5 Strawberry mousse
page 371
PREP 20 MINS, PLUS CHILLING

6 Moroccan orange salad
page 356
PREP 15 MINS

20-30 minutes

7 Vanilla pudding with raspberries
page 368
PREP 10 MINS   COOK 10 MINS, PLUS CHILLING

8 Warm fruit compote page 362
PREP 10 MINS   COOK 10 MINS

9 Banana and cranberry ice cream
page 378
PREP 10 MINS, PLUS FREEZING   COOK 10 MINS

10 Sweet spiced freekeh with fresh
figs page 358
PREP 5 MINS   COOK 25 MINS

BREAKFASTS

Protein-packed

Feelgood fillers

Mint frittata

Mint is a popular herb in southern Italy where the Middle Eastern influence is strong. It flavors this Italian version of the Spanish tortilla beautifully.

Low carb

Gluten free

Low salt

SERVES 8
PREP 5 MINS
COOK 10–15 MINS

8 large eggs

3 tbsp grated pecorino or Parmesan cheese

salt and freshly ground black pepper

3–4 tbsp olive oil

1 small onion, finely chopped

generous handful of mint leaves, roughly torn

1 Beat the eggs with the cheese and season. Set aside.

2 Heat 2 tablespoons of the oil in a frying pan. Add the onion, salt lightly to get the juices running, and cook gently until just soft—do not let it brown. Stir in the mint and cook for another minute.

3 Remove the pan from the heat and allow the mixture to cool. In a bowl, mix the onion and mint with the eggs.

4 Reheat the pan with the remaining oil. As soon as the oil is lightly smoking, pour in the egg mixture.

5 As soon as the first layer sets, pull the edges to the middle, then let cook gently, running a palette knife or offset spatula around the rim to loosen the edge. Shake the pan to keep the bottom from burning.

6 As soon as the top begins to look set, remove the pan from the heat. Slide the tortilla onto a plate, place a second plate on top, and invert so that the cooked side is on top. Slide the tortilla back into the pan and cook for another 1–2 minutes.

try this....
Pea, salmon, and mint frittata

Add 5½oz (150g) cooked **peas** and 5½oz (150g) flaked, poached **salmon** at the end of step 3.

NUTRITION PER SERVING	
Energy	156kcals/653kJ
Carbohydrate	0.75g
of which sugar	0.5g
Fat	12g
of which saturates	3.5g
Salt	0.35g
Fiber	0.2g

Turkish eggs

There are many interpretations of *shakshouka*, but it is primarily a bell pepper and tomato dish to which eggs are added. Known as *menemen* in Turkey, this particular dish is popular in Syria, Lebanon, and Jordan.

| Low carb |
| Low saturated fat |
| Dairy free |
| Gluten free |
| Low salt |

SERVES 4
PREP 10 MINS
COOK 15 MINS

2 tbsp olive oil

1 onion, halved and
    finely sliced

2 red or green bell peppers,
    finely sliced

2 garlic cloves, finely chopped

1 red chile, seeded and
    finely chopped

1 tsp sugar

1 x 14oz (400g) can
    chopped tomatoes

salt and freshly ground black
    pepper

4 large eggs

small bunch of flat-leaf
    parsley, finely chopped

1 Heat the oil in a heavy-bottomed frying pan and cook the onion and peppers for 2–3 minutes, until soft. Toss in the garlic and chile and cook until the vegetables begin to color.

2 Add the sugar and tomatoes, and cook over medium heat for 3–4 minutes, until the mixture is slightly pulpy. Season well.

3 Using a wooden spoon, make 4 indentations in the tomato mixture and crack an egg into each one. Reduce the heat, cover the pan, and cook until the whites are set. Scatter with the parsley and serve.

NUTRITION PER SERVING	
Energy	203kcals/848kJ
Carbohydrate	11g
of which sugar	10g
Fat	14g
of which saturates	3g
Salt	0.4g
Fiber	3g

Poached eggs in garlic yogurt

This Turkish classic is accompanied by garlic-flavored yogurt. It can be enjoyed as a snack, as a hot mezze dish, or as a supper dish with a salad.

Low carb

Gluten free

Low salt

SERVES 4
PREP 5 MINS
COOK 10 MINS

2¼ cups thick, creamy yogurt

2 garlic cloves, finely chopped

salt and freshly ground black pepper

2–3 tbsp white wine vinegar

4 large eggs

1–2 tbsp butter

1 tsp pimentón (Spanish paprika) or dried red chiles, finely chopped

a few dried sage leaves, crumbled

1 In a bowl, beat the yogurt with the garlic. Season to taste. Spoon the yogurt into a serving dish or individual plates, spreading it flat to create a thick base for the eggs.

2 Fill a pan with 3½ cups water, add the vinegar, and bring to a rolling boil. Stir the water with a spoon to create a mini whirlpool in the center. Crack one egg into a small bowl and gently slip it into the water. As the egg spins and the white sets around the yolk, stir the water again for the next one. Poach each egg for 2–3 minutes, so that the yolks are still soft. Drain the eggs using a slotted spoon and place on top of the yogurt base.

3 Quickly melt the butter in a small pan. Stir in the paprika and sage leaves, then spoon in the eggs and sprinkle a little salt over the top. Serve immediately.

NUTRITION PER SERVING

Energy	288kcals/1205kJ
Carbohydrate	6g
of which sugar	5g
Fat	22g
of which saturates	12g
Salt	0.5g
Fiber	0.1g

Fava bean tortilla

This tortilla is made with fava beans instead of potatoes and is flavored with marjoram, an herb that works well with all members of the bean family.

| Low carb |
| Low saturated fat |
| Dairy free |
| Gluten free |
| Low salt |

SERVES 6
PREP 5 MINS
COOK 10–15 MINS

1lb 2oz (500g) fava beans, shelled

4 tbsp olive oil

2 tbsp white wine or dry sherry

4 large eggs

salt and freshly ground black pepper

1 tsp fresh marjoram leaves

1 Slide the beans out of their skins, unless they are very tiny and the skins are unwrinkled and tender. Heat 1 tablespoon of the oil in a small frying pan, add in the beans, and turn them. Add the wine, allow the alcohol to evaporate, then cover the pan and let simmer gently for 5–6 minutes, until the beans are just soft and the liquid has almost evaporated. Let cool.

2 In a bowl, season the eggs and beat together with the marjoram leaves, then add the beans and stir.

3 Reheat the pan with the remaining oil. Pour in the egg-bean mixture and cook gently as a thick pancake, neatening the edges with a spatula and lifting up the edges to let the uncooked egg run underneath.

4 Cook until the top is beginning to set and the bottom is golden brown. Then slide the tortilla onto a plate, remove the pan from the heat, place a second plate on top, and invert so that the cooked side is on top. Slide back into the pan and cook for 2–3 minutes more on low heat, until the tortilla is firm but still juicy in the middle. Serve warm or cool.

NUTRITION PER SERVING	
Energy	194kcals/812kJ
Carbohydrate	6g
of which sugar	1g
Fat	12g
of which saturates	2g
Salt	0.2g
Fiber	6g

Classic omelet

The ultimate fast food, omelets are extremely quick to make and very tasty too—perfect for a nutritious and satisfying breakfast or brunch.

Low carb

Dairy free

Gluten free

Low salt

MAKES 1
PREP 2–3 MINS
COOK 5 MINS

2 large eggs

salt and freshly ground
  black pepper

pat of butter

1 Beat the eggs in a bowl and season to taste. Melt the butter in a frying pan over moderate heat and pour in the egg mixture.

2 Tilt the pan to spread the egg mixture evenly. Stir the eggs with a fork, stopping as soon as they are set. Fold the side of the omelet closest to the handle halfway over itself.

3 Sharply tap the handle so the bottom side of the omelet curls over. Slide the omelet to the edge of the pan. Transfer to a serving plate, and serve with a fresh green salad on the side.

NUTRITION PER SERVING

Energy	221kcals/925kJ
Carbohydrate	0g
of which sugar	0g
Fat	17g
of which saturates	6g
Salt	0.6g
Fiber	0g

Greek tomato omelet

This juicy egg cake, a breakfast and supper dish in the Peloponnese, is flavored with dill and melted cubes of salty *kefalotiri*, a cheese made with ewe's or goat's milk.

Low carb

Gluten free

Low salt

SERVES 4–5
PREP 15 MINS
COOK 15 MINS

4 tbsp olive oil

2 large ripe, firm tomatoes, thickly sliced

1 garlic clove, chopped

3½oz (100g) kefalotiri, mozzarella, or taleggio cheese, diced

6 large eggs

1 tbsp chopped dill

salt and freshly ground black pepper

1 Heat the oil in a small frying pan. Spread the tomato slices in an even layer over the surface, sprinkle with garlic, and cook gently until the tomato is soft and slightly dry. Top with the cheese but do not stir.

2 Meanwhile, beat the eggs with dill and a little seasoning. As soon as the cheese has melted a little, pour in the egg, turn up the heat, cover loosely, and cook until the top begins to look set. Flip the cake over and cook the other side. You can also slide the pan under the broiler.

NUTRITION PER SERVING	
Energy	312kcals/1305kJ
Carbohydrate	2g
of which sugar	1.8g
Fat	26g
of which saturates	8g
Salt	0.7g
Fiber	0.7g

Scrambled eggs with smoked salmon

This is the ultimate feel-good brunch recipe. Smoked salmon is rich in omega-3 fats and a source of iron—but do remember, it is high in salt.

SERVES 4
PREP 10 MINS
COOK 10 MINS

6 eggs

2 tbsp whole milk

salt and freshly ground black
    pepper

½oz (15g) unsalted butter

5¾oz (160g) smoked salmon,
    cut into thin strips, or hot
    smoked salmon, flaked

2 tbsp finely chopped chives

4 whole wheat muffins, split
    and toasted

1 Beat the eggs with the milk, and season with salt and pepper.

2 Heat the butter in a medium nonstick frying pan over medium heat until foaming. Add the eggs and stir with a wooden spoon until almost set. Stir in the smoked salmon and cook until just set.

3 Sprinkle with the chives. Spoon over the toasted muffin halves and serve hot.

NUTRITION PER SERVING	
Energy	392kcals/1640kJ
Carbohydrate	30g
of which sugar	2g
Fat	17g
of which saturates	5.5g
Salt	2.5g
Fiber	2g

Poached eggs with chargrilled asparagus

For a grown-up breakfast, dip the asparagus in the egg yolk as if it were a toast stick.

| Low carb |
| Dairy free |
| Gluten free |
| Low salt |

SERVES 4
PREP 5 MINS
COOK 10 MINS

1 bunch of asparagus, woody ends removed

1 tbsp olive oil

salt and freshly ground black pepper

4 large eggs

1 Heat a grill pan and rub the asparagus spears with the oil. Cook on the grill pan over medium heat for 5–7 minutes (depending on thickness), turning occasionally, until they are tender and charred in places. Sprinkle them with salt and pepper.

2 When the asparagus is nearly ready, bring a large pan of salted water to a boil. Crack an egg into a teacup and gently slide into the bubbling water. Repeat for all the eggs (using a teacup helps them maintain their shape). Poach the eggs in very gently simmering water for about 3 minutes until the white is set but the yolk is still runny. (The trick to perfect poached eggs is that they must be very fresh; this helps the white to stay together in a neat shape.)

3 Transfer the asparagus to warmed plates, place an egg on top of each pile, and sprinkle with black pepper.

NUTRITION PER SERVING	
Energy	128kcals/530kJ
Carbohydrate	1g
of which sugar	1g
Fat	10g
of which saturates	2g
Salt	0.2g
Fiber	1.5g

Fried eggs with garlic

Boiled, fried, or scrambled egg dishes are very popular in the Middle East, where they are served for breakfast, as street snacks in busy markets, or as a late-night snack at home. This recipe is often served in Lebanon, Syria, and Jordan.

Low salt

SERVES 4
PREP 5 MINS
COOK 6–8 MINS

2 tbsp olive oil

pat of butter, plus extra to serve

2–3 garlic cloves, crushed

1–2 tsp sumac

8 eggs

1 tsp dried mint salt

1 In a heavy-bottomed frying pan, heat the oil and the butter. Add the garlic and sumac and cook for 1–2 minutes, until it begins to color. Crack the eggs into a bowl and pour into the pan.

2 Sprinkle the mint over the eggs and cover the pan with a lid. Reduce the heat and cook until the whites are just set.

3 Sprinkle a little salt over the eggs, divide into four portions, and serve with toast or flatbread.

NUTRITION PER SERVING

Energy	243kcals/1007kJ
Carbohydrate	0g
of which sugar	0g
Fat	21g
of which saturates	5.5g
Salt	0.7g
Fiber	0g

Cuban-style rice

Cuban rice, named for the fried bananas served on the side, is loved by Spanish children as much for its pretty colors as for the sweet-salty combination of flavors. Leftover paella makes a particularly good version.

Low saturated fat

Dairy free

Gluten free

Low salt

SERVES 4
PREP 10 MINS
COOK 10 MINS

about 1¾ cups cooked rice

3–4 tbsp olive oil

4–8 eggs

4 small bananas, peeled and halved lengthwise

1lb 2oz (500g) fresh or canned tomatoes

1 thick slice of onion, chopped

1 garlic clove, chopped

1 fresh red chile, seeded and chopped (optional)

1 Heat the rice through in a low oven or microwave and transfer to a warm serving dish.

2 Heat the oil in a large frying pan. Crack the eggs in and cook sunny-side up. Remove with a slotted spoon, arrange on top of the rice, and keep warm.

3 In the same pan, cook the bananas just enough to caramelize them a little. Remove and arrange them with the eggs.

4 Meanwhile, liquidize the tomatoes, onion, and garlic with the chile, if using. Pour the tomato mix into the same frying pan and bubble up for 1–2 minutes to concentrate the juices and develop the flavors. Serve the rice with its toppings, and the tomato sauce on the side.

NUTRITION PER SERVING	
Energy	393kcals/1644kJ
Carbohydrate	48g
of which sugar	22g
Fat	15g
of which saturates	3g
Salt	0.5g
Fiber	3g

Mexican eggs

A cheap, filling breakfast. Add chile if you want more heat.
If you don't have any tomato sauce, simply blend a can of
tomatoes in a food processor, then strain.

SERVES 4
PREP 5 MINS
COOK 25 MINS

1 tbsp olive oil

2 garlic cloves, crushed

1 x 14oz (400ml)
 tomato sauce

1 tsp smoked paprika

salt and freshly ground
 black pepper

1 tbsp chopped
 cilantro leaves

4 large eggs

4 thick slices of country-
 style bread

1 Heat the oil in a 10in (25cm) heavy-bottomed,
ovenproof frying pan over medium heat and cook
the garlic for 1 minute until it begins to color. Add the
tomato sauce and smoked paprika and season well.
Bring to a boil, reduce to a gentle simmer, and cook
for 20 minutes until thickened and reduced.

2 Five minutes before it is ready, preheat the broiler
to its highest setting. Stir most of the cilantro into the
tomato mixture.

3 When the sauce is ready, take it off the heat. Make
four holes in the sauce with the back of a spoon. Crack
an egg into each hole and put the pan under the hot
broiler for 2–3 minutes, until the eggs have just set.
Meanwhile, broil or toast the slices of bread.

4 Scoop a little of the tomato sauce over the top of
each piece of toast, then top it with an egg and sprinkle
over the reserved cilantro to serve.

NUTRITION PER SERVING

Energy	228kcals/958kJ
Carbohydrate	22g
of which sugar	4g
Fat	10g
of which saturates	2.5g
Salt	1.2g
Fiber	2g

Potato, pancetta, and red onion hash

A hash is perfect if you crave something a little more substantial in the morning. Try serving each portion topped with a fried egg—keep the yolks runny, if you like them that way, as they will form a "sauce" for the hash.

Gluten free

High fiber

SERVES 2
PREP 10 MINS
COOK 20 MINS

salt and freshly ground
  black pepper

1lb 2oz (500g) floury potatoes,
  such as Russet, peeled and
  cut into bite-sized chunks

2 tsp olive oil

1 red onion, finely chopped

½ red bell pepper, diced

1¾oz (50g) chopped pancetta

1 tbsp finely chopped chives

1¾oz (50g) grated mature
  Cheddar cheese, to serve

1 Bring a pan of salted water to a boil, add the potatoes, and cook for 10 minutes. Drain.

2 Meanwhile, heat the oil in a large, nonstick frying pan over medium heat and cook the onions and red bell pepper for 5 minutes. Add the pancetta, season well, and cook for another 5 minutes, stirring occasionally.

3 Add the boiled potatoes to the frying pan and cook over high heat for about 10 minutes, stirring frequently.

4 Divide the hash between warmed plates and sprinkle with the chives. Serve with a grating of Cheddar cheese or, if you prefer, baked beans and ketchup.

NUTRITION PER SERVING	
Energy	347kcals/1452kJ
Carbohydrate	52g
of which sugar	7g
Fat	17g
of which saturates	7.5g
Salt	1.3g
Fiber	9g

Roasted mushrooms with scrambled eggs on toast

A lovely way to serve eggs, this makes an unusual and luxurious breakfast or supper dish.

SERVES 4
PREP 10 MINS
COOK 20 MINS

2 tbsp olive oil

2 tbsp chopped parsley leaves

salt and freshly ground
    black pepper

4 large flat mushrooms, such as
    Portobello, stems discarded

4 large eggs

¼ cup reduced fat milk

1 heaping tbsp finely
    chopped chives

1 tbsp butter

4 thick slices of country-style
    bread

1 Preheat the oven to 400°F (200°C). In a bowl, mix the oil and parsley and season. Brush the mixture all over the mushrooms, place on a baking sheet, and roast for 20 minutes until tender.

2 Just before the mushrooms are ready, whisk together the eggs, milk, and chives and season well.

3 Heat a large, heavy-bottomed frying pan and melt the butter. Scramble the eggs in the pan over low heat for 3–4 minutes, using a wooden spoon and a slow, scraping motion to move them around so all the egg comes in contact with the heat. Be sure to get into every area of the bottom and the corners of the pan so the egg cooks evenly.

4 Meanwhile, broil or toast the bread. When the toast is ready, spoon over the juices from the mushrooms and top each piece with a mushroom, gill-side up.

5 While the egg is still a little soft or liquid (it will continue to cook off the heat), place one-quarter of it into each mushroom to serve.

NUTRITION PER SERVING	
Energy	306kcals/1280kJ
Carbohydrate	21g
of which sugar	2g
Fat	16g
of which saturates	5g
Salt	0.9g
Fiber	4g

French toast with blueberries

Blueberries are low in calories and high in antioxidants - more so than any other fruit. Many studies have also shown that they help reduce blood pressure.

SERVES 2
PREP 10 MINS
COOK 10 MINS

4 eggs

1 cup skim milk

$1/4$ tsp ground cinnamon

4 slices thick whole wheat bread, cut into triangles

1 tbsp sunflower oil

9oz (250g) blueberries

maple syrup, to serve

1 Crack the eggs into a mixing bowl. Add the milk and cinnamon and whisk together.

2 Pour the mixture into a shallow dish. Soak the bread in the mixture for about 30 seconds.

3 Heat half a tablespoon of the oil in a frying pan on low heat. Carefully place two triangles in the pan.

4 Fry the triangles on both sides until they turn golden brown. Repeat steps 3 and 4 for the remaining bread triangles.

5 Serve the French toast warm, with blueberries and maple syrup or try it with butter and jam.

NUTRITION PER SERVING	
Energy	243kcals/1017kJ
Carbohydrate	26g
of which sugar	10g
Fat	9g
of which saturates	2g
Salt	0.7g
Fiber	2g

Quinoa and polenta muffins with eggs, bacon, and avocado

Rich in whole grains, these deliciously savory muffins make a perfect start to your day. Serve the muffins with eggs, bacon, and avocado for a hearty breakfast.

SERVES 8
PREP 10 MINS
COOK 20 MINS

1 tbsp light olive oil

4 large eggs

8 bacon slices

1 tbsp butter, to serve

2 avocados, pitted and cut
  into thin slices

FOR THE BATTER

¾ cup polenta or corn grits

½ cup whole wheat flour

¾ cup prepared quinoa

1 tbsp baking powder

½ tsp baking soda

¾ tsp sea salt

1 cup milk

3½ tbsp light olive oil

1 tbsp honey

3 large eggs

1 Preheat the oven to 400°F (200°C). Grease and line an 8-hole muffin pan with baking cups. For the batter, place the polenta, flour, quinoa, baking powder, baking soda, and salt in a large bowl and mix to combine.

2 In a separate bowl, whisk together the milk, oil, honey, and eggs until well combined. Then gently fold the liquid mixture into the dry ingredients and mix until just combined.

3 Divide the batter equally between the eight baking cups and transfer the pan to the oven. Bake for about 20 minutes or until a toothpick inserted into the center comes out clean.

4 Meanwhile, heat the oil in a frying pan over medium heat and fry the eggs. Then add the bacon and fry until crisp. Split the muffins, top with some butter, and serve with the fried eggs, bacon, and avocado.

NUTRITION PER SERVING

Energy	499kcals/1871kJ
Carbohydrate	30g
of which sugar	5g
Fat	28g
of which saturates	7g
Salt	2.3g
Fiber	3.1g

Buttermilk biscuits

These biscuits are a staple served at breakfast with bacon, sausage, or scrambled eggs.

MAKES 6
PREP 10 MINS
COOK 10–12 MINS

1⅔ cups self-rising flour, sifted, plus extra for dusting

2 tsp baking powder

½ tsp fine salt

8 tbsp butter, chilled and cut into cubes

¾ cup buttermilk

1 large egg, lightly beaten

1 Preheat the oven to 450°F (230°C). In a large bowl, or the bowl of a food processor, mix together the flour, baking powder, and salt. Add the butter and rub it in, or pulse-blend, until the mixture resembles fine breadcrumbs.

2 Make a well in the center of the flour mixture and stir in the buttermilk. You will need to use your hands to bring the dough together. Gently knead the mixture on a floured work surface to form a soft dough.

3 Gently roll the dough out to a thickness of 1in (3cm). Cut rounds out of the dough with a 3in (7cm) biscuit cutter. Gently bring the dough back together and re-roll it to cut out as many as possible.

4 Brush each biscuit with a little of the egg. Bake in the top of the oven for 10–12 minutes, until they have risen and are golden brown.

NUTRITION PER SERVING	
Energy	318kcals/1336kJ
Carbohydrate	37g
of which sugar	2g
Fat	16g
of which saturates	9g
Salt	1.5g
Fiber	2g

Savory cheese and bacon muffins

The perfect breakfast on the go or handy snack, bacon adds a delicious twist to these cheesy mini-cakes that will keep you full all morning.

SERVES 4

PREP 10 MINS

COOK 25 MINS

4 bacon slices

5½oz (150g) Cheddar cheese, cut into small pieces

1½ cups fresh breadcrumbs

small bunch of scallions, finely chopped

3 eggs

½ cup reduced fat milk

handful of fresh chives, chopped

salt and freshly ground black pepper

butter, for greasing

1 Preheat the oven to 375°F (190°C). Heat a frying pan over medium-high heat and add the bacon slices. Fry until cooked, but not too crispy, then cut into bite-sized pieces and set aside.

2 In a large bowl, mix together the cheese, breadcrumbs, scallions, eggs, and milk. Stir through the bacon and chives, and season well.

3 Grease four 5fl oz (150ml) ramekins or a muffin pan with the butter and divide the batter equally between them. Bake in the oven for about 25 minutes, or until the muffins are well risen and golden and a skewer inserted into the middle comes out clean. Transfer to a wire rack and leave to cool slightly. Serve warm.

NUTRITION PER SERVING	
Energy	221kcals/925kJ
Carbohydrate	6g
of which sugar	2g
Fat	21g
of which saturates	5g
Salt	1.5g
Fiber	1g

Banana and oatbran muffins

These muffins are a healthy choice for a leisurely brunch; delicious eaten when they're still warm. One muffin offers a good amount of fiber.

MAKES 12
PREP 20 MINS
COOK 20 MINS

1¼ cups all-purpose flour

1 tsp baking soda

1 tsp baking powder

1 tsp ground cinnamon

¾ cup oatbran

1¾oz (50g) chopped walnuts (optional)

8 tbsp butter, softened, plus extra
for greasing (if using a pan)

½ cup brown sugar

2 large eggs, lightly beaten

3 ripe bananas, mashed

½ cup skim milk

1 Preheat the oven to 375°F (190°C). Place 12 paper muffin liners in a 12-hole muffin pan, or simply place the liners on a baking sheet, or grease a 12-hole muffin pan with butter.

2 Sift the flour, baking soda, baking powder, cinnamon, and oatbran into a large bowl. Pour in any bran left in the sieve. Add the walnuts (if using). Stir well.

3 Place the butter and brown sugar in a separate mixing bowl and cream together, using an electric hand-held mixer, until light and fluffy. Add the eggs and mix well. Stir in the bananas and milk.

4 Pour the wet mixture into the dry and stir to combine. Do not over-mix or the muffins will be heavy. Divide the mixture between the paper liners or muffin pan holes.

5 Bake for 20 minutes (start checking after 15), or until a toothpick inserted into a muffin comes out clean. Transfer to a wire rack to cool.

NUTRITION PER SERVING	
Energy	254kcals/1063kJ
Carbohydrate	30g
of which sugar	13g
Fat	12g
of which saturates	5.5g
Salt	0.5g
Fiber	2g

Banana and yogurt pancake stack

Try stacking pancakes for a luxurious breakfast treat. Younger children especially love their sweet fluffiness.

Low salt

SERVES 6
PREP 10 MINS
COOK 15–20 MINS

1½ cups self-rising flour, sifted

1 tsp baking powder

2 tbsp granulated sugar

1 cup whole milk

2 large eggs, lightly beaten

½ tsp vanilla extract

2 tbsp unsalted butter, melted and cooled, plus extra for cooking

2–3 bananas

¾ cup (7oz) Greek yogurt

honey, to serve

1 Sift the flour and baking powder into a large bowl and add the sugar. In a bowl, whisk together the milk, eggs, and vanilla extract. Make a well in the center of the flour mixture and whisk in the milk mixture, a little at a time, bringing in the flour as you go. Finally, whisk in the cooled, melted butter until the mixture is smooth.

2 Melt a pat of butter in a large, nonstick frying pan. Pour tablespoons of the batter into the pan, leaving space between them for the batter to spread. Each pancake should become about 3¼–4in (8–10cm) in diameter, but don't worry too much.

3 Cook over medium heat, reducing the heat if they seem to be cooking too fast. Turn the pancakes when small bubbles appear on the surface and pop. Cook for another 1–2 minutes until golden brown and cooked through.

4 Slice the bananas diagonally to produce 2in- (5cm-) long strips. Place a warm pancake on a plate and top with a spoonful of yogurt and slices of banana. Top with another pancake, more yogurt, banana, and honey. Finish the stack with a third pancake, topped with a spoonful of yogurt and drizzled generously with honey.

NUTRITION PER SERVING	
Energy	317kcals/1336kJ
Carbohydrate	40g
of which sugar	17g
Fat	13g
of which saturates	7g
Salt	0.8g
Fiber	2g

Potato pancakes with smoked salmon

Cook extra mashed potatoes during the week and you'll have the basis of this fabulous weekend brunch dish. Dill helps with digestion and also has antibacterial properties.

SERVES 4
PREP 10 MINS
COOK 10–15 MINS

1lb (450g) cooked, cold mashed potatoes

1 large egg, beaten

1 tbsp all-purpose flour, plus extra for dusting

salt and freshly ground black pepper

2 tbsp olive oil

3½oz (100g) smoked salmon, thinly sliced

¼ cup sour cream

2 tbsp chopped dill

lemon wedges, to serve

1 Place the potato, egg, and flour in a mixing bowl. Season well and stir to combine. Divide into eight equal portions and, with flour-dusted hands, shape into rounds about 3in (7cm) in diameter.

2 Heat the oil in a large, nonstick frying pan over medium heat. Carefully add the pancakes to the pan. Cook for 10–15 minutes, occasionally turning the pancakes carefully with a metal spatula, until they are browned and heated through.

3 Transfer the pancakes to warmed plates. Top each with smoked salmon, sour cream, and dill. Season well with black pepper and serve with lemon wedges.

try this....
Green potato pancakes

Rinse 7oz (200g) **kale** and steam for 6–8 minutes. Squeeze the excess water from the kale, then roughly chop the leaves and stir into the mashed potato. Alternatively, replace white potatoes with **sweet potatoes**.

NUTRITION PER SERVING	
Energy	288kcals/1199kJ
Carbohydrate	21g
of which sugar	2g
Fat	18g
of which saturates	7g
Salt	0.9g
Fiber	2g

Buckwheat pancakes with cherry almond sauce

Buckwheat makes an incredible gluten-free flour and is even kinder on your digestion when soaked overnight. A good source of B vitamins, it is also rich in magnesium, copper, and easily-digestible protein.

SERVES 8
PREP 10 MINS,
PLUS SOAKING
COOK 30 MINS

FOR THE BATTER

1¼ cups buckwheat flour

2¼fl oz (65ml) plain yogurt

¾ cup milk

2 eggs

¾ tsp baking soda

¼ tsp baking powder

½ tsp vanilla extract

⅛ tsp salt

1–2 tbsp coconut oil, plus extra if needed

Greek yogurt, to serve

FOR THE SAUCE

12oz (350g) cherries, pitted

3 tbsp sugar

1 tsp almond extract

FOR A GLUTEN-FREE OPTION

use gluten-free baking powder

Low salt

1 For the batter, place the flour, yogurt, and milk in a large bowl. Mix to combine, cover with a paper towel, and leave at room temperature for 8 hours or up to 24 hours.

2 Place the eggs, baking soda, baking powder, vanilla, and salt in a large bowl. Whisk lightly until well blended. Then gradually pour the egg mixture into the flour mixture and whisk until well combined.

3 Heat a large nonstick frying pan over medium-high heat and add the oil once the pan is hot. Pour tablespoons of the batter into the pan, leaving space between them for the pancakes to spread. Each pancake should spread to about 6in (15cm) in diameter.

4 Cook the pancakes until small bubbles appear on the surface and the underside is firm. Then turn them over and cook for another 1–2 minutes or until cooked through. Transfer the cooked pancakes to a warm oven. Continue cooking until all the batter is used up, adding more oil to the pan as needed.

5 For the sauce, place the cherries in a large, lidded saucepan and cover with ½ cup of water. Add the sugar and place the pan over medium-high heat. Cover and simmer until the cherries have broken down. Then uncover and cook until the liquid becomes syrupy. Remove from the heat and stir in the almond extract. Serve the cherry almond sauce with the pancakes and Greek yogurt.

NUTRITION PER SERVING	
Energy	181kcals/758kJ
Carbohydrate	27g
of which sugar	12g
Fat	6g
of which saturates	4g
Salt	0.6g
Fiber	1g

Pumpkin and cinnamon waffles

Adding canned pumpkin and spices to these waffles gives them a wonderfully autumnal taste. Particularly low in calories, pumpkin is also rich in fiber, minerals, and vitamins.

SERVES 6
PREP 20 MINS
COOK 5 MINS

1½ cups self-rising flour, sifted

¼ cup light brown sugar

1 tsp baking powder

2 tsp ground cinnamon

2 large eggs, separated

1¼ cups skim milk

1 tsp vanilla extract

1½oz (40g) butter, melted and cooled

⅔ cup (5oz) canned pumpkin

vegetable oil, for greasing (optional)

maple syrup, apple wedges, or sliced bananas, to serve

1 In a bowl, use a balloon whisk to mix the flour, brown sugar, baking powder, and cinnamon.

2 Whisk together the egg yolks, milk, vanilla extract, melted butter, and pumpkin. Using a clean whisk, whisk the egg whites to firm peaks. Stir the pumpkin mixture into the flour mixture until evenly combined.

3 Preheat the waffle maker or iron, and oil it if that is suitable for the model you own. Gently fold the egg whites into the batter until they are well combined. Spoon a ladleful of the batter onto the hot waffle iron (or the amount that is recommended by the manufacturer) and spread it almost to the edge. Close the lid and bake until golden.

4 Serve immediately with maple syrup, apple wedges, or sliced bananas.

NUTRITION PER SERVING	
Energy	256kcals/1071kJ
Carbohydrate	35g
of which sugar	9g
Fat	9g
of which saturates	5g
Salt	0.7g
Fiber	2g

Quick stovetop granola

Making your own granola ensures that it is packed with your favorite ingredients, which you can mix and match to your heart's desire. Seeds are rich in omega-3 fats, while nuts offer good levels of protein.

SERVES 6
PREP 15 MINS, PLUS COOLING
COOK 10–12 MINS

1½ cups rolled oats

½ cup mixed seeds, such as sunflower, sesame, pumpkin, and golden flaxseed

⅓ cup mixed unsalted nuts, such as cashews, almonds, hazelnuts, and walnuts

1 tbsp light olive oil, plus extra for greasing

2 tbsp honey

3½ tbsp maple syrup

¼ cup dried blueberries

¼ cup dried cranberries

¼ cup dried cherries

2 tbsp dried coconut

Greek yogurt or milk, to serve

1 Place the oats, seeds, and nuts in a large deep-sided frying pan. Heat over medium heat, stirring frequently, for 3–5 minutes or until lightly browned. Transfer to a baking sheet and set aside.

2 Heat the oil, honey, and syrup in the frying pan until melted and well combined. Return the toasted oats, nuts, and seeds to the pan and heat for another 5 minutes, stirring frequently, until warmed through and evenly coated.

3 Mix together the berries, cherries, and coconut, add to the pan, and combine well.

4 Pour the mixture onto the baking sheet, spread it out, and let cool completely. When cold, break the granola into small pieces and transfer to an airtight container. To serve, layer Greek yogurt and granola into four glass dishes. Alternatively, serve with milk.

NUTRITION PER SERVING	
Energy	303kcals/1268kJ
Carbohydrate	36g
of which sugar	20g
Fat	13.5g
of which saturates	3g
Salt	trace
Fiber	4g

Fall fruit compôte

When the temperature is cooler, try this seasonal fruit salad for breakfast, served hot or cold. Dried fruits contain both soluble and insoluble fiber.

Low saturated fat

Gluten free

High fiber

SERVES 4
PREP 10 MINS, PLUS SOAKING
COOK 15 MINS

3½oz (100g) dried apples
3½oz (100g) dried figs
3½oz (100g) dried prunes
1 cinnamon stick
½ vanilla bean, halved lengthwise
finely grated zest and juice of 1 orange
1 tbsp brown sugar
Greek yogurt, to serve

1 Place all the dried fruits in a mixing bowl. Add the cinnamon, vanilla bean, and orange zest and juice. Pour in ¾ cup of boiling water. Cover the bowl and set aside overnight.

2 In the morning, transfer the contents of the bowl to a saucepan. Add the sugar and ⅔ cup of cold water and bring to a boil.

3 Reduce the heat and simmer very gently, uncovered, for 15 minutes. Remove the vanilla bean and cinnamon stick. Serve with a dollop of Greek yogurt.

NUTRITION PER SERVING	
Energy	165kcals/703kJ
Carbohydrate	38g
of which sugar	38g
Fat	trace
of which saturates	trace
Salt	trace
Fiber	8g

Overnight oats

Prepare these no-cook oats the night before, then enjoy a delicious instant breakfast the next morning. Oats are rich in beta-glucan, a fiber that lowers cholesterol.

Gluten free

Low salt

SERVES 2
PREP 10 MINS,
PLUS SOAKING

1¾oz (50g) rolled oats

⅔ cup coconut milk

1 tbsp honey

fresh cherries

toasted walnuts

1 Combine the oats and coconut milk. Transfer the mixture to a sealed jar and leave to soak in the refrigerator overnight.

2 In the morning, top off with a little more milk, if necessary. Drizzle over the honey, add the cherries, and top with the walnuts. Serve at once.

try this....
Banana and cinnamon overnight oats

Mash 1 **banana** with 2 tablespoons **cocoa powder**, 1 tablespoon **brown sugar**, and 1 teaspoon **cinnamon**. Spoon over the oats, then sprinkle with 1 tablespoon **chia seeds** and some toasted **coconut flakes**. Serve at once.

NUTRITION PER SERVING

Energy	653kcals/2372kJ
Carbohydrate	52g
of which sugar	22g
Fat	43g
of which saturates	26g
Salt	0g
Fiber	5.5g

LUNCHES

Soups
....

Salads
....

Sandwiches and wraps
....

Broccoli soup with cheesy croutons

Broccoli has an impressive nutritional profile. Low in calories and high in fiber, it is also rich in calcium and potassium, and a good source of Vitamin C.

SERVES 4
PREP 10 MINS
COOK 15–20 MINS

1 large head broccoli, about 1lb 2oz (500g)

1 tbsp olive oil

1 large onion, finely chopped

2 garlic cloves, crushed or finely chopped

4 cups vegetable or chicken stock

5 tbsp reduced-fat sour cream or crème fraîche

FOR THE CROUTONS

3 thick slices slightly stale whole wheat bread, crusts removed

2 tbsp olive oil, plus extra for greasing

1¾oz (50g) Parmesan cheese, grated

1 To make the croutons, preheat the oven to 425°F (220°C). Cut the bread into small cubes and place in a bowl, drizzle over the oil and Parmesan, and mix well. Transfer the croutons to a greased ovenproof dish and cook for 7–10 minutes, or until golden and crispy. Remove and cool.

2 Divide the broccoli into florets, then slice and coarsely chop the stalks.

3 Heat the oil in a large pan, add the onion and sauté for 1–2 minutes. Then add the broccoli and garlic, and cook for another 1–2 minutes.

4 Add the stock, bring to a boil, then reduce the heat, and simmer for 10 minutes, or until the broccoli is soft. Pulse the mixture in a food processor or process using a hand-held blender to form a purée.

5 Return the soup to the pan and gently reheat, then stir in the crème fraîche. Divide between four bowls, then scatter over the croutons, and serve.

NUTRITION PER SERVING	
Energy	235kcals/1320kJ
Carbohydrate	20g
of which sugar	7g
Fat	16g
of which saturates	6g
Salt	0.9g
Fiber	8g

Pea, mint, and avocado soup with quinoa

This light and creamy chilled soup is enhanced with the addition of the nutty-flavored and protein-packed quinoa. Quick and easy to prepare, it's the perfect summer lunch.

Dairy free

Low salt

High fiber

SERVES 4
PREP 10 MINS
COOK 20–25 MINS

⅓ cup uncooked quinoa

2 avocados, pitted

1lb 2oz (500g) frozen peas

¾ cup chopped mint, plus extra to garnish

1 quart unsweetened almond milk

1 Rinse the quinoa under running water, drain, and place in a lidded saucepan. Cover with 1 cup of water and bring to a boil.

2 Reduce the heat to a simmer, cover, and cook for 15–20 minutes or until almost all the liquid has been absorbed and the quinoa is fluffy. Remove from the heat, drain any remaining water, and set aside to cool.

3 Scoop out the flesh from the avocados and place in a food processor. Add the peas, mint, and half the milk and pulse until smooth. Then add the remaining milk and pulse until fully incorporated.

4 Divide the soup equally between four soup bowls. Top with equal quantities of the cooled quinoa. Garnish with some mint and serve immediately.

NUTRITION PER SERVING	
Energy	420kcals/1757kJ
Carbohydrate	28g
of which sugar	10g
Fat	22g
of which saturates	4.5g
Salt	0g
Fiber	11g

15-minute soup

This simple soup is prepared with a premade broth in Spain—leftovers from one of the bean soups popular at midday, flavored with diced Serrano ham and parsley, and fortified with hard-boiled egg.

Low carb

Low saturated fat

Dairy free

SERVES 4
PREP 5 MINS
COOK 25 MINS

3½ cups hot chicken or beef broth

2 tbsp rice

4 tbsp diced Serrano ham

2 eggs, hard-boiled and chopped

1 tbsp finely chopped flat-leaf parsley

1 tbsp finely chopped mint (optional)

FOR A GLUTEN-FREE OPTION
use gluten-free stock

1 In a large pan, bring the broth, rice, and ham to a boil. Reduce the heat and simmer for 15 minutes, or until the rice is nearly tender.

2 Add the eggs and simmer for another minute. Remove from the heat, then stir in the parsley and mint, if using. Serve piping hot.

NUTRITION PER SERVING	
Energy	126kcals/532kJ
Carbohydrate	6g
of which sugar	0g
Fat	6g
of which saturates	1.5g
Salt	2.8g
Fiber	0g

Butternut squash soup

Make this rich, velvety soup more sophisticated with a garnish of sage leaves, quickly fried in light oil. Butternut squash contains antioxidants that are known to promote good eyesight.

Dairy free

SERVES 4–6
PREP 5 MINS
COOK 20 MINS

3 tbsp olive oil

1 onion, chopped

1 leek, white part only, chopped

1 celery stalk, chopped

1lb 2oz (500g) butternut squash, peeled and cut into 1in (3cm) cubes

2½ cups vegetable or chicken stock

½ tbsp chopped sage leaves

salt and freshly ground black pepper

1 Heat the oil in a large, heavy-bottomed saucepan with a lid. Add the onion, leek, and celery and cook for 5 minutes until they soften, but do not brown.

2 Add the squash, stock, and sage, and season well.

3 Bring to a boil, then reduce to a gentle simmer, cover, and cook for 15 minutes until the squash is tender.

4 Blend the soup, either in a blender or using a hand-held blender, until completely smooth. Check the seasoning and serve.

NUTRITION PER SERVING	
Energy	208kcals/870kJ
Carbohydrate	19g
of which sugar	11g
Fat	10g
of which saturates	6g
Salt	2g
Fiber	5g

Lettuce soup with peas

For the best flavor choose very fresh, crisp lettuce for this refreshing chilled soup. Peas are a good source of Vitamin C and other antioxidants.

Low carb

Low saturated fat

Gluten free

Low salt

SERVES 4
PREP 20 MINS,
PLUS CHILLING

4½oz (125g) peas
  (shelled weight)

1 small garlic clove

sea salt and freshly ground
  black pepper

2 round heads of lettuce,
  torn into pieces and solid
  cores discarded

1 cup plain yogurt

¾in (2cm) piece fresh
  ginger, peeled and
  finely grated

handful of mint leaves

juice of ½ lemon

1 Bring a small amount of water to a boil in a pan, add the peas, and cook for 1 minute. Drain (reserving the cooking water), cool under cold running water, and chill in the refrigerator.

2 Halve the garlic clove and crush the halves with a pinch of coarse salt. Combine the garlic with all the other ingredients (except the peas) in a blender or food processor, adding just enough of the reserved cooking water to get the blades moving or until the desired consistency is achieved—it is best if you can get it fairly smooth, with a bit of texture.

3 Transfer the soup to a large bowl and chill for 30 minutes. When ready to serve, stir in the cooked peas, leaving a few to garnish.

NUTRITION PER SERVING	
Energy	88kcals/368kJ
Carbohydrate	9g
of which sugar	6g
Fat	2.5g
of which saturates	1.5g
Salt	0.1g
Fiber	2.5g

Italian meatball soup

A strong beef or chicken broth enriched with tiny meatballs is traditionally served at the start of a southern Italian Christmas feast. Fresh broth is a good source of calcium.

SERVES 6
PREP 20–30 MINS
COOK 10 MINS

14oz (400g) lean ground beef

1¾ cups fresh breadcrumbs

1 garlic clove, finely chopped

2 tbsp finely chopped flat-leaf parsley, plus extra to garnish

2 large eggs, beaten

a little milk

salt and freshly ground black pepper

2–3 heaping tbsp all-purpose flour

5½ cups hot strong chicken or beef broth

1 Work the ground beef with the breadcrumbs, garlic, parsley, and eggs to a soft paste—you may need a little milk or more breadcrumbs. Season.

2 Spread the flour on a plate. With damp hands, pinch off little pieces of the mixture and form into balls no bigger than a marble. Season the flour and roll the balls through it to coat.

3 Bring the broth gently to a boil and slip in the meatballs. Reduce the heat to a steady simmer and poach the meatballs until firm, for about 10 minutes. Garnish with parsley.

NUTRITION PER SERVING

Energy	301kcals/1259kJ
Carbohydrate	26g
of which sugar	2g
Fat	11g
of which saturates	4.5g
Salt	2g
Fiber	0.2g

Wild garlic soup

Sweet potato, wheatgrass, and wild garlic will boost you if you are feeling run-down. Wild garlic is available only in the spring, but you could use a mixture of wild arugula and spinach at other times of the year.

SERVES 4
PREP 5–10 MINS
COOK 25–30 MINS

1 tbsp sunflower or vegetable oil

4 shallots, chopped

1 sweet potato
(about 14oz/400g), peeled
and chopped into small cubes

2½ cups vegetable stock

1 tbsp wheatgrass juice or 1 tsp
wheatgrass powder (optional)

¼ cup crème fraîche or plain yogurt,
to serve (optional)

7oz (200g) wild garlic leaves

salt and freshly ground black pepper

FOR A GLUTEN-FREE OPTION
use gluten-free stock

1 Heat the oil in a medium saucepan over low heat, add the shallots and a little water, and allow the shallots to soften. Add the sweet potato and sauté for 5 minutes. Pour in the hot vegetable stock, bring to a boil, and simmer for about 15 minutes, or until the sweet potato softens.

2 Meanwhile, if using the wheatgrass juice or powder, mix it with the crème fraîche or yogurt in a small bowl.

3 Remove the pan from the heat, pour the mixture into a blender or food processor, and purée until smooth. Add the wild garlic and purée again until smooth. Season to taste. Pour the soup into four individual serving bowls, swirl a tablespoon of crème fraîche or yogurt into each portion, and serve.

NUTRITION PER SERVING	
Energy	209kcals/874kJ
Carbohydrate	22g
of which sugar	7g
Fat	9.5g
of which saturates	4.5g
Salt	1.5g
Fiber	4.5g

Moroccan fish soup

In the Middle East, fish is generally broiled or grilled, fried, or baked. It only appears in a few classic stews and soups, such as this North African recipe, which is popular in the coastal regions of Morocco, Tunisia, Libya, and Egypt.

Low carb

Low saturated fat

Dairy free

SERVES 6
PREP 10 MINS
COOK 20 MINS

2–3 tbsp olive oil

1 onion, finely chopped

2–3 garlic cloves, finely chopped

2–3 tsp harissa paste

small bunch of flat-leaf parsley, finely chopped

4 cups hot fish stock

⅔ cup white wine (optional)

1 x 14oz (400g) can chopped tomatoes, drained

2¼lb (1kg) fresh firm-fleshed fish fillets, such as cod, haddock, ling, grouper, sea bass, or snapper, cut into bite-sized chunks

salt and freshly ground black pepper

small bunch of cilantro, coarsely chopped, to garnish

FOR A GLUTEN-FREE OPTION
use gluten-free stock

1 Heat the oil in a large, deep, heavy-bottomed pan and stir in the onion and garlic, until they begin to color. Add the harissa and parsley and pour in the fish stock. Bring to a boil, reduce the heat, and simmer, uncovered, for 10 minutes to let the flavors mingle.

2 Add the wine, if using, and the tomatoes. Gently stir in the fish chunks and bring to a boil again. Reduce the heat, season to taste, and simmer uncovered for about 5 minutes to make sure the fish is cooked through. Scatter the chopped cilantro over the top and serve immediately.

NUTRITION PER SERVING	
Energy	218kcals/912kJ
Carbohydrate	4g
of which sugar	4g
Fat	5g
of which saturates	0.8g
Salt	2g
Fiber	0.9g

Sweet potato soup

This sophisticated soup is rich and velvety, and can be ready in minutes. The crispy croutons add a satisfying crunch and make this hearty dish even more substantial.

SERVES 6
PREP 10 MINS
COOK 20 MINS

5 tbsp olive oil

1 onion, chopped

1 leek, white part only, chopped

1 celery stalk, chopped

1lb 2oz (500g) sweet potatoes, peeled and cut into 1in (3cm) cubes

½ tbsp chopped sage leaves

2½ cups vegetable or chicken stock

salt and freshly ground black pepper

2 tbsp unsalted butter

4 slices of day-old white bread, crusts removed and cut into ½in (1cm) dice

1 Heat 3 tablespoons of oil in a large, heavy-based saucepan. Add the onion, leek, and celery and cook for 5 minutes, or until the vegetables are softened but not browned.

2 Add the sweet potatoes, sage, and stock to the pan. Season to taste and bring to the boil.

3 Reduce the heat to a gentle simmer and cover the saucepan with the lid. Cook for 10 minutes, or until the sweet potatoes are tender.

4 While the soup is simmering, in a large frying pan, heat the remaining oil and butter until hot. Add the bread pieces, then fry, stirring constantly for 10 minutes, or until golden.

5 Using a slotted spoon, remove the croutons from the frying pan and drain off the excess oil on a paper towel.

6 Using an electric hand-held blender, process the soup until smooth. Season again, if needed.

7 Ladle the soup into serving bowls, garnish with the croutons, and serve warm.

NUTRITION PER SERVING	
Energy	309kcals/1293kJ
Carbohydrate	35g
of which sugar	7.5g
Fat	14.5g
of which saturates	4g
Salt	1.4g
Fiber	5g

Salmorejo

A fresh soup from southern Spain, similar to gazpacho. Tomatoes help regulate blood sugar.

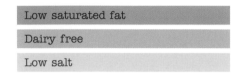

Low saturated fat

Dairy free

Low salt

SERVES 4
PREP 15 MINS, PLUS
SOAKING AND CHILLING

4oz (115g) day-old rustic bread, crusts removed

3 tbsp olive oil, plus more to garnish

2 tbsp red wine vinegar

4 ripe large tomatoes, skinned and seeded

1 cucumber, peeled, seeded, and chopped

1 red bell pepper, seeded and quartered

1 onion, roughly chopped

3 garlic cloves

salt and freshly ground black pepper

2 hard-boiled eggs, peeled and chopped

2 slices Serrano ham or prosciutto, cut into thin strips

1 Break the bread into pieces and place in a bowl. Add the oil and vinegar, mix well, and let stand for about 10 minutes, until softened.

2 Purée the tomatoes, cucumber, red bell pepper, onion, and garlic with ½ cup water in a food processor. Add the bread and process. Season.

3 Transfer to a bowl and chill at least 2 hours. Ladle into bowls and top each with hard-boiled eggs, ham, and a drizzle of olive oil.

NUTRITION PER SERVING	
Energy	280kcals/1172kJ
Carbohydrate	22g
of which sugar	9.5g
Fat	16g
of which saturates	2.5g
Salt	0.7g
Fiber	4.5g

Watercress soup

For extra flavor, serve this velvety soup with shredded Parmesan cheese. Watercress is a powerhouse of nutrients.

SERVES 4
PREP 10 MINS
COOK 15 MINS

1¾ tbsp oil

1 onion, finely chopped

6oz (175g) watercress

3 ripe pears, peeled, cored, and roughly chopped

1.4 quarts (1.3 liters) chicken stock

salt and freshly ground black pepper

3½fl oz (100ml) half-fat crème fraîche

1 tbsp fresh lemon juice

Parmesan cheese, grated, to serve

olive oil, to drizzle

FOR A GLUTEN-FREE OPTION
use gluten-free stock

1 Melt the oil in a large saucepan over medium-low heat. Add the onion and cover. Cook, stirring occasionally, about 10 minutes, or until tender.

2 Meanwhile, trim the watercress and pluck off the leaves. Add the watercress stems to the pot with the pears and stock. Bring to a boil over high heat.

3 Cover and simmer gently for 15 minutes, or until the pears are tender. Season with salt and pepper. Reserving a few watercress leaves for garnish, purée the soup and watercress leaves in a blender. Add the crème fraîche and lemon juice, and adjust the seasoning.

4 Serve hot, garnished with Parmesan shavings and drizzled with a little olive oil.

NUTRITION PER SERVING	
Energy	277kcals/1159kJ
Carbohydrate	16g
of which sugar	15g
Fat	12g
of which saturates	5g
Salt	2g
Fiber	4g

Gazpacho

The vegetables are the stars of the show, so use the freshest you can find—
the no-cook approach will celebrate their ripe flavor.

Low carb

Low saturated fat

Dairy free

Gluten free

Low salt

SERVES 4
PREP 15 MINS, PLUS CHILLING

2¼lb (1kg) tomatoes, plus extra
   to serve

1 small cucumber, peeled and finely
   chopped, plus extra to serve

1 small red bell pepper, seeded and
   chopped, plus extra to serve

2 garlic cloves, crushed

¼ cup sherry vinegar

salt and freshly ground black pepper

½ cup extra virgin olive oil, plus
   extra to serve

1 hard-boiled egg, white and yolk
   separated and chopped, to serve

1 Bring a pan of water to a boil. Place the tomatoes in a heatproof bowl, pour over enough boiling water to cover, and leave for 20 seconds, or until the skins split. Drain and cool under cold running water. Gently peel off the skins and cut the tomatoes in half, then seed and chop the flesh.

2 Place the tomato flesh, cucumber, red bell pepper, garlic, and vinegar in a food processor or blender. Season to taste and process until smooth. Pour in the oil and process again. Dilute with a little cold water or a few ice cubes if too thick. Transfer the soup to a serving bowl, cover with plastic wrap, and chill.

3 When ready to serve, finely chop the extra cucumber and red bell pepper. Place the cucumber, bell pepper, and egg yolk and white in individual bowls and arrange on the table, along with a bottle of olive oil. Ladle the soup into bowls and serve, letting each diner add their own garnish. If the soup hasn't had enough time to chill properly, add an ice cube or two to each bowl.

try this....
Green gazpacho

Place 3½oz (100g) **baby spinach**, 2 **garlic cloves**, 1 large **cucumber**, large handful of fresh **basil leaves**, flesh from 1 ripe **avocado**, 4 **spring onions**, 7oz (200g) **plain yogurt**, and 2 tablespoons **sherry vinegar** in a blender and process until smooth. To serve, divide between four bowls, add a couple of ice cubes, and garnish with diced **avocado** and **pea shoots.**

NUTRITION PER SERVING	
Energy	279kcals/1167kJ
Carbohydrate	9.5g
of which sugar	9.5g
Fat	24g
of which saturates	3.5g
Salt	0.1g
Fiber	4g

Mango and curry leaf soup

Alphonso mangoes, renowned for their fragrant flesh and creamy texture, have a short season in India from early April through May. Other varieties work well too.

SERVES 4
PREP 15 MINS
COOK 20 MINS

FOR THE GARNISH
small handful of curry leaves
vegetable oil for deep frying

FOR THE SOUP
4 ripe mangoes, Alphonso if in season
2 tbsp vegetable oil
1 tsp black mustard seeds
handful of fresh curry leaves
1 red chile, seeded, finely chopped
2 tsp palm sugar or dark brown (muscovado) sugar
½ tsp turmeric
2 tsp rice flour
1¼–1¾ cups vegetable stock
1¼ cup half-fat coconut milk
juice of 1 lime, to taste
salt and freshly ground black pepper
2 tbsp chopped fresh cilantro

FOR A GLUTEN-FREE OPTION
use gluten-free stock

1 First make the garnish: deep-fry the curry leaves in hot oil until crisp—it only takes a few seconds. Drain on paper towels and set aside.

2 Coarsely chop the flesh of three mangoes into small pieces and finely dice the fourth. Set aside. Heat the oil in a medium pan and, when hot, fry the mustard seeds for a few seconds before adding the curry leaves and chile. Continue frying for 30 seconds, until the leaves stop sputtering.

3 Add the chopped mango to the pan, reserving the diced mango. Turn the heat to low and simmer the fruit until softened. Stir in the sugar and cook until the mango begins to caramelize. Sprinkle over the turmeric and rice flour and cook for 30 seconds, stirring all the time. Pour over 1¼ cups of the stock and simmer for 10 minutes.

4 Add the coconut milk and simmer for 2–3 minutes. Sharpen with lime juice, season with salt and pepper, and stir in the cilantro and diced mango. If the soup is too thick, add a little hot vegetable stock. Divide the soup between the bowls and sprinkle with a few crisp-fried curry leaves.

NUTRITION PER SERVING	
Energy	226kcals/946kJ
Carbohydrate	26g
of which sugar	23g
Fat	11g
of which saturates	5.5g
Salt	0.6g
Fiber	5g

Chilled melon and ginger soup

This is a soup to make in a hurry. All that's needed to bring out its fruity flavor is a seriously good chill—and a perfectly ripe melon.

Low saturated fat

Gluten free

Low salt

SERVES 4
PREP 15 MINS,
PLUS CHILLING

1 ripe Galia melon, peeled and seeded

1in (2.5cm) piece of fresh ginger, peeled

1 tsp fennel seeds

7oz (200g) white seedless grapes

grated zest and juice of 1 lime

1 tsp dried mint

¼ cup Greek yogurt, beaten

salt and freshly ground black pepper

FOR THE GARNISH

2 tbsp mint leaves

pinch of sugar

1oz (25g) crystallized ginger, finely chopped

1 Coarsely chop three-quarters of the melon flesh into bite-sized chunks. Finely chop the remainder and set aside. Grate the ginger and squeeze any juice over the melon chunks. Discard the leftover ginger.

2 Heat a heavy-bottomed frying pan over low heat and lightly toast the fennel seeds for about 30 seconds, until you smell an aniseedlike aroma. Grind the seeds to a coarse powder using a mortar and pestle.

3 Put the ground fennel seeds into a blender or food processor with the coarsely chopped melon and ginger juice. Add the grapes, lime juice and zest, and dried mint. Pulse until smooth and push through a sieve to remove the skins.

4 Stir in the yogurt, season, and chill thoroughly—it's best to half-freeze this soup, then blend it well just before serving. Spoon into bowls, adding a small pile of the reserved melon to each one. Shred the fresh mint, mix with the sugar and crystallized ginger, and scatter over the soup. Serve immediately

NUTRITION PER SERVING	
Energy	106kcals/444kJ
Carbohydrate	19g
of which sugar	19g
Fat	2g
of which saturates	1g
Salt	0.1g
Fiber	1.4g

Mango and red snapper broth

This is a complete meal in a bowl. Raw mangoes add bite to a citrusy broth flecked with fiery red chiles. Raw mangoes are available in many Asian markets.

Low saturated fat

Dairy free

High fiber

SERVES 4
PREP 15 MINS, PLUS MARINATING
COOK 15 MINS

1lb (500g) skinless red snapper fillets, cut into 1in (2.5cm) cubes

2 stalks lemongrass, finely chopped

2 tbsp vegetable oil

4 bird's eye red chiles, finely sliced

4 scallions, finely sliced

2in (5cm) fresh ginger, finely shredded

4 garlic cloves, coarsely chopped

4 small raw green mangoes, or under-ripe mangoes, peeled and finely chopped

2 tsp palm sugar or brown sugar

2 tbsp rice wine vinegar

1 quart (1 liter) fish stock

8 kaffir lime leaves, torn in half

1 tbsp Asian fish sauce

4oz (100g) medium egg noodles

4oz (100g) thin green beans, halved

salt to season

juice of 1 lime, to taste

2 tbsp chopped fresh cilantro leaves

1 tbsp shredded fresh mint leaves

FOR THE MARINADE

1 tbsp light soy sauce

2 tsp fish sauce

1 tbsp toasted sesame oil

1 tbsp mirin

1 tsp sugar

juice of 1 lime

1 Combine the soy and fish sauce, sesame oil, mirin, sugar, and lime juice, and spoon over the fish. Refrigerate for 20 minutes. Pound the lemongrass to a paste with a dash of water, using a mortar and pestle. Set aside.

2 Heat the oil in a wok or large pan and cook the chiles, scallions, ginger, and garlic for 30 seconds over high heat. Add the mangoes and cook for 1 minute. Stir in the sugar until it begins to caramelize. Add the vinegar, lemongrass, stock, lime leaves, and fish sauce. Bring to a boil.

3 Stir in the noodles, beans, and fish pieces (not the marinating liquid). Simmer for 3–5 minutes, until the noodles are cooked and the fish flakes easily. Season with salt, sharpen with lime juice, and add the herbs.

NUTRITION PER SERVING	
Energy	402kcals/1682kJ
Carbohydrate	35g
of which sugar	12g
Fat	11g
of which saturates	2g
Salt	3.2g
Fiber	6g

Mussel soup

Mussels, cultivated since ancient times in the Bay of Taranto in the far south of Italy, are an excellent source of fatty acids, vitamins, and minerals. They are the most nutrient-dense seafood.

Low carb

Low saturated fat

Dairy free

SERVES 4–6
PREP 10 MINS
COOK 10–20 MINS

3lb (1.35kg) large mussels in shells

⅔ cup dry white wine

2–3 tbsp olive oil

1 medium onion, finely chopped

1 garlic clove, finely chopped

3½ cups hot fish stock

1lb 2oz (500g) ripe tomatoes, peeled and diced

1–2 bay leaves

1 tbsp crumbled fresh or dried oregano

1 tsp capers, drained

salt

bunch of basil, shredded, to serve

FOR A GLUTEN-FREE OPTION
use gluten-free stock

1 Scrub the mussels and trim off the beards. They will close themselves tightly—but if they do not, they are dead and should not be used.

2 In a large soup pan, bring the wine to a boil and pack in the mussels. Cover and steam for 2–3 minutes, giving the pan a shake to move the shellfish around, until all the shells are open. Reject any that remain shut and reserve the ones in their shells. Strain the broth through a fine sieve to remove the grit and set aside.

3 In the same pan, heat the oil and cook the onion and garlic until soft but not browned. Add the stock and the reserved broth, tomatoes, bay leaves, and oregano and bring to a boil. Simmer for 5 minutes, then pour in the mussels and capers. Reheat and season with salt.

4 Sprinkle the basil and serve in deep soup bowls.

NUTRITION PER SERVING	
Energy	222–148kcals/
	936–624kJ
Carbohydrate	6–4g
of which sugar	5.5–4g
Fat	8.5–6g
of which saturates	1.3–0.8g
Salt	2.8–1.8g
Fiber	2–1.4g

Avocado, cilantro, and lime tabbouleh

Tabbouleh is a traditional part of a mezze in the Middle East, but it also makes an excellent salad. The lime and avocado in this version give it a fresh dimension.

Low saturated fat

Dairy free

SERVES 4
PREP 15 MINS, PLUS
SOAKING AND CHILLING

1½ cups bulgur wheat

1½ tsp rock salt

2 tomatoes, diced

1 avocado, peeled, pitted, and diced

1 small red bell pepper, seeded and diced

⅓ cup red onion, diced

handful of cilantro leaves, roughly chopped

½ cup lime juice

2 tbsp extra virgin olive oil

salt and freshly ground black pepper

1 Place 1½ cups of water in a large saucepan and bring to a boil. Place the bulgur wheat and rock salt in a large bowl. Pour the boiling water in the bowl, cover, and leave to soak for about 30 minutes.

2 Drain any excess water from the bulgur wheat and place it in a large bowl. Then add the tomatoes, avocado, red bell peppers, onions, and cilantro. Mix well to combine. Transfer the mixture to a large serving bowl.

3 Drizzle the lime juice and oil over the mixture. Toss well to coat. Season to taste with salt and black pepper, if needed. Mix well and chill the tabbouleh in the refrigerator for about 20 minutes before serving.

try this....
Shrimp and avocado salad with freekeh

Replace the bulgur wheat with 2 x 250g packs **ready-to-eat freekeh** and 7oz (200g) cooked, peeled **shrimp**.

NUTRITION PER SERVING	
Energy	306kcals/1275kJ
Carbohydrate	38g
of which sugar	5g
Fat	14g
of which saturates	2.5g
Salt	1.9g
Fiber	2.4g

Jeweled couscous in a jiffy

A salad that needs no cooking at all. Make the evening before, then pack in a lunchbox for a healthy weekday meal.

Low saturated fat

Dairy free

Low salt

SERVES 4–6
PREP 12 MINS,
PLUS COOLING

2 cups couscous

1½ tbsp olive oil

1 tbsp powdered vegetable stock or 2 cups hot vegetable stock

1¾oz (50g) pine nuts

3½oz (100g) dried apricots, finely chopped

large handful of cilantro, finely chopped

4½ tbsp extra virgin olive oil

juice of 1 large lemon

salt and freshly ground black pepper

2 or 3 tbsp pomegranate seeds, to serve

1 Bring a small saucepan of water to a boil. Put the couscous into a bowl, then drizzle over the olive oil. Rub it into the couscous, scatter with the powdered vegetable stock (if using), and mix it in.

2 Pour in 2 cups of boiling water (if using powdered stock) or hot vegetable stock, and stir briefly. The liquid should just cover the couscous. Immediately seal with plastic wrap.

3 Leave for 5 minutes, then test the grains, which should be nearly soft, and all the water soaked in. Fluff the couscous with a fork and let it cool, fluffing it occasionally to separate the grains.

4 Meanwhile dry-fry the pine nuts in a nonstick frying pan over medium heat, stirring, until they color. Be careful, as they can burn quickly. Set aside to cool.

5 Toss together the cooled couscous, pine nuts, apricots, and cilantro. Mix in the extra virgin olive oil and lemon juice and season to taste. Scatter with the pomegranate seeds to serve.

NUTRITION PER SERVING	
Energy	396kcals/1657kJ
Carbohydrate	46g
of which sugar	9g
Fat	18g
of which saturates	2g
Salt	0.7g
Fiber	4g

Chorizo, chickpea, and mango salad

A hearty, main meal salad with great variety of flavor. Chorizo is an excellent source of selenium.

Dairy free

Gluten free

SERVES 2
PREP 15 MINS
COOK 15 MINS

1 tbsp olive oil

5½oz (150g) chorizo, roughly chopped

14oz (400g) can of chickpeas, drained and rinsed

3 cloves of garlic, finely chopped

handful of flat-leaf parsley, finely chopped

1 tbsp dry sherry

2 ripe mangos, stoned, and flesh diced

small handful of fresh basil, roughly chopped

small handful of fresh mint leaves, roughly chopped

small handful of fresh cilantro leaves, roughly chopped

9oz (250g) baby spinach leaves

1 Heat the olive oil in a frying pan, add the chorizo and chickpeas and cook over low heat for 1 minute, then add the garlic and parsley and cook for a further minute. Add the sherry and cook for 10 minutes, stirring occasionally.

2 Put the mango and remaining herbs in a bowl and toss together, then add the chickpea mixture and combine well. Spoon onto a bed of spinach to serve.

NUTRITION PER SERVING	
Energy	504kcals/2106kJ
Carbohydrate	31g
of which sugar	5.5g
Fat	24g
of which saturates	8g
Salt	1.5g
Fiber	2.5g

try this....
Spicy chicken, chickpea, and mango salad

Replace chorizo with 12oz (350g) **rotisserie chicken**, roughly chopped into bite-sized pieces, and a dash of **jerk seasoning**.

Mexican quinoa salad

Crunchy tortilla chips and spicy chiles create a salad that packs a real punch in flavor and texture, and which everyone can enjoy.

Low saturated fat

Dairy free

Low salt

High fiber

SERVES 2
PREP 10–15 MINS,
PLUS COOLING
COOK 20 MINS

⅓ cup uncooked quinoa

14oz (400g) can red kidney beans, drained

¼ cup canned corn

½ red onion, finely chopped

1 red bell pepper, seeded and finely chopped

4–6 slices pickled jalapeño chiles, finely chopped

1 avocado, pitted and cut into cubes

1 head of romaine lettuce

1¾oz (50g) plain corn tortilla chips, crumbled, plus extra to serve

1 lemon or lime, halved, to serve

FOR A GLUTEN-FREE OPTION
use gluten-free tortillas

1 Rinse the quinoa under running water, drain, and place in a lidded saucepan. Cover with 1 cup of water and bring to a boil.

2 Reduce the heat to a simmer, cover, and cook for 15–20 minutes or until almost all the liquid has been absorbed and the quinoa is fluffy. Remove from the heat, drain any remaining water, and set aside to cool.

3 Place the quinoa, kidney beans, corn, onions, peppers, and jalapeños in a large bowl. Mix until well combined. Then add the avocado and mix lightly to combine.

4 Roughly shred the lettuce and add to the bowl. Sprinkle the tortillas over the mixture and toss lightly. Transfer the salad to a serving platter or plate. Serve immediately with tortilla chips and lemons or limes to squeeze over the dish.

NUTRITION PER SERVING	
Energy	555kcals/2322kJ
Carbohydrate	57g
of which sugar	10g
Fat	24g
of which saturates	4g
Salt	0.5g
Fiber	20g

Couscous with pine nuts and almonds

A tasty alternative to rice; serve either hot or cold. Couscous makes a good source of low-fat protein for vegetarians.

| Low saturated fat |
| Dairy free |
| Low salt |
| High fiber |

SERVES 4
PREP 15 MINS, PLUS STANDING

1 cup couscous

1 red bell pepper, seeded and chopped

½ cup raisins

½ cup chopped dried apricots

½ cucumber, seeded and diced

¼ cup chopped pitted Kalamata olives

¼ cup blanched almonds, lightly toasted

¼ cup pine nuts, lightly toasted

¼ cup olive oil

2 tbsp fresh lemon juice

1 tbsp chopped mint

salt and freshly ground black pepper

1 Put the couscous in a heatproof bowl. Add enough boiling water to cover the couscous by 1in (2.5cm). Let stand for 15 minutes, or until the couscous has absorbed all the water. Fluff up the grains with a fork.

2 Stir in the pepper, raisins, apricots, cucumber, olives, almonds, and pine nuts.

3 Whisk together the oil, lemon juice, and mint. Pour over the couscous and toss. Season with salt and pepper. Serve warm, or let cool and serve at room temperature.

NUTRITION PER SERVING	
Energy	619kcals/2590kJ
Carbohydrate	63g
of which sugar	31g
Fat	33g
of which saturates	3g
Salt	0.3g
Fiber	7g

Quinoa salad with mango, lime, and toasted coconut

A healthy salad full of big, tropical flavors and bright colors. Try to get Alphonso mangoes, if possible, which are famed for their sweetness.

SERVES 4
PREP 15 MINS
COOK 10 MINS

1¾oz (50g) unsweetened
  or flaked coconut

10oz (300g) quinoa

14oz (400g) can butter beans,
  drained and rinsed

½ red onion, finely chopped

1 large mango, peeled, pitted,
  and cut into bite-sized pieces

1 lime, peeled, segmented,
  and segments halved

handful of mint, finely chopped

handful of flat-leaf parsley,
  finely chopped

FOR THE DRESSING

3 tbsp olive oil

1 tbsp white wine vinegar

pinch of sugar

salt and freshly ground pepper

1 Toast the coconut by dry frying it in a pan over medium heat for 2–3 minutes until golden, stirring so that it doesn't burn. Set aside and cool.

2 To make the dressing, place all the ingredients in a small bowl or liquid measuring cup and whisk. Taste and adjust the seasoning as needed.

3 Cook the quinoa according to the instructions on the package. Drain well and place into a large serving bowl. While the quinoa is still warm, stir in the butter beans, onion, mango, lime, mint, and parsley, and season.

4 Pour over the dressing and stir well. Sprinkle the toasted coconut on top and serve immediately.

try this....
Spicy chicken and quinoa salad with mango and lime

Omit the coconut and butter beans. Cook 7oz (200g) **green beans** in a pan of boiling water for 3–4 minutes. Plunge into cold water to cool, then drain well and slice in half. Continue as above from step 2, adding the beans and 12oz (350g) diced **rotisserie chicken,** sprinkled with **curry powder**.

NUTRITION PER SERVING	
Energy	460kcals/1935kJ
Carbohydrate	54g
of which sugar	12.5g
Fat	20g
of which saturates	8g
Salt	0.8g
Fiber	7.5g

Quinoa and fennel salad

The peppery and licorice notes of fennel in this salad contrast well with the nuttiness of the quinoa and the juicy and sweet pomegranate seeds.

Low saturated fat

Dairy free

Low salt

High fiber

SERVES 4
PREP 10 MINS,
PLUS STANDING
COOK 15 MINS

1 cup uncooked quinoa

1½ cups vegetable stock

1 tsp ground cumin

1 whole fennel bulb

3 tbsp olive oil

1 tbsp lemon juice

salt and freshly ground
   black pepper

4 scallions, trimmed
   and thinly sliced

3 tbsp chopped cilantro
   leaves

2 tbsp chopped mint leaves

3½oz (100g) pomegranate
   seeds

FOR A GLUTEN-FREE OPTION
use gluten-free stock

1 Rinse the quinoa under cold running water. Drain and place in a large saucepan. Add the stock and cumin and bring to a boil, stirring frequently. Then cover and cook over medium heat for about 10 minutes. Remove from the heat and drain. Return the quinoa to the pan and leave for about 10 minutes, covered, to fluff up.

2 To prepare the fennel, trim the stalks, root end, and any tough outer pieces from the bulb and reserve the fronds. Cut the bulb in half lengthwise. Then set each half on a cutting board, flat-side down, and cut into thin slices lengthwise.

3 Heat 2 tablespoons of the oil in a large frying pan over medium heat. Add the fennel slices and cook for about 5 minutes, turning over once, until golden. Remove from the heat and transfer to a bowl. Add the lemon juice and remaining oil, season to taste, and mix well to combine.

4 Add the onions, cilantro, mint, and reserved fennel fronds to the bowl. Then add the quinoa and half the pomegranate seeds. Stir to mix; taste and adjust the seasoning, if needed. Divide the salad between four plates and sprinkle the remaining pomegranate seeds over it. Serve at room temperature or cold.

NUTRITION PER SERVING

Energy	525kcals/2197kJ
Carbohydrate	28g
of which sugar	7.5g
Fat	11g
of which saturates	1.5g
Salt	0.8g
Fiber	7g

Herbed mackerel salad

Throw together this fragrant salad for a light dinner packed with flavor—and then mop up the delicious dressing with a crispy baguette. Smoked mackerel is great to have in the refrigerator because it's inexpensive and high in protein.

Low saturated fat

Dairy free

SERVES 4
PREP 10–15 MINS
COOK 15–20 MINS

salt and freshly ground black pepper

1¼lb (550g) new potatoes, well scrubbed and chopped into bite-sized chunks

7oz (200g) hot-smoked mackerel fillets, skinned

2oz (60g) baby salad leaves

2 tbsp chopped dill

2 tbsp chopped chives

7oz (200g) cooked beets (not in vinegar), roughly chopped

baguette, to serve

FOR THE DRESSING
¼ cup extra virgin olive oil

juice of 1 lemon

1 tsp whole-grain mustard

1 tsp honey

1 garlic clove, finely chopped

1 Bring a large pan of salted water to a boil, add the potato chunks, and cook for 10–15 minutes, or until tender. Drain and set aside.

2 Meanwhile, break the mackerel into bite-sized pieces, removing any bones you find as you go, and place in a large serving bowl. Add the salad leaves and herbs and gently toss together.

3 Place the dressing ingredients in a small bowl, season, and whisk together with a fork.

4 Add the warm potatoes to the serving bowl, pour in the dressing, and stir gently. Add the beets and serve immediately with the baguette.

NUTRITION PER SERVING

Energy	279kcals/1167kJ
Carbohydrate	26g
of which sugar	6g
Fat	12g
of which saturates	2.5g
Salt	1.1g
Fiber	4g

Panzanella

Good-quality bread is a joy, and even when it is past its best it can be used in this delectable Italian salad. The oil and vinegar moisten the bread and stop it from tasting stale.

Low saturated fat

Dairy free

SERVES 4–6
PREP 15 MINS,
PLUS STANDING

12oz (350g) unsliced stale dense-textured white bread, such as ciabatta or sourdough, roughly torn into bite-sized pieces

1lb 5oz (600g) mixed tomatoes, at room temperature, such as red, yellow, green, purple, baby plum, cherry, or beefsteak, all roughly chopped into bite-sized chunks

1 red onion, finely chopped

2 garlic cloves, finely chopped

2 tbsp capers in brine, drained

salt and freshly ground black pepper

leaves from 1 bunch of basil, roughly torn

FOR THE DRESSING

6 tbsp extra virgin olive oil

3 tbsp red wine vinegar

½ tsp ground mustard

½ tsp granulated sugar

1 Place the bread, tomatoes, onion, garlic, and capers in a large serving bowl. Season well and stir to combine.

2 Place the dressing ingredients in a small bowl, season, and stir well. Pour over the bread and tomato mixture and stir to coat.

3 Set aside for at least 10 minutes and up to 2 hours, at room temperature, to allow the flavors to mingle. Stir the basil leaves into the salad just before serving.

NUTRITION PER SERVING	
Energy	396kcals/1664kJ
Carbohydrate	47g
of which sugar	8.5g
Fat	19g
of which saturates	3g
Salt	1.7g
Fiber	4.5g

Mixed bean and goat cheese salad

The robust beans complement the rich cheese. They are a low-calorie food that is high in protein and a good source of B vitamins.

Gluten free
Low salt
High fiber

SERVES 4
PREP 10 MINS

14oz can of butter beans, drained and rinsed

14oz can of flageolet beans, drained and rinsed

scant 1oz (25g) bunch of chives, finely chopped

2 tsp white wine vinegar

1 tbsp of fruity olive oil, plus extra to serve

1 tbsp of fresh thyme leaves

pinch of red pepper flakes

salt and freshly ground black pepper

1¾oz (50g) package of pea shoots

lemon juice, to season (optional)

3½oz (100g) semi-hard goat cheese, broken up into pieces

1 Put the beans in a large bowl and add the chives, vinegar, olive oil, thyme, and red pepper flakes and stir to combine. Season well with salt and black pepper.

2 Stir through the pea shoots, taste, and add a squeeze of lemon if you wish. Transfer to a shallow serving dish and top with the goat cheese, a drizzle of olive oil, and a twist of freshly ground black pepper. If you are a meat eater, you might try a little Serrano ham as an accompaniment.

try this....
Lentils with goat cheese and tomatoes

Replace both types of beans with 2 cans **dried lentils**, and add 2½oz (75g) roughly chopped **sun-blushed tomatoes**.

NUTRITION PER SERVING	
Energy	280kcals/1170kJ
Carbohydrate	30g
of which sugar	3g
Fat	11g
of which saturates	5g
Salt	0.2g
Fiber	8.5g

Tomato salad with red onion and mozzarella

Versatile and easy to prepare, this simple salad of tomatoes, red onion, and mozzarella bursts with vibrant colors and delicious Italian flavors.

Low carb

Gluten free

Low salt

SERVES 4
PREP 10 MINS

8 ripe plum tomatoes, sliced

6 cherry tomatoes, halved

1 small red onion, peeled and sliced

handful of basil leaves, torn

extra virgin olive oil, to drizzle

salt and freshly ground black pepper

2 handfuls of arugula

balsamic vinegar, to drizzle

2 balls of half-fat mozzarella, torn

1 Place the tomatoes, onion, and half of the basil leaves in a bowl. Drizzle with plenty of olive oil, season well, and toss through.

2 Arrange the arugula on a serving platter and drizzle with a little oil and some balsamic vinegar. Season and add the tomato and basil mixture. Add the torn mozzarella. Scatter the remaining basil leaves over the top and drizzle again with a little oil and balsamic vinegar. Serve immediately.

NUTRITION PER SERVING	
Energy	159kcals/664kJ
Carbohydrate	9g
of which sugar	9g
Fat	12g
of which saturates	5.5g
Salt	0.4g
Fiber	3g

Fattoush

You can vary the ingredients in this tangy salad, but sumac, pomegranate molasses, and toasted flatbread are essential to this traditional dish.

Low saturated fat

Dairy free

Low salt

SERVES 6
PREP 15 MINS

handful of fresh lettuce leaves

2–3 tomatoes, peeled and sliced

1 red or green bell pepper, seeded and sliced

4–5 scallions, trimmed and sliced

small bunch of flat-leaf parsley, coarsely chopped

2 thin flatbreads, such as pita breads

2–3 tbsp olive oil

juice of 1 lemon

1–2 garlic cloves, crushed

1 tsp cumin seeds, crushed

salt and freshly ground black pepper

1–2 tbsp pomegranate molasses

2 tsp sumac

1 Arrange the lettuce leaves, tomatoes, peppers, and scallions in a wide, shallow bowl and sprinkle the parsley over the top. Lightly toast the flatbreads, break them into bite-sized pieces, and scatter them over the salad.

2 In a small bowl, combine the oil and lemon juice with the garlic and cumin seeds. Season well and pour over the salad. Drizzle the pomegranate molasses over the top and sprinkle with sumac. Toss the salad gently just before serving.

NUTRITION PER SERVING	
Energy	120kcals/502kJ
Carbohydrate	17g
of which sugar	5g
Fat	4g
of which saturates	0.6g
Salt	0.2g
Fiber	2g

Chicken salad with radicchio and asparagus

This French salade tiède, or warm salad, is quick to cook and easy to assemble. Crunchy lettuce and garlicky chicken with a punchy dressing makes for a healthy dinner you can put together in minutes.

| Low carb |
| Low saturated fat |
| Dairy free |
| Gluten free |
| Low salt |

SERVES 4
PREP 5–10 MINS
COOK 10–15 MINS

4 tbsp extra virgin olive oil

4 chicken breasts, about 5½oz (150g) each, cut into thin strips

1 garlic clove, finely chopped

2oz (60g) roasted red bell peppers, thinly sliced

salt and freshly ground black pepper

1 small head of radicchio, torn into small pieces

9oz (250g) asparagus spears, each trimmed and cut into 3 pieces

2 tbsp raspberry vinegar

½ tsp sugar

1 Heat 2 tablespoons of the oil in a large nonstick frying pan over medium-high heat. Add the chicken and garlic and cook, stirring, for 5–7 minutes, or until the chicken is tender and cooked through. Stir in the roasted red bell peppers, and season to taste with salt and pepper.

2 Meanwhile, put the radicchio leaves in a large serving bowl. Remove the chicken from the pan using a slotted spoon and place in the bowl with the radicchio.

3 Add the asparagus to the oil remaining in the pan and cook, stirring constantly, for 1–2 minutes, or until just tender. Transfer to the bowl with the chicken.

4 Whisk together the remaining 2 tablespoons of the oil, the vinegar, and sugar, then pour into the pan and stir over high heat until well combined. Pour this dressing over the salad and toss quickly so that all the ingredients are well mixed and coated with the dressing. Serve immediately.

NUTRITION PER SERVING

Energy	284kcals/1190kJ
Carbohydrate	3g
of which sugar	3g
Fat	13g
of which saturates	2g
Salt	0.2g
Fiber	2g

try this....
Chicken salad with lentils and asparagus

Heat 1 tablespoon **oil** in a pan, add 2 finely sliced sticks of **celery**, 1 finely chopped **red onion**, and 1 diced **red bell pepper**, then sauté over medium heat for 5 minutes, or until the onion is starting to soften. Add another 1 tablespoon oil and the chicken, asparagus, and garlic, and cook for another 5–7 minutes, or until the chicken is cooked through. Allow the chicken mixture to cool, then mix with 1 can **green lentils**. Make the dressing as directed in step 4, pour over the chicken and lentils, and serve.

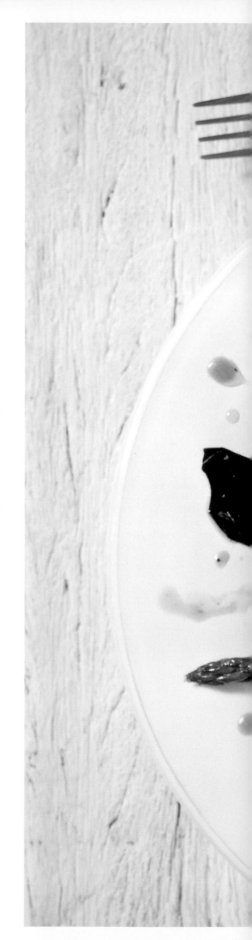

Chicken Caesar salad with polenta croutons

Using baked polenta to make the crunchy croutons for this perennially popular salad gives it a twist by providing extra texture to complement the succulence of the chicken and the freshness of the lettuce.

SERVES 4
PREP 20 MINS
COOK 10 MINS

2 tbsp olive oil

1 cup prepared polenta, cut into 1in (2.5cm) cubes

½ tsp rock salt

¼ tsp freshly ground black pepper

1 large or 2 small heads romaine lettuce, washed, dried, and torn into bite-sized pieces

8oz (225g) cooked chicken, cut into bite-sized pieces

¾ cup freshly grated Romano cheese

FOR THE DRESSING

½ cup extra virgin olive oil

1 tbsp Dijon mustard

3 tbsp good-quality mayonnaise

4 anchovy fillets, chopped

½ tsp Worcestershire sauce

1 garlic clove, crushed

2 tbsp finely grated Parmesan cheese, plus extra to serve

pinch of sugar

1 Heat the oil in a large frying pan over medium heat. Add the polenta and season with ½ teaspoon of salt and ¼ teaspoon of pepper. Cook for 10 minutes, turning over the polenta cubes occasionally, until crisp and lightly browned. Remove from the heat and set aside.

2 For the dressing, place all the ingredients in the small bowl of a food processor and pulse until emulsified into a thick and creamy dressing. Alternatively, place the ingredients in a large bowl and blend well with a handheld blender. Season with pepper, mix well to combine, and set aside.

3 Place the lettuce, chicken, and cheese in a large bowl and toss lightly to combine. Drizzle over the dressing, a little at a time, and toss until well coated. Arrange the salad on a serving dish and scatter the polenta croutons over it. Sprinkle over some Parmesan and serve immediately.

NUTRITION PER SERVING	
Energy	521kcals/2180kJ
Carbohydrate	1.5g
of which sugar	1.5g
Fat	44g
of which saturates	10g
Salt	1.5g
Fiber	0.8g

Spicy Asian chicken salad

This colorful salad requires very little cooking. Toss with the dressing at the last minute to prevent wilting.

Low carb

Low saturated fat

Dairy free

Gluten free

SERVES 4–6
PREP 10 MINS
COOK 7–10 MINS

14oz (400g) boneless, skinless chicken breasts

salt

¼ cup fresh lime juice

4 tsp Thai fish sauce

1 tbsp granulated sugar

pinch of red pepper flakes (optional)

1 Little Gem lettuce, shredded

3½oz (100g) beansprouts

1 large carrot, shaved using a vegetable peeler

6in (15cm) piece of cucumber, seeded and finely sliced

½ red bell pepper, finely sliced

½ yellow bell pepper, finely sliced

approx. 15 cherry tomatoes, halved

small handful of mint leaves, chopped

small handful of cilantro leaves, chopped

1¾oz (50g) salted peanuts, chopped (optional)

1 Poach the chicken in a large saucepan in plenty of simmering salted water or chicken stock for 7–10 minutes, depending on thickness, until cooked through. Let cool, then thinly slice.

2 Whisk the lime juice, fish sauce, sugar, a pinch of salt, and the red pepper flakes (if using) together, until the sugar dissolves.

3 Mix together the salad vegetables, most of the herbs, and the chicken. Mix in the dressing and scatter with the remaining herbs and the peanuts (if using), to serve.

try this....
Asian chicken salad with a peanut dressing

Make the salad as directed above. To make the peanut dressing, place 3½oz (100g) **crunchy peanut butter**, 1 tablespoon **toasted sesame oil**, 1 tablespoon **soy sauce**, 1 tablespoon **rice wine vinegar**, 1 teaspoon **honey**, 1 crushed **garlic clove**, and ⅓ cup leftover poaching liquid or chicken stock in a saucepan. Gently simmer until the sauce starts to thicken, then season to taste. Leave to cool and spoon over the salad.

NUTRITION PER SERVING	
Energy	243–162kcals/ 1019–679kJ
Carbohydrate	12–8g
of which are sugar	11–7.5g
Fat	8.5–5.5g
of which are saturates	1.5–1g
Salt	1.4–0.9g
Fiber	4.5–3g

Bean thread noodle salad

This light yet vibrant summer salad is refreshing and perfect as part of an Asian-inspired meal or buffet lunch.

Low saturated fat

Dairy free

Gluten free

SERVES 4
PREP 20 MINS

7oz (200g) dried Chinese bean thread noodles or thin rice noodles

1 large carrot, shaved using a vegetable peeler

4in (10cm) cucumber, halved lengthwise, seeded, and finely sliced on the diagonal

4 scallions, white parts only, finely sliced on the diagonal

1 mango, not too ripe, finely julienned

handful of mint leaves, roughly chopped

handful of cilantro leaves, roughly chopped

FOR THE DRESSING
juice of 2 limes

2 tbsp white wine vinegar or rice wine vinegar

1 tsp granulated sugar

pinch of salt

1 Put the noodles in a large bowl and cover with boiling water. Leave for 4 minutes, or according to the package instructions, until they are soft but still have a bite to them. Stir and separate the strands with chopsticks when you first pour the water over them, and once or twice afterward. Drain and refresh under cold water, then drain thoroughly.

2 Meanwhile, assemble the rest of the salad ingredients in a bowl, keeping back a few herbs to serve. Preparing the salad vegetables over the bowl means you will capture all the juices. Pat the noodles completely dry with paper towels and add the cold, drained noodles to the bowl.

3 Whisk together the dressing ingredients and toss it through the salad. Serve, scattered with the reserved herbs.

try this....
Shrimp and mango salad

In step 2, add 12 oz (350g) cooked, peeled **shrimp** to the salad ingredients and continue as above.

NUTRITION PER SERVING	
Energy	228kcals/957kJ
Carbohydrate	48g
of which sugar	10g
Fat	0.5g
of which saturates	0.1g
Salt	0.5g
Fiber	3g

Grilled halloumi and roast tomato salad

A perfect balance of rich and fresh flavors. Halloumi is rich in protein, and will melt only at high temperatures. Soak in buttermilk if you find it too salty.

Low carb

Gluten free

SERVES 4
PREP 5 MINS
COOK 15 MINS

7oz (200g) cherry tomatoes, halved

3 tbsp olive oil

salt and freshly ground black pepper

9oz (250g) half-fat halloumi, cut into ¼in- (5mm-) thick slices

3 cloves of garlic, finely chopped

small handful of flat-leaf parsley, finely chopped

½ tsp paprika

small handful of fresh basil, roughly chopped

9oz (250g) fresh baby spinach leaves

1 Preheat the oven to 350°F (180°C). Place the tomatoes in a small roasting pan, drizzle with 1 tablespoon of the oil, and season with salt and pepper. Toss together using your hands, then roast in the oven for 15 minutes with the tomatoes sitting skin side down.

2 While they are cooking, put the halloumi, garlic, parsley, paprika, and the remaining oil into a bowl and combine well. Heat a griddle pan until hot then carefully add a slice of halloumi, letting it drain before adding it to the pan. Repeat, adding the halloumi slices one by one until they are all in the griddle pan. When you have added the last one, go back to the first one and begin turning them over to cook on the other side. They should be golden brown. When you have turned them all, go back to the first one and begin removing them from the griddle pan.

3 Put the halloumi slices back into the bowl with the garlic, herb, and spice mix and stir gently. Add the cooked tomatoes to the mix along with the basil and stir to combine so everything is well coated. Add the spinach leaves, toss together, and serve immediately on a shallow platter.

NUTRITION PER SERVING	
Energy	264kcals/1105kJ
Carbohydrate	3g
of which sugar	2g
Fat	19g
of which saturates	9g
Salt	1.7g
Fiber	1.5g

Thai-spiced lamb salad with lime dressing

The bright, vibrant colors of this spicy lamb salad really sing out, making it perfect for a summer lunch. The limes disguise the flavor of Thai fish sauce.

Dairy free

Gluten free

SERVES 4
PREP 10 MINS
COOK 7–10 MINS,
PLUS RESTING

grated zest and juice of 5 limes

3 tsp palm sugar or brown sugar

1 red chile, seeded and
    finely chopped

½ tsp Thai fish sauce

1 tsp tamarind

3 tbsp peanut oil

1lb 2oz (500g) boneless lamb
    chump or leg

3½oz (100g) Thai glass noodles,
    cooked

3 shallots, finely sliced

handful of cilantro leaves

12 Thai basil leaves

small handful of mint leaves

⅓ cup roasted peanuts,
    coarsely ground

1 For the dressing, place the lime zest and juice, sugar, chile, fish sauce, tamarind, and 1 tablespoon of oil in a small bowl. Mix to combine all the ingredients and dissolve the sugar. Set aside.

2 Cut the lamb into six equal strips. Heat a grill pan and add the remaining oil. Sear the lamb for about 2 minutes on each side. Do not overcook the lamb; it should be rare. Let rest for 3 minutes.

3 Slice the lamb thinly and place in a large bowl. Add the glass noodles, dressing, shallots, herbs, and peanuts, and toss to combine. Divide the salad between four plates and serve immediately.

NUTRITION PER SERVING	
Energy	391kcals/1636kJ
Carbohydrate	12g
of which sugar	5g
Fat	25g
of which saturates	7g
Salt	0.6g
Fiber	1.6g

Watermelon salad with feta and pumpkin seeds

This salad is fast becoming a modern classic. The sweetness of the ripe melon contrasts wonderfully with the salty feta and the nuttiness of the pumpkin seeds.

Low carb

Gluten free

SERVES 4
PREP 10 MINS
COOK 5 MINS

2oz (60g) pumpkin seeds

sea salt and freshly ground black pepper

¼ tsp chili powder

¼ cup light olive oil

juice of 1 lemon

1lb 2oz (500g) watermelon, peeled, seeded if preferred, and cut into ¾in (2cm) squares

½ red onion, finely sliced

4 large handfuls of mixed salad leaves, such as watercress, arugula, or baby spinach

10oz (300g) feta cheese, cut into ½in (1cm) squares

1 Dry-fry the pumpkin seeds for 2–3 minutes until they start to pop. Add a pinch of sea salt and the chili powder, stir, and cook for another minute. Set aside to cool.

2 In a large bowl, whisk together the oil, lemon juice, and sea salt and pepper to taste. Add the watermelon, red onion, and salad leaves, and toss well to coat with the dressing.

3 Scatter the feta cheese and the seeds over the top of the salad and serve immediately.

NUTRITION PER SERVING	
Energy	419kcals/1742kJ
Carbohydrate	13g
of which sugar	11g
Fat	33g
of which saturates	13g
Salt	2.8g
Fiber	1.8g

Orange salad with olives

Refreshing orange salads are popular in the southern Mediterranean and are served alongside stews and grilled meat or fish.

Low carb

Low saturated fat

Dairy free

Gluten free

SERVES 4
PREP 15–20 MINS

1 small-medium red onion, thinly sliced

2 ripe oranges

8–10 black olives

juice and finely grated zest of ½ lemon

2 tbsp fruity olive oil

salt and freshly ground black pepper

a few leaves of arugula (optional)

1 Place the onion in a bowl of cold water. Using a sharp knife, remove the peel and pith from the oranges and slice thinly.

2 Place the oranges in a shallow serving dish. Drain the onion slices, place on a double layer of paper towels, and pat dry. Arrange the slices on the oranges. Scatter the olives on top.

3 In a small cup, combine the lemon juice and zest and the oil. Season to taste and drizzle over the salad. If you like, scatter with the arugula. Let stand for 5 minutes before serving.

NUTRITION PER SERVING	
Energy	97kcals/406kJ
Carbohydrate	8g
of which sugar	7g
Fat	6.5g
of which saturates	1g
Salt	2g
Fiber	1.6g

Fennel salad

This pretty fennel and peach salad from the French Riviera makes a refreshing appetizer on a hot summer day. Peaches contain Vitamins A, C, E, and K, plus six B vitamins.

| Low carb |
| Low saturated fat |
| Gluten free |
| Low salt |

SERVES 4
PREP 15–20 MINS

2 small fennel bulbs, trimmed at the bottom and very thinly sliced

juice and finely grated zest of ½ lemon

1 tbsp extra virgin olive oil

salt and freshly ground black pepper

2 ripe peaches or nectarines, halved, cored, and sliced

1 tbsp chopped flat-leaf parsley

½ tbsp chopped mint leaves

1 slice of cured ham (about ¼in–½in/ 5mm–1cm thick), such as prosciutto crudo, Serrano, or smoked ham, diced

1 In a shallow bowl, toss the fennel with the lemon juice and zest, oil, and a little salt. Add the peaches or nectarines, sprinkle with half the herbs, and season with pepper. Toss lightly.

2 Arrange on a serving platter. Scatter the ham and the remaining herbs over the top. Serve immediately.

NUTRITION PER SERVING	
Energy	78kcals/326kJ
Carbohydrate	7g
of which sugar	6.5g
Fat	3.5g
of which saturates	0.5g
Salt	0.3g
Fiber	4g

Swiss chard and sweet potato salad

Fiber-rich Swiss chard's slightly bitter taste fades with cooking, and marries well with the sweet potato in this recipe. This also makes a great side dish.

Low saturated fat

Dairy free

Low salt

SERVES 4
PREP 5–10 MINS
COOK 25 MINS

1 tbsp olive oil, plus extra to drizzle

2 shallots, peeled and finely chopped

1 tsp coriander seeds, crushed

1 chile, seeded and finely chopped

2 garlic cloves, minced

2 large sweet potatoes, peeled and cubed

9oz (250g) Swiss chard, stalks removed and finely chopped, and leaves finely sliced

salt and freshly ground black pepper

1 Heat the olive oil with a tablespoon of water over low heat in a medium saucepan with a lid. Add the shallots and coriander seeds and cook, stirring occasionally, until the shallots soften.

2 Add the chile and garlic, and cook for 1 minute. Add the sweet potato and cook over medium heat for about 5 minutes, adding a dash of water if necessary. Then add the chopped chard stalks, cover with the lid, and cook for 10 minutes.

3 When the sweet potato is almost cooked, add the shredded chard leaves, cover, and let wilt for about 3 minutes. Season with salt and pepper, drizzle over a few drops of olive oil, and serve.

try this....
Pumpkin, spinach, and feta salad

Toss 1lb 5oz (600g) diced **butternut squash** with 2 tablespoons olive oil, then season with salt, pepper, and **red pepper flakes**. Roast at 400°F (200°C) for 20 minutes, or until soft. Leave to cool, then mix with 2 handfuls of **baby spinach**, 1 handful of coarsely chopped **almonds**, and 7oz (200g) crumbled **reduced-fat feta**.

NUTRITION PER SERVING	
Energy	194cals/823kJ
Carbohydrate	33g
of which sugar	9g
Fat	6g
of which saturates	1g
Salt	0.5g
Fiber	5g

Greek salad

A classic, deeply refreshing combination that needs very ripe, flavorful tomatoes. Make sure you use very tasty, pungent black olives, and an aromatic, strong extra virgin olive oil.

Low carb

Gluten free

Low salt

SERVES 6–8
PREP 25–30 MINS,
PLUS STANDING

2 small cucumbers

2½lb (1kg) tomatoes

1 red onion

2 green bell peppers, cored, seeded, and cubed

4½oz (125g) Kalamata or other Greek olives

6oz (175g) feta cheese, cubed

FOR THE HERB VINAIGRETTE

3 tbsp red wine vinegar

salt and freshly ground black pepper

½ cup extra virgin olive oil

3–5 sprigs of mint, leaves picked and finely chopped

3–5 sprigs of oregano, leaves picked and finely chopped

7–10 sprigs of parsley, leaves picked and finely chopped

1 To make the vinaigrette, whisk together the vinegar, salt, and pepper. Gradually whisk in the oil, so the vinaigrette emulsifies and thickens slightly. Add the herbs, then whisk again and taste for seasoning.

2 Peel the cucumbers and cut each in half lengthwise. Scoop out the seeds with a teaspoon. Discard the seeds. Cut the cucumbers lengthwise into 2–3 strips, then into ½in (1cm) slices.

3 With the tip of a small knife, core the tomatoes. Cut each one into eight wedges, then cut each wedge in half. Peel and trim the red onion and cut into very thin rings. Gently separate the concentric circles within each ring with your fingers.

4 Put the cucumbers, tomatoes, onion rings, and peppers in a large bowl. Briskly whisk the dressing, pour it over, and toss thoroughly. Add the olives (they may be either left whole or pitted) and feta and gently toss again. Taste for seasoning. Allow the flavors to mellow for about 30 minutes before serving.

NUTRITION PER SERVING

Energy	211kcals/883kJ
Carbohydrate	7.5g
of which sugar	7g
Fat	17g
of which saturates	5g
Salt	1g
Fiber	3.5g

Shrimp, sweet chili, and Greek yogurt wraps

Sweet, fresh-tasting pea shoots, juicy shrimp, and sharp yogurt make a wonderful combination. Pea shoots are a rich source of Vitamins A and C and folic acid.

Low saturated fat

Low salt

SERVES 4
PREP 10 MINS

4 large wraps

1¾oz (50g) pea shoots, mixed baby salad leaves, or arugula

½ cucumber, halved, seeded, and finely sliced

6oz (175g) package of cooked, shelled large shrimp, sliced in half horizontally and deveined

3 heaping tbsp Greek yogurt

4 tsp Thai sweet chili sauce

salt and freshly ground black pepper

FOR A GLUTEN-FREE OPTION
use gluten-free wraps

1 Lay the wraps on a work surface and divide the pea shoots between them, starting at the edge nearest you and covering about one-third of the wrap. Layer one-quarter of the cucumber, then the shrimp, along the pea shoots, and top each with ½ tbsp of yogurt and 1 tsp of chili sauce. Season.

2 Take the remaining yogurt and smear a little, with the back of a spoon, all over the piece of each wrap farthest from you (it should cover one-third of the wrap). This helps it stick together.

3 Fold the side nearest to you over the filling. Roll it away from you until it sticks together with the yogurt. Slice each end off and halve on a diagonal to serve, or pack for transportation.

try this....
Crab and spicy tomato wraps

Replace the shrimp with 7oz (200g) flaked **white crabmeat** and replace the yogurt with fresh **tomato salsa**. Serve with a dip made from 7oz (200g) **2% fat Greek yogurt**, diced **cucumber**, and 1 crushed **garlic clove**.

NUTRITION PER SERVING	
Energy	249kcals/1054kJ
Carbohydrate	43g
of which sugar	5g
Fat	2g
of which saturates	1g
Salt	1.2g
Fiber	3g

Double-decker turkey and avocado sandwiches

Layering a sandwich is an easy way to make it more attractive. Use wholegrain, multigrain bread for the highest fiber content.

SERVES 4
PREP 10 MINS

3 heaping tbsp good-quality mayonnaise

1 heaping tsp Dijon mustard

salt and freshly ground black pepper

butter, softened, for spreading

12 large slices of multigrain bread

2 handfuls of salad leaves

5½oz (150g) thinly sliced turkey breast

2 avocados, thinly sliced

½ lemon

1 Mix the mayonnaise and mustard together and season well. Butter eight slices of bread on one side only, and four slices carefully on both sides.

2 Lay four of the single-side-buttered slices on a cutting board, buttered sides up. Top each slice with one-quarter of the salad leaves, pressing them into the bread gently. Lay one-quarter of the turkey on top of each and spread with a thin layer of the mayonnaise.

3 Put a double-side-buttered slice of bread on each sandwich, then layer one-quarter of the avocado over each, drizzle with a little lemon juice, and season well.

4 Top each with a final slice of bread, buttered side down, and press down well to hold everything together. Carefully trim the crusts off the bread and cut into halves on a diagonal to serve, or pack into a container for transportation.

NUTRITION PER SERVING	
Energy	614kcals/2572kJ
Carbohydrate	55g
of which sugar	4g
Fat	32g
of which saturates	9g
Salt	2g
Fiber	10g

Crayfish panini with herbed mayonnaise

Crayfish is low in fat and a good source of selenium and zinc. Its mild flavor makes a good foil for the strong herbs.

SERVES 4
PREP 15 MINS

2¼lb (1kg) cooked crayfish tails

4 Italian-style crusty bread rolls

1 head oakleaf or other butter lettuce, leaves separated

2 fresh peaches, pitted and sliced

FOR THE HERBED MAYONNAISE

½ cup mayonnaise

juice of 1 lime

small handful of fresh cilantro, chopped

small handful of fresh mint leaves, chopped

small handful of fresh chives, chopped

1 anchovy fillet in olive oil, drained and minced

freshly ground black pepper

1 Remove all the meat from the crayfish tails, leaving it in large chunks, if possible. Divide into four equal portions and set aside.

2 To make the herbed mayonnaise, combine the mayonnaise, lime juice, herbs, and anchovy in a bowl. Season with pepper and stir to blend well.

3 Slice the rolls in half, but without cutting all the way through. Open them up and spread with the herbed mayonnaise. Arrange some of the lettuce leaves over the rolls, then put the crayfish on top. Arrange peach slices between the crayfish, then spoon a little more of the mayonnaise over the top. Close up the rolls and serve immediately

NUTRITION PER SERVING	
Energy	527kcals/2204kJ
Carbohydrate	38g
of which sugar	8g
Fat	27g
of which saturates	4g
Salt	1.2g
Fiber	4g

Spicy turkey burgers

Turkey is an excellent source of selenium, iron, zinc, and B vitamins. It spoils quickly, so store it in the refrigerator after shaping the burgers.

Low saturated fat

Low salt

SERVES 4
PREP 15 MINS,
PLUS CHILLING
COOK 10 MINS

14oz (400g) ground turkey

⅓ cup fresh white bread crumbs

1 tbsp sweet chili sauce

4 scallions, white part only, finely sliced

¼ cup finely chopped cilantro leaves

¾in (2cm) fresh ginger, finely grated

1 red chile, seeded and finely chopped

salt and freshly ground black pepper

TO SERVE
4 hamburger buns

lettuce

tomato

finely sliced red onions

mayonnaise

Greek yogurt

sweet chili sauce

1 Prepare the grill for cooking. In a large bowl, mix together all the ingredients until well combined.

2 With damp hands (to help keep the mixture from sticking to your fingers), divide the mixture into four balls and roll each one between your palms until smooth. Flatten each ball out to a large, fat disk, 1in (3cm) high, and pat the edges in to tidy them up. Place the burgers on a plate, cover with plastic wrap, and chill for 30 minutes (this helps them keep their shape while cooking).

3 Cook over a hot grill for 6–7 minutes, turning as needed, until the meat is springy to the touch and the edges charred.

4 Serve with a selection of buns and accompaniments, and let everyone build their own burgers.

NUTRITION PER SERVING	
Energy	244kcals/1027kJ
Carbohydrate	16g
of which sugar	2.5g
Fat	7g
of which saturates	3g
Salt	0.5g
Fiber	0.8g

Zucchini and pea mini tortillas

Bursting with fresh green summer vegetables, these mini tortillas make a great appetizer. Alternatively, for a tasty packed lunch, simply wrap them in foil for transportation.

Dairy free

Low salt

MAKES 20
PREP 20 MINS
COOK 5 MINS

3 zucchini, grated

2oz (50g) baby spinach leaves

grated zest and juice of 1 lemon

9oz (250g) peas (shelled weight)

2oz (50g) pine nuts, toasted

salt and freshly ground
  black pepper

10 flour tortillas, halved

2 tbsp reduced-fat mayonnaise

large handful of snow peas

large handful of pea shoots

FOR A GLUTEN-FREE OPTION
use gluten-free tortillas

1 In a large bowl, mix the zucchini, spinach, lemon zest and juice, peas, and pine nuts together. Season well.

2 Heat a frying pan over high heat. Place two tortilla halves in the pan at a time and heat for 15 seconds on each side. Cover the heated tortillas with a paper towel to keep warm.

3 Brush one of the tortilla halves with mayonnaise. Place a little of the filling in the center. Arrange some snow peas and pea shoots on top, so that they stick out at one end, then roll up the tortilla. Repeat to make 20 mini tortillas.

try this....
Carrot and red pepper hummus tortilla

Grate 2 large **carrots**, mix with 10oz (300g) **red pepper hummus**. Heat the tortilla as suggested in step 2. Spread a little of the hummus mixture over 1 tortilla, top with a handful of pea shoots or **watercress**, and then roll. Repeat with the remaining tortilla.

NUTRITION PER SERVING	
Energy	144kcals/602kJ
Carbohydrate	20g
of which sugar	1g
Fat	5g
of which saturates	2g
Salt	0.5g
Fiber	2.5g

Falafel

Using a can of chickpeas, instead of dried chickpeas soaked in advance, will give you all the flavor with none of the fuss in this Middle Eastern classic.

MAKES 12
PREP 25 MINS, PLUS
SOAKING AND STANDING
COOK 15 MINS

1 x 14oz (400g) can of chickpeas

1 tbsp tahini

1 garlic clove, crushed

1 tsp salt

1 tsp ground cumin

1 tsp turmeric

1 tsp ground coriander

½ tsp cayenne pepper

2 tbsp finely chopped flat-leaf parsley

juice of 1 small lemon

vegetable oil, for frying

1 Drain the soaked chickpeas and place them in a food processor with the remaining ingredients. Process until finely chopped but not puréed.

2 Transfer the mixture to a bowl and set aside for at least 30 minutes (and up to 8 hours), covered, in the refrigerator.

3 Wet your hands and shape the mixture into 12 balls. Press down slightly to flatten.

4 Heat 2in (5cm) of oil in a deep pan or wok. Fry the balls in batches for 3–4 minutes, or until lightly golden. Drain on paper towels and serve immediately.

NUTRITION PER SERVING	
Energy	162kcals/678kJ
Carbohydrate	21g
of which sugar	2g
Fat	5.5g
of which saturates	1.5g
Salt	0.8g
Fiber	2.3g

Ostrich burgers

A lean alternative to the beef burger, served with savory ingredients that complement the richness of the meat.

SERVES 4
PREP 15 MINS,
PLUS CHILLING
COOK 10 MINS

1¾lb (800g) ground ostrich meat

1 onion, finely chopped

2 tbsp chopped flat-leaf parsley

1 tbsp capers, drained and chopped

4 anchovy fillets, chopped

salt and freshly ground black pepper

FOR A GLUTEN-FREE OPTION
use gluten-free hamburger buns, mustard, and pickles

1 Place all the ingredients in a large bowl, season well, and mix to combine. Divide the meat mixture into four equal-sized balls and gently flatten to make patties. Chill the patties in the refrigerator for at least 1 hour to help firm them up.

2 Cook the patties on a hot grill or a griddle pan for 2 minutes on each side for medium-rare, or reduce the heat and cook for about 5 minutes, on each side, for well-done. Do not cook the patties for long over high heat since they will dry out fast. Serve with hamburger buns, mustard, and pickles.

NUTRITION PER SERVING	
Energy	269kcals/1126kJ
Carbohydrate	2.5g
of which sugar	2g
Fat	9g
of which saturates	4g
Salt	0.9g
Fiber	0.7g

Roast beet, goat cheese, and arugula sandwiches

These are fabulous for a picnic or packed lunch, or try them at home with toasted bread instead. Beets provide several nutrients, notably folic acid and potassium.

SERVES 4
PREP 10 MINS
COOK 20 MINS

4 small beets, approx. 2½oz (75g) each, peeled and sliced ¼in (5mm) thick

1 tbsp olive oil

salt and freshly ground black pepper

8 large slices sourdough or other rustic bread

butter, softened, for spreading

7oz (200g) soft goat cheese

2 handfuls of arugula leaves

1 Preheat the oven to 400°F (200°C). Place the beet slices on a baking sheet, brush them with the olive oil, and season them well. Bake them at the top of the oven for 20 minutes, turning once, until they are lightly browned and cooked through. Remove them from the oven and set aside to cool.

2 Spread the slices of bread with butter on one side only. Spread four slices with one-quarter each of the goat cheese, season with a little pepper, then add a layer of the cooled beet slices.

3 Top the beets with a layer of the arugula and finish the sandwich with a final slice of bread, buttered side down. Cut in half to serve, or pack into a container for transportation.

NUTRITION PER SERVING

Energy	436kcals/1832kJ
Carbohydrate	41g
of which sugar	8g
Fat	22g
of which saturates	12g
Salt	2g
Fiber	4.5g

White bean purée, alfalfa, and carrot pita pockets

A delicious mix of moist softness and crunch makes these portable pockets ideal to pack for lunch.

Low saturated fat

Dairy free

High fiber

SERVES 4

PREP 15 MINS

- 1 x 14oz (400g) can of cannellini beans, drained and rinsed (reserve 2 tbsp of the liquid)
- 2 large garlic cloves, crushed
- 2 heaping tbsp finely chopped flat-leaf parsley leaves
- 1 tbsp olive oil
- ¼ tsp salt
- freshly ground black pepper
- 2 tbsp lemon juice
- 4 whole wheat pita breads
- 1 large carrot, coarsely grated
- 1¾oz (50g) alfalfa shoots or other shoots

1 To make the bean purée, put the beans, garlic, parsley, olive oil, salt, pepper, lemon juice, and 1 tablespoon of the bean liquid into a food processor and process to a rough paste. If it is too thick, add another tablespoon of the liquid (but remember this needs to be a thick paste to hold up well in the pita bread).

2 Cut each pita in half and open to make eight small pockets. Spread a layer of bean purée on both inside faces of the pockets.

3 Sprinkle a little carrot and alfalfa into each. Serve layered on top of each other with the stuffing showing, or pack into a container for transportation.

NUTRITION PER SERVING	
Energy	287kcals/1203kJ
Carbohydrate	45g
of which sugar	6.5g
Fat	5g
of which saturates	0.7g
Salt	1.8g
Fiber	12g

Deluxe peanut butter sandwiches

This "dressed-up" version of the popular peanut butter and jelly sandwich makes a nutritious, delicious snack. Marmalade is high in sugar but relatively low-calorie.

Dairy free

SERVES 4
PREP 10 MINS

½ cup creamy or chunky peanut butter

2 tbsp orange marmalade

3 ripe medium bananas

8 slices whole wheat bread, toasted

1 In a small bowl, combine the peanut butter and marmalade until well mixed. Peel the bananas and cut them in half lengthwise, and then crosswise in half to make twelve pieces total.

2 Spread the peanut butter equally over four slices of toast. Top each with 3 pieces of banana, and top with remaining toast.

3 Cut each sandwich in half diagonally, if you like.

NUTRITION PER SERVING	
Energy	458kcals/1916kJ
Carbohydrate	53g
of which sugar	21g
Fat	17g
of which saturates	3g
Salt	1g
Fiber	9g

Stuffed ciabatta with grilled vegetables

This is incredibly tasty and simple to transport, and will easily feed a family of four.

SERVES 4
PREP 10 MINS, PLUS CHILLING
COOK 15 MINS, PLUS COOLING

½ eggplant, cut into ½in (1cm) slices

2 zucchini, cut into ½in (1cm) slices

4–6 tbsp olive oil

salt and freshly ground black pepper

1 large beefsteak tomato

1 ciabatta loaf

2 roasted red bell peppers from a jar, drained, and sliced

ball of mozzarella, approx. 4½oz (125g), thinly sliced

handful of basil leaves

1 Preheat a large grill pan or a broiler to its highest setting. Brush the slices of eggplant and zucchini on both sides with olive oil and season them well. Either grill or broil them for 2–4 minutes each side, until they are charred in places and cooked through. Put them on a large plate in a single layer to cool.

2 Slice about ½in (1cm) off each end of the tomato, reserving these pieces. Slice the remaining tomato as thinly as possible.

3 Cut the ciabatta in half, leaving a hinge so you can open it out flat. Drizzle both sides with a little olive oil. Take the ends of the tomato and rub both sides of the bread with the cut side, to soften and flavor the bread, then discard the ends.

4 Cover one side of the loaf with the eggplant, zucchini, and red bell peppers, then top with mozzarella. Sprinkle with the basil, season, then add the tomato.

5 Close the loaf and press down on it hard. Wrap it very tightly in plastic wrap, going around it a few times until it is completely covered and compressed. Leave in the refrigerator with a weight (such as a cutting board and some cans) on top for at least 4 hours, turning once. Unwrap and slice to serve, or transport wrapped and slice at a picnic.

NUTRITION PER SERVING	
Energy	435kcals/1812kJ
Carbohydrate	36g
of which sugar	4g
Fat	25g
of which saturates	6.5g
Salt	1.2g
Fiber	8g

MAINS

Lean meat

Plant-based

Wholesome pastas

Fish

Seafood

Sushi and ceviche

Grains as mains

Harissa-spiced lamb chops

Spice up some lamb chops with Moroccan-inspired seasoning, add mashed chickpeas and chopped tomatoes tossed with olive oil and balsamic vinegar, and you've got a tasty feast on the table in less than half an hour.

Dairy free

High fiber

SERVES 4
PREP 5 MINS
COOK 15–20 MINS

FOR THE LAMB

8 x 3½oz (100g) lamb loin
  chops

1 cup fresh white bread
  crumbs

finely grated zest
  of 1 lemon

1 tbsp harissa paste

2 tbsp finely chopped
  cilantro leaves

2 tsp olive oil

salt and freshly ground
  black pepper

FOR THE CHICKPEA MASH

1 tbsp olive oil

1 red onion, finely chopped

2 garlic cloves,
  finely chopped

2 x 14oz (400g) cans
  chickpeas, drained
  and rinsed

1½ tbsp lemon juice

2 tbsp extra virgin olive oil

2 tbsp finely chopped
  cilantro leaves

tomato salad, to serve

FOR A GLUTEN-FREE OPTION
use gluten-free bread crumbs

1 Preheat the broiler to its medium setting. Place the chops on a foil-lined baking sheet and broil on one side for 8 minutes.

2 While the chops are broiling, place the bread crumbs, zest, harissa, cilantro, and olive oil in a bowl, season with salt and pepper, and stir well to combine evenly.

3 Turn the chops when ready, and press the bread crumb and harissa mixture onto the uncooked side of each chop. Broil for another 8 minutes.

4 Meanwhile, make the chickpea mash. Heat the oil in a saucepan over medium heat, add the onion, and cook for 5 minutes. Add the garlic and cook for 2 minutes. Stir in the chickpeas, lemon juice, and extra virgin olive oil, and gently heat.

5 Remove from the heat and mash roughly with a potato masher; it should not be smooth. Stir in the cilantro and season generously. Serve the chops with the chickpea mash and a dressed tomato salad.

NUTRITION PER SERVING	
Energy	594kcals/2489kJ
Carbohydrate	31g
of which sugar	2.5g
Fat	30g
of which saturates	9g
Salt	1.3g
Fiber	8g

Lamb kebabs with yogurt and pomegranate

These Greek-inspired kebabs are easy to make and are traditionally served with a refreshing yogurt dressing.

SERVES 4
PREP 30 MINS,
PLUS MARINATING
COOK 10 MINS

12oz (350g) lean lamb shoulder, cut into cubes

½ tsp ground cumin

½ tsp ground coriander

½ tsp garam masala

¼ tsp ground cinnamon

olive oil, for brushing

seeds from 1 pomegranate, to serve

FOR THE DRESSING

1 shallot, finely chopped

1 garlic clove, chopped

1 tbsp chopped mint

½ cucumber, peeled, seeded, and chopped

1¼ cup Greek-style yogurt

pinch of salt

1 Place the lamb in a large bowl. Add the cumin, coriander, garam masala, and cinnamon to the bowl and mix to coat the meat in the spices. Leave to marinate for 30 minutes.

2 For the dressing, place the shallots, garlic, mint, cucumber, and yogurt in a large serving bowl. Add the salt, mix well to combine, and set aside.

3 Heat a large heavy-bottomed frying pan or a grill pan. Divide the lamb cubes into four equal portions and thread them onto four skewers. Brush the pan with a little oil and grill the meat for 8 minutes, turning regularly, until well-browned.

4 Remove from the heat. Sprinkle over the pomegranate seeds, remove the kebabs from the skewers, and transfer to a serving platter. Serve with a dollop of the yogurt dressing, couscous, and pita bread.

NUTRITION PER SERVING	
Energy	280kcals/1172kJ
Carbohydrate	7g
of which sugar	6.5g
Fat	18g
of which saturates	8.5g
Salt	0.5g
Fiber	1.5g

Spicy lamb and feta meatballs

These are good with rice or couscous, or even wrapped up with salad in a tortilla for a quick lunch.

Low carb

Low salt

SERVES 4
PREP 10 MINS, PLUS CHILLING
COOK 10 MINS

14oz (400g) ground lamb

½ cup fresh white bread crumbs

1 large egg, beaten

1 tsp ground cumin

1 tsp paprika

handful of mint leaves, finely chopped

salt and freshly ground black pepper

2oz (60g) crumbled feta cheese

2 tbsp sunflower or vegetable oil

couscous, to serve

1 Mix together the ground lamb, bread crumbs, egg, spices, and mint, and season well. Gently mix in the feta cheese. Cover and chill for 30 minutes.

2 With damp hands, shape walnut-sized balls with the lamb mixture.

3 Heat the oil in a large frying pan and cook the meatballs over medium heat for 5–7 minutes, until browned all over and cooked through. Serve with couscous.

NUTRITION PER SERVING	
Energy	350kcals/1455kJ
Carbohydrate	9g
of which sugar	0.5g
Fat	24g
of which saturates	9g
Salt	1g
Fiber	0.5g

Marinated lamb chops with broccoli in lemon juice

This meal is simplicity itself. The marinade is quick to prepare, and you can leave it to flavor the lamb for as much, or as little, time as you have.

Low carb

Dairy free

Low salt

SERVES 4
PREP 5 MINS, PLUS MARINATING
COOK 30 MINS

4 lean lamb loin chops, excess
 fat removed

sea salt and freshly ground black pepper

handful of fresh rosemary sprigs

1 head broccoli, about 1lb (450g),
 florets and stems chopped small

juice of 1 lemon

pinch of crushed red pepper flakes

mint jelly, to serve

FOR THE MARINADE

2 tbsp sherry vinegar, cider vinegar,
 or white wine vinegar

pinch of sugar

splash of dark soy sauce

FOR A GLUTEN-FREE OPTION

use gluten-free tamari to replace
 dark soy sauce

1 First, prepare the marinade. Mix together the vinegar, sugar, and dark soy sauce, then pour over the lamb. Let marinate at room temperature for at least 5 minutes, or up to 2 hours if time permits.

2 Preheat the oven to 400°F (200°C). Place the lamb chops in a roasting pan, season well with salt and pepper, and add the rosemary sprigs. Roast in the oven for 20–30 minutes until cooked to your liking.

3 While the lamb is cooking, add the broccoli to a pan of boiling salted water and cook for about 10 minutes until soft. Drain, keeping the broccoli in the pan, then mash gently with a fork. Now squeeze in the lemon juice and stir in the pepper flakes, a pinch of salt, and some black pepper. Serve immediately with the lamb chops and a dollop of mint jelly on the side.

NUTRITION PER SERVING	
Energy	258kcals/1079kJ
Carbohydrate	2g
of which sugar	2g
Fat	13g
of which saturates	5g
Salt	0.5g
Fiber	2.5g

Grilled lamb with tomato salsa

Chermoula is a classic North African marinade for seafood, but it also pairs well with grilled meats. In Morocco, it is used liberally in tagines.

Low carb

Dairy free

Gluten free

SERVES 6

PREP 15 MINS, PLUS MARINATING

COOK 15 MINS

12 lamb cutlets, trimmed

salt and freshly ground black pepper

4 ripe plum tomatoes, chopped

1 tbsp olive oil

1 tbsp balsamic vinegar

cilantro leaves, chopped, to garnish

small bunch of mint leaves, chopped, to garnish

FOR THE MARINADE

2–3 garlic cloves, chopped

1 red chile, seeded and chopped

1 tsp coarse salt

small bunch of cilantro, chopped

small bunch of flat-leaf parsley, chopped

2 tsp ground cumin

1 tsp paprika

4–5 tbsp olive oil

juice of 1 lemon

1 For the marinade, place the garlic, red chile, and coarse salt in a mortar and pestle and pound until they form a paste. Add the cilantro and parsley and pound to a coarse paste. Add the cumin and paprika, then pour in the oil and lemon juice. Mix well.

2 Place the cutlets in a dish. Rub the marinade over the lamb and marinate for 30 minutes.

3 Season the tomatoes and drizzle with the olive oil, balsamic vinegar, cilantro, and mint. Set aside.

4 Preheat the broiler to its highest setting. Remove the cutlets from the marinade and broil for 5 minutes on each side, or until cooked through and crisp. Serve the lamb with the tomato salad on the side.

NUTRITION PER SERVING	
Energy	325kcals/1360kJ
Carbohydrate	2.5g
of which sugar	2.5g
Fat	21g
of which saturates	6.5g
Salt	1.1g
Fiber	0.7g

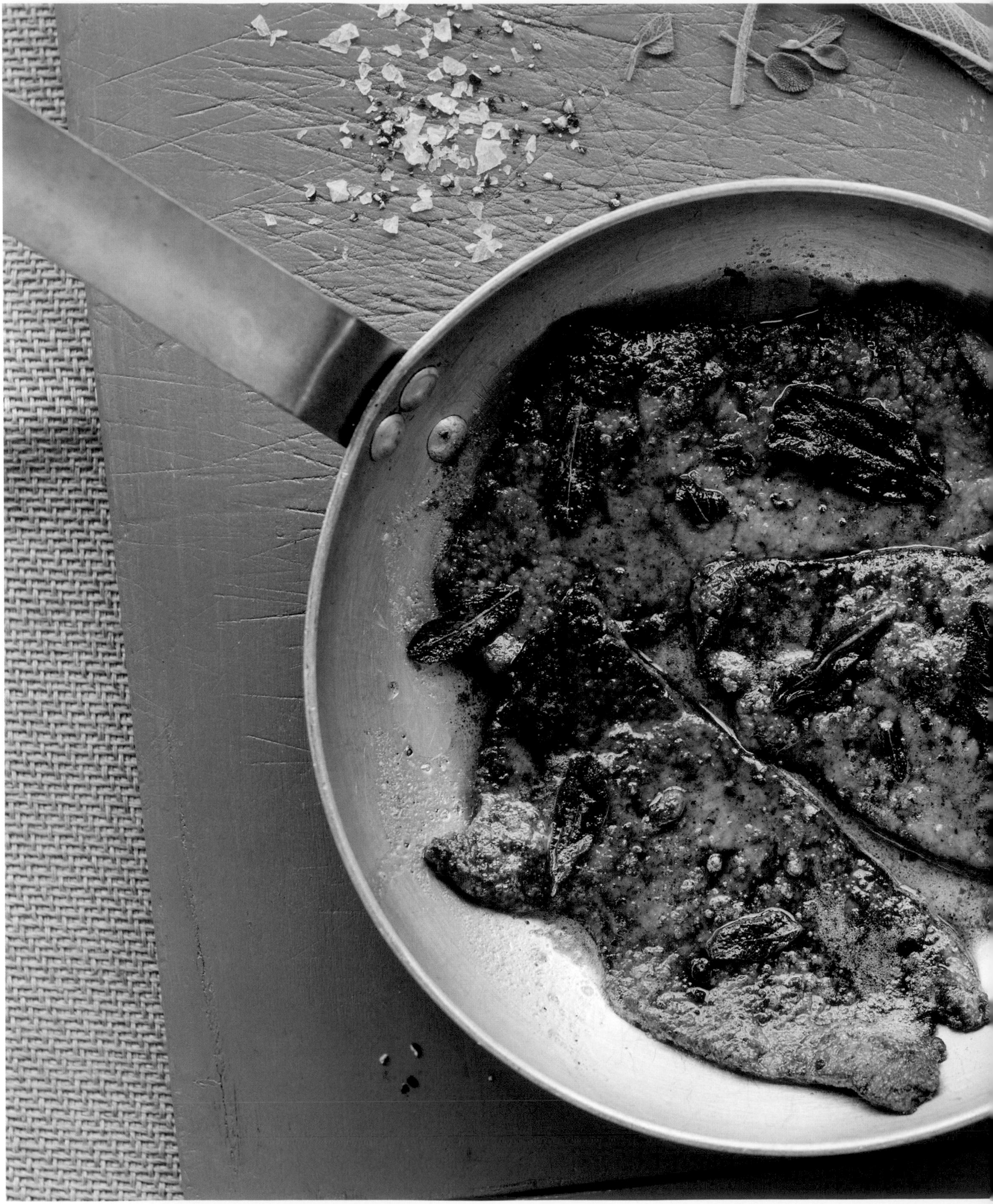

Calf's liver with sage

The aroma of sage leaves permeates the quickly cooked liver in this classic dish. Replace the lemon juice with balsamic vinegar for a sweet and sour twist. Serve immediately—liver is tender when hot.

Low carb

Low salt

SERVES 4
PREP 15 MINS
COOK 5 MINS

2 tbsp all-purpose flour, seasoned with salt and pepper

1lb (450g) calf's liver, trimmed and sliced

1 tsp olive oil

1 tbsp butter, plus a pat of butter extra

handful of sage leaves

juice of 1 lemon

1 Place the flour in a shallow dish. Add the liver, toss to coat lightly, and shake off any excess.

2 Heat the oil and 1 tablespoon of butter in a large frying pan over medium-high heat. As the butter starts to foam, add the liver, making sure the pieces do not touch, and cook for about 2 minutes on each side. Do this in batches to avoid overcrowding the pan. Remove the liver from the pan, place on a serving dish, and keep warm.

3 Reduce the heat and add a pat of butter to the pan. Then add the sage leaves and, as soon as they start to sizzle, add the lemon juice.

4 Place the sage leaves over the liver, pour in the buttery juices, and serve hot.

NUTRITION PER SERVING

Energy	206kcals/862kJ
Carbohydrate	6g
of which sugar	0.1g
Fat	11g
of which saturates	4g
Salt	0.3g
Fiber	0.3g

Veal scaloppine with salsa verde

A typical Italian dish, it is traditionally served with salsa verde—a simple sauce that goes well with meat, fish, and vegetables. Try experimenting with different herbs.

Gluten free

SERVES 4
PREP 15–20 MINS
COOK 5 MINS,
PLUS RESTING

4 x 6¼oz (180g) veal sirloin medallions

8 slices prosciutto

12 sage leaves

freshly ground black pepper

2 tbsp unsalted butter

a dash of olive oil (optional)

FOR THE SALSA

3 tbsp finely chopped flat-leaf parsley

grated zest and juice of 1 small lemon

2 tbsp capers, drained and rinsed, if in salt, and finely chopped

2 garlic cloves, crushed

⅔ cup olive oil

½ tsp Dijon mustard

sea salt

1 Place the veal between two sheets of plastic wrap and flatten slightly using a rolling pin or mallet. Remove from the plastic wrap and set aside. Spread out two slices of prosciutto on a plate and top with three sage leaves. Place the veal on top of the sage leaves and season with pepper. Wrap the prosciutto around the veal and repeat with each medallion.

2 Meanwhile, for the salsa, place the parsley, lemon zest, capers, and garlic in a bowl. Add the lemon juice, oil, and mustard. Toss well to coat, and taste and adjust the seasoning, if needed.

3 Heat the butter in a large frying pan. Add the veal, and when the butter starts to foam, cook until golden on both sides. Add the oil, if required. Let the veal rest for 2 minutes and serve with the salsa verde.

NUTRITION PER SERVING	
Energy	541kcals/2265kJ
Carbohydrate	0.4g
of which sugar	0.1g
Fat	39g
of which saturates	10g
Salt	1.6g
Fiber	0g

Pork steaks with fried apples

A super-quick, tasty meal; the fried apples make a near-instant accompaniment to the pork.

SERVES 4
PREP 5 MINS
COOK 15 MINS

4 x 3½oz (100g) boneless
  pork chops

salt and freshly ground black pepper

2 tbsp olive oil

1 tbsp butter

4 small apples, peeled, cored,
  and quartered

1 tbsp lemon juice

½ tsp granulated sugar

1 Season the pork well with salt and pepper. Heat 1 tablespoon of the oil in a large frying pan and cook the pork for 3–5 minutes on each side, depending on thickness, until cooked through. Set it aside, loosely covered in foil to keep it warm.

2 Add the remaining 1 tablespoon of oil and the butter to the pan and allow it to bubble up. Add the apple pieces, pour in the lemon juice, sprinkle with the sugar, and season with salt and pepper.

3 Cook the apples over medium heat for 5–7 minutes, turning occasionally, until they soften and start to caramelize. Turn them gently using 2 spatulas, so the pieces don't break up. Serve each pork steak topped with one-quarter of the apples.

NUTRITION PER SERVING

Energy	255kcals/1073kJ
Carbohydrate	13g
of which sugar	13g
Fat	12.5g
of which saturates	4g
Salt	0.3g
Fiber	3g

Cinnamon and ginger beef with noodles

A quick dish with punchy flavors. Cinnamon and ginger, both from China, have a reputation for health benefits that science is now investigating.

Low saturated fat

Dairy free

SERVES 4
PREP 10 MINS
COOK 15 MINS

1lb 2oz (500g) lean steak, thinly sliced

2 tsp ground cinnamon

1 tbsp sunflower oil

1 onion, sliced

2in (5cm) piece of fresh ginger, peeled and shredded

1 red chile, seeded and finely chopped

2 garlic cloves, finely chopped

1 tbsp fish sauce

1 tbsp sesame oil

7oz (200g) mixed exotic mushrooms, such as oyster, shiitake, and hon shimeji, trimmed or chopped

7oz (200g) snow peas

14oz (400g) medium or thick straight-to-wok udon noodles

FOR A GLUTEN-FREE OPTION
use gluten-free noodles

1 Put the steak in a bowl, sprinkle over the cinnamon, and stir to coat. Heat the sunflower oil in a wok, add the onion, and stir-fry over high heat for 1 minute. Add the ginger and chile and stir-fry for another minute.

2 Now add the steak, garlic, fish sauce, and sesame oil and continue to cook, stirring, until the meat is no longer pink. Add the mushrooms and snow peas and continue to stir-fry for another 1–2 minutes.

3 Add the noodles and stir-fry for about 3 minutes until the noodles become sticky. Serve immediately.

NUTRITION PER SERVING

Energy	378kcals/1584kJ
Carbohydrate	33g
of which sugar	2.5g
Fat	12g
of which saturates	3g
Salt	1.2g
Fiber	2.2g

Wasabi beef and bok choy

Wasabi has antibacterial, antimicrobial, and antiparasitic qualities. Little wonder that the Japanese have cultivated it for thousands of years.

Low carb

Low salt

SERVES 4
PREP 10 MINS
COOK 10 MINS

2 tbsp olive oil

2 tsp wasabi paste

4 sirloin steaks, about 7oz (200g) each

7oz (200g) bok choy, cut lengthwise into 8 pieces

5 garlic cloves, finely chopped

1 tbsp dark soy sauce

sea salt and freshly ground black pepper

FOR A GLUTEN-FREE OPTION
use gluten-free tamari to replace dark soy sauce

1 Heat the barbecue grill until it is hot and any flames have subsided. Mix together 1 tbsp of the olive oil and the wasabi paste. Use the mixture to coat the sirloin steaks thinly and evenly.

2 Put the steaks on the barbecue and grill over high heat for about 3 minutes on each side. Transfer to a plate and leave to rest in a warm place for 5 minutes.

3 Meanwhile, toss the bok choy in the remaining olive oil with the garlic and soy sauce. Grill on the barbecue for 2–3 minutes until charred and just wilted.

4 To serve, cut the steak into ½in (1cm) slices, season with salt and pepper, and serve with the bok choy.

NUTRITION PER SERVING

Energy	323kcals/1352kJ
Carbohydrate	2g
of which sugar	1.5g
Fat	14.5g
of which saturates	5g
Salt	0.9g
Fiber	1g

Steak glazed with mustard and brown sugar

Tenderloin is a very lean cut of beef, and has very little fat running through it. This means that it is a very good choice in a balanced diet.

Low carb

Low saturated fat

Dairy free

Gluten free

Low salt

SERVES 4
PREP 5 MINS
COOK 10 MINS

4 x 3½–5½oz (100–150g) steaks, preferably tenderloin filet, approx. 1in (3cm) thick, at room temperature

1 tbsp olive oil

salt and freshly ground black pepper

1 tbsp Dijon mustard

1 tbsp light brown sugar

1 Rub the steaks with the oil and season well with salt and pepper. Pan-fry or grill over high heat until cooked as you like. For rare, allow 2–3 minutes each side; for medium, 3–4 minutes each side; and for well done, 4–5 minutes each side. Allow the meat to rest for about 5 minutes, loosely covered with foil to keep warm.

2 Meanwhile, preheat the broiler to its highest setting. Brush each steak on one side with a thin layer of mustard, then sprinkle with an even layer of the sugar.

3 Broil the steaks for a minute or two only, until the sugar has melted and caramelized over the top. You don't want to cook them any further, just to create a great glazed effect.

NUTRITION PER SERVING	
Energy	184kcals/767kJ
Carbohydrate	4g
of which sugar	4g
Fat	9g
of which saturates	3g
Salt	0.4g
Fiber	0g

Beef with soy and lime, and a grapefruit and ginger salsa

Soy sauce has up to ten times the level of antioxidants found in red wine, chiles have comparatively more vitamin C than citrus fruits, and rump steak is a lean cut of beef. Enjoy!

Low saturated fat

Dairy free

Low salt

SERVES 4
PREP 10 MINS
COOK 15 MINS

1 tbsp peanut or sunflower oil

1 red onion, cut into 8 wedges

1½lb (675g) boneless sirloin (rump) steak, cut into strips

1 red jalapeño chile pepper, seeded and cut into thin strips

splash of soy sauce

juice of 1 lime

1 tbsp honey

7oz (200g) mushrooms, sliced

handful of fresh cilantro, to serve

rice or noodles, to serve

FOR THE GRAPEFRUIT AND GINGER SALSA

2 grapefruit, peeled, segmented, and chopped

1in (2.5cm) piece of fresh ginger, finely grated

1 red jalapeño chile pepper, seeded and finely chopped

pinch of sugar (optional)

freshly ground black pepper

1 First, make the salsa. Put all the ingredients in a bowl, stir, and taste. Add a little freshly ground black pepper if you wish. Set aside.

2 Heat the oil in a wok over high heat until hot. Add the onion and stir-fry for about 5 minutes until tender, then add the beef and chile strips. Continue to stir-fry for another 5 minutes or so, keeping everything moving in the wok. Add the soy sauce, lime juice, and honey, and continue stirring and tossing.

3 Add the mushrooms and stir-fry for a few minutes until they are tender and begin to release their juices.

4 To serve, transfer the beef mixture to a platter and pile the cilantro on top. Serve with rice or noodles and the grapefruit salsa on the side.

NUTRITION PER SERVING	
Energy	326kcals/1365kJ
Carbohydrate	12g
of which sugar	12g
Fat	2.5g
of which saturates	4g
Salt	0.4g
Fiber	2.6g

Dry-rubbed barbecued steak

Rubbing the steak with this spicy mix and allowing it to rest lets the flavors really permeate the meat.

Low carb

Low saturated fat

Dairy free

Gluten free

Low salt

SERVES 4
PREP 5–10 MINS, PLUS CHILLING
COOK 5–10 MINS, PLUS RESTING

2 tsp smoked paprika

2 tsp ground mustard

1 tsp garlic salt

1 tsp dried thyme

1 tbsp light brown sugar

freshly ground black pepper

4 steaks, such as flank or sirloin, approx. 5½oz (150g) each

1 tbsp olive oil

1 In a mortar and pestle or a spice grinder, mix the dry ingredients together to form a fine powder.

2 Rub each steak all over with the spice mix and wrap each one with plastic wrap. Let rest in the refrigerator for 4–6 hours. Prepare the grill for cooking.

3 Unwrap the steaks and allow them to come to room temperature. Drizzle with a little oil and grill on a hot barbecue for 2–3 minutes on each side if you want medium-rare (3–4 minutes for medium, or 4–5 for well done), turning only after the underside has crusted up.

4 Remove from the heat and allow to rest for 5 minutes, covered with foil, before serving.

NUTRITION PER SERVING	
Energy	226kcals/949kJ
Carbohydrate	4g
of which sugar	4g
Fat	9g
of which saturates	3g
Salt	1.2g
Fiber	0g

Thai-style stir-fried ground beef

Using ground meat is an easy way to introduce young children to Asian flavors—just leave out the chiles.

Low carb

Dairy free

SERVES 4–6
PREP 5 MINS
COOK 10 MINS

salt

3½oz (100g) broccoli florets, cut very small

2 tbsp sunflower or vegetable oil

bunch of scallions, finely chopped

2 garlic cloves, crushed

1in (3cm) fresh ginger, finely chopped

1 tbsp finely chopped cilantro stalks, plus a handful of cilantro leaves, roughly chopped

1 red chile, seeded and finely chopped (optional)

14oz (400g) ground beef

1 tbsp fish sauce

2 tbsp soy sauce

1 tbsp lime juice

1 tsp granulated sugar

rice, to serve

FOR A GLUTEN-FREE OPTION
use gluten-free tamari to replace soy sauce

1 Bring a large pan of salted water to a boil and blanch the broccoli for 1 minute, then drain and refresh it under cold water. Set aside.

2 Heat the sunflower oil in a wok or a large, deep-sided frying pan. Add the scallions, garlic, ginger, cilantro stalks, and chile (if using), and cook for a couple of minutes until colored slightly.

3 Add the ground beef and continue to cook over high heat until the meat is well browned.

4 Return the broccoli and add the fish sauce, soy sauce, lime juice, and sugar. Mix well, cooking for a minute or 2 until the broccoli is piping hot. Stir in the cilantro leaves and serve with rice.

NUTRITION PER SERVING

Energy	300kcals/1244kJ
Carbohydrate	4g
of which sugar	4g
Fat	22g
of which saturates	8g
Salt	2.3g
Fiber	1.5g

Flatbreads topped with lamb and hummus

This tasty Middle Eastern–style recipe is the perfect use for any leftovers from a roast joint of lamb.

Dairy free

Low salt

SERVES 2
PREP 10 MINS
COOK 20 MINS

1 tbsp olive oil, plus extra for drizzling

1 onion, finely chopped

3 garlic cloves, grated or finely chopped

7oz (200g) leftover roast lamb, shredded

pinch of ground allspice

pinch of ground cinnamon

salt and freshly ground black pepper

2 flatbreads or plain naan

handful of pine nuts, toasted

handful of mint leaves, coarsely chopped

hummus, to serve

1 Preheat the oven to 400°F (200°C). Heat the oil in a frying pan over medium heat, add the onion, and cook for about 5 minutes until the onion is soft and translucent.

2 Stir in the garlic and cook for a few more seconds. Now add the leftover lamb and stir through. Sprinkle over the allspice and cinnamon and cook for a few minutes, stirring occasionally. Season with salt and pepper.

3 Lay the flatbreads or naan on a baking sheet and drizzle with a little oil. Spoon over the lamb mixture and cook in the oven for about 10 minutes until the lamb is heated through. Scatter over the pine nuts and mint leaves, and top each flatbread or naan with a dollop of hummus. Serve immediately.

NUTRITION PER SERVING	
Energy	624kcals/2611kJ
Carbohydrate	33g
of which sugar	7g
Fat	38g
of which saturates	12g
Salt	0.8g
Fiber	3.5g

Seared duck with raspberry cardamom glaze

The tangy, slightly tart raspberry sauce perfectly complements the rich flavors of the crisp duck breast. Duck fat is relatively healthy, with less saturated fat than butter.

Low carb

Gluten free

Low salt

SERVES 4
PREP 20 MINS
COOK 20 MINS

1lb 5oz (600g) skin-on duck breasts
salt and freshly ground black pepper

FOR THE SAUCE
1 tbsp butter
1 tbsp brown sugar
3½oz (100g) shallots, finely chopped
7oz (200g) fresh raspberries, chopped
1 tsp cardamom seeds, crushed
1 tbsp red wine vinegar

1 Use a sharp knife to score the skin on the duck breasts. Rub the meat generously with salt and pepper.

2 Place the duck skin-side down in a heavy-bottomed frying pan over medium-low heat. Allow the duck fat to render for about 10–12 minutes. Flip and cook for an additional 3–5 minutes. Set aside to rest. Keep warm.

3 Drain off the duck fat. In the same pan, melt the butter. Add the brown sugar and shallots and cook until caramelized.

4 Add the raspberries, cardamom, and vinegar. Cook, stirring frequently, for 5–7 minutes. Transfer the duck to a serving plate and serve topped with the raspberry sauce.

NUTRITION PER SERVING	
Energy	429kcals/1794kJ
Carbohydrate	7g
of which sugar	7g
Fat	25g
of which saturates	8g
Salt	trace
Fiber	2g

Venison steak with blackberries

This simple method cooks the lean meat quickly, while the blackberries provide a tangy accompaniment.

Low carb

Gluten free

Low salt

SERVES 4
PREP 5 MINS
COOK 15 MINS

4 venison haunch steaks, about 7oz (200g) each

salt and freshly ground black pepper

1 tbsp sunflower oil

4 tbsp butter, chilled and diced

¼ cup blackberry wine or red wine

2 tbsp red currant jelly

5½oz (150g) blackberries

1 Pat the steaks dry with paper towels to remove any excess blood. Season well. Heat the oil and 1 teaspoon of butter in a heavy-bottomed pan over medium heat. Place the steaks in the hot pan and cook for 4–5 minutes on each side.

2 Reduce the heat and cook for another 5 minutes, turning once, until well-browned. Remove the meat from the pan, cover with foil, and set aside. Then add the wine, red currant jelly, and blackberries to the pan. Bring to a boil, stirring gently to melt the jelly.

3 Once the sauce has thickened, remove from the heat and whisk in the remaining butter. Do not boil the sauce again, or else the butter will separate. Serve the steaks with the sauce poured over them.

NUTRITION PER SERVING	
Energy	366kcals/1532kJ
Carbohydrate	6.5g
of which sugar	6.5g
Fat	16g
of which saturates	8.5g
Salt	0.5g
Fiber	1.6g

Spicy chicken meatballs

These are perfect alongside a vegetable and noodle stir-fry. Finely chopped chile can be added for more heat.

Low saturated fat

Low salt

SERVES 4
PREP 10 MINS
COOK 10 MINS

14oz (400g) ground chicken

¼ cup fresh white bread crumbs

2 scallions, finely chopped

1 garlic clove, crushed

¾in (2cm) fresh ginger, finely grated

1 tbsp finely chopped cilantro leaves

1 tbsp sweet chili sauce

1 tsp lime juice

1 tsp fish sauce

2 tbsp sunflower or vegetable oil

1 Mix all the ingredients, except the oil, together in a large bowl until evenly incorporated. It's easiest to use your fingers for this; you may prefer to wear plastic food preparation gloves. Cover and refrigerate for at least 30 minutes..

2 With damp hands, shape walnut-sized balls with the chicken mixture, placing them on a plate. At this point, you may cover and chill the meatballs for up to 1 day, if that is more convenient.

3 Heat the sunflower oil in a large frying pan and cook the meatballs over medium-high heat for about 3–5 minutes, turning to color all sides, until golden and cooked through (cut one through to the center to make sure there is no trace of pink). You may need to do this in batches, depending on the size of the pan. Serve.

NUTRITION PER SERVING	
Energy	211kcals/888kJ
Carbohydrate	11.5g
of which sugar	3g
Fat	7g
of which saturates	1g
Salt	0.8g
Fiber	0.5g

Pad Thai

Originating from roadside food stands in Thailand, this zingy noodle dish is designed to be quick to cook and easy to assemble—ideal for the time-limited chef! Experiment with different kinds of rice noodles to find your favorite.

Dairy free

Low salt

SERVES 4
PREP 5 MINS
COOK 15 MINS

10oz (300g) medium or thick dried rice noodles

3 tbsp sunflower oil

2 eggs, lightly beaten

1 tsp shrimp paste (optional)

2 hot red chiles, seeded and finely chopped

3 boneless, skinless chicken breasts, cut into ¼in (5mm) slices

bunch of scallions, finely chopped

splash of Thai fish sauce, such as nam pla

juice of 1 lime

1 tbsp brown sugar

salt and freshly ground black pepper

5½oz (150g) unsalted peanuts, toasted in a dry wok or frying pan

handful of cilantro leaves, finely chopped

lime wedges, to serve

FOR A GLUTEN-FREE OPTION
use gluten-free noodles

1 Put the noodles in a large bowl, cover with boiling water, and leave for 8 minutes, or until soft. Drain and set aside.

2 Meanwhile, put 1 tablespoon of the oil in a large wok over high heat and swirl around the pan. Add the beaten egg and swirl it around the wok for about a minute, or until it begins to set—don't let it set completely—then remove, chop, and set aside.

3 Add the remaining 2 tablespoons of oil to the pan, then add the shrimp paste (if using) and chiles and stir. With the heat still high, add the chicken and stir vigorously for 5 minutes, or until no longer pink.

4 Stir in the scallions, fish sauce, lime juice, and sugar and toss together well. Cook for a few minutes until the sugar has dissolved, then season well with salt and pepper. Return the egg to the pan.

5 Add the noodles to the pan and toss together to coat with the sauce, then add half the peanuts and half the cilantro and toss again. Transfer to a large, shallow warmed serving bowl and scatter with the rest of the peanuts and cilantro. Garnish with lime wedges to serve.

NUTRITION PER SERVING	
Energy	740kcals/3092kJ
Carbohydrate	68g
of which sugar	7.5g
Fat	30g
of which saturates	5.5g
Salt	1g
Fiber	0.5g

Spicy stir-fried chicken with vegetables

This dish incorporates three different green vegetables, but it is quite spicy, so to reduce the heat for young or sensitive palates, cut down the amount of chile used.

Low carb

Low saturated fat

Dairy free

SERVES 4
PREP 15 MINS, PLUS MARINATING
COOK 10 MINS

3 tbsp soy sauce

2 tbsp rice wine or dry sherry

1 tsp sugar

2½ tbsp sunflower or vegetable oil

14oz (400g) boneless, skinless chicken thighs, cut into ½in (1cm) strips

1¾oz (50g) thin green beans, halved

salt

1¾oz (50g) broccoli florets

2 garlic cloves, crushed

1in (3cm) fresh ginger, finely chopped

1 red chile, seeded and finely chopped

bunch of scallions, cut into ¾in (2cm) pieces

3½oz (100g) sugarsnap peas, halved on the diagonal

1 tbsp oyster sauce

1 Mix 1 tablespoon of the soy sauce, 1 tablespoon of the rice wine, the sugar, and ½ tablespoon of the oil in a bowl. Stir in the chicken, cover, and refrigerate for 30 minutes.

2 Cook the green beans in a pan of boiling salted water for 1 minute. Add the broccoli and cook for another minute. Drain and refresh under cold water. Set aside.

3 Heat the remaining oil in a wok, add the garlic, ginger, and chile, and cook for 1 minute. Now add the chicken and stir for 2–3 minutes. Add the scallions and peas and stir-fry for another 2–3 minutes. Pour in the remaining soy sauce, rice wine, and the oyster sauce, and bubble up. Add in the blanched vegetables and heat through to serve.

NUTRITION PER SERVING	
Energy	216kcals/904kJ
Carbohydrate	6g
of which sugar	5g
Fat	10g
of which saturates	1.5g
Salt	2.6g
Fiber	2g

Sweet and sour chicken

Removing the pineapple chunks of the take-out version makes this a more sophisticated alternative.

Low carb

Low saturated fat

Dairy free

SERVES 4
PREP 15 MINS,
PLUS MARINATING
COOK 10 MINS

FOR THE MARINADE
1 tsp cornstarch
1 tbsp soy sauce
1 tbsp rice wine or dry sherry
1 tsp granulated sugar

FOR THE CHICKEN
1lb 2oz (500g) boneless, skinless chicken breast, cut into ½in (1cm) slices
2 tbsp sunflower or vegetable oil
2 garlic cloves, finely chopped
1in (3cm) fresh ginger, finely chopped
3½oz (100g) raw, unsalted cashews, roughly chopped

FOR THE SAUCE
2 tbsp rice wine vinegar or white wine vinegar
2 tbsp rice wine or dry sherry
3 tbsp ketchup
2 tbsp soy sauce
½ cup chicken stock
1 tbsp granulated sugar

1 Mix the marinade ingredients in a bowl and turn the chicken to coat. Cover and refrigerate for at least 30 minutes.

2 Whisk together all the sauce ingredients and set aside.

3 Heat the oil in a wok, add the garlic and ginger, and stir-fry for 1 minute. Add the chicken and stir-fry until it turns pale.

4 Add the sauce and bring to a boil. Add the cashews and cook for 2–3 minutes until the mixture has thickened and the chicken is coated in a glossy sauce. Serve.

NUTRITION PER SERVING	
Energy	386kcals/1616kJ
Carbohydrate	14g
of which sugar	10g
Fat	19g
of which saturates	3.5g
Salt	2.7g
Fiber	1g

Turkey scallops stuffed with prunes and pecans

Turkey scallops are very easy to make from the breasts.
Serve these sweetened versions with sautéed potatoes
and wilted spinach.

| Low saturated fat |
| Dairy free |
| Gluten free |
| Low salt |

SERVES 4
PREP 15 MINS
COOK 15–20 MINS

2 boneless, skinless turkey breasts,
   about 14oz (400g) each

large handful of pitted prunes, chopped

handful of roasted pecans,
   finely chopped

handful of flat-leaf parsley, chopped

1 tbsp olive oil

1 Preheat the oven to 400°F (200°C). Cut each turkey breast in half and sandwich the four pieces between sheets of plastic wrap. Pound them with a meat hammer or the edge of a rolling pin until they are an even thickness of about ¼in (5mm). Remove the plastic wrap and slice the breasts in half so that you now have eight scallops.

2 Mix the prunes and nuts with the parsley in a bowl, then spoon the mixture into the middle of each turkey scallop. Roll up from one narrow end and secure with a toothpick.

3 Set the turkey rolls in a roasting pan, drizzle with the oil, and roast in the oven for 15–20 minutes, until cooked through. Serve with sautéed potatoes and wilted spinach.

NUTRITION PER SERVING

Energy	298kcals/1248kJ
Carbohydrate	4.5g
of which sugar	4.3g
Fat	9g
of which saturates	1.3g
Salt	0.3g
Fiber	1.3g

Cajun chicken with corn salsa

Avocados give the salsa a wonderfully creamy flavor, which helps to balance the fieriness of the chicken.

Low carb

Low saturated fat

Dairy free

Low salt

SERVES 2

PREP 10 MINS

COOK 15 MINS

2 skinless chicken breasts

1 tbsp of Cajun seasoning

1 tbsp olive oil

FOR THE SALSA

1 large fresh corn on the cob, stripped of husks and threads

½ small red onion, finely chopped

½ red pepper, seeded and diced

1 red chile, seeded and finely chopped

1 small Hass avocado, diced

1 tbsp olive oil

juice of 1 lime

1 Put the chicken breasts between two pieces of plastic wrap and pound with a rolling pin until flattened evenly. Mix the Cajun seasoning with the oil and brush over the flattened chicken. Leave to marinate for at least 15 minutes.

2 To make the salsa, add the corn to a large pan of boiling water and cook for 5 minutes, then immediately transfer to a bowl of ice water to cool. Drain well, then, using a sharp knife, scrape off all the kernels. Combine with the remaining salsa ingredients, mix well, and set aside.

3 Heat a griddle pan and cook the chicken for 4–5 minutes on one side, pressing the pieces down on the griddle pan, then turn and cook for 4–5 minutes on the other side, or until cooked through.

4 Spoon the salsa onto serving plates and top with the griddled chicken.

NUTRITION PER SERVING	
Energy	442kcals/1846kJ
Carbohydrate	18g
of which sugar	5g
Fat	23g
of which saturates	4g
Salt	0.3g
Fiber	3.5g

Chicken liver with Marsala

This sauce from the Piedmont region of Italy, where wild mushrooms, including truffles, grow in abundance. Mushrooms have good amounts of trace minerals.

Low carb

Gluten free

Low salt

SERVES 4
PREP 15 MINS,
PLUS SOAKING
COOK 10 MINS

4 tbsp butter

14oz (400g) chicken livers, trimmed

2 shallots, finely chopped

1oz (30g) dried porcini mushrooms, soaked in water for 30 minutes and the water reserved

1 tsp tomato paste

4 tbsp Marsala

1 Heat the butter in a large saucepan over medium heat. Add the livers and cook for about 2 minutes. Remove with a slotted spoon, place on a plate lined with paper towels, and set aside.

2 Add the shallots to the pan and cook until soft. Then add the mushrooms and tomato paste and stir to combine. Stir in the Marsala and shake the pan lightly to mix through.

3 Return the livers to the pan and mix well to coat with the sauce. Taste and adjust seasoning, if needed, and add a little of the reserved soaking water if the sauce seems too thick. Serve hot with tagliatelle mixed with a little truffle oil.

NUTRITION PER SERVING	
Energy	236kcals/988kJ
Carbohydrate	2g
of which sugar	1.7g
Fat	15g
of which saturates	9g
Salt	0.5g
Fiber	1.6g

Cashew nut paella

Cashews are expensive nuts, but they make a delicious paella. Try substituting chopped cooked chestnuts or even toasted hazelnuts for a change.

Dairy free

High fiber

SERVES 4
PREP 10 MINS
COOK 25 MINS

large pinch of saffron strands

2½ cups hot vegetable stock

2 tbsp olive oil

1 leek, chopped

1 onion, chopped

2 garlic cloves, crushed

1 red bell pepper, seeded and chopped

1 carrot, chopped

9oz (250g) paella rice

⅔ cup dry white wine

4oz (115g) cremini mushrooms, sliced

4oz (115g) roasted, unsalted cashew nuts

salt and freshly ground black pepper

4oz (115g) fresh shelled or frozen peas

1½ tbsp chopped thyme

4 tomatoes, quartered

½ tsp smoked paprika

sprig of flat-leaf parsley and lemon wedges, to garnish

FOR A GLUTEN-FREE OPTION
use gluten-free stock

1 Put the saffron in the stock to infuse. Heat the oil in a paella pan or large frying pan and cook the leek, onion, garlic, red bell pepper, and carrot, stirring, for 3 minutes until softened but not browned. Add the rice and stir until coated in oil and glistening.

2 Add the wine and boil until it has been absorbed, stirring. Stir in the saffron-infused stock, mushrooms, nuts, and some salt and pepper. Bring to a boil, stirring once, then reduce the heat, cover, and simmer very gently for 10 minutes.

3 Add the peas and thyme, stir gently, then distribute the tomatoes over the top. Cover and simmer very gently for a further 10 minutes until the rice is just tender and has absorbed most of the liquid but is still creamy.

4 Sprinkle the paprika over and stir through gently, taking care not to break up the tomatoes. Taste and adjust the seasoning, if necessary.

5 Garnish with a sprig of parsley and lemon wedges and serve hot.

NUTRITION PER SERVING	
Energy	582kcals/2435kJ
Carbohydrate	68g
of which sugar	11g
Fat	21g
of which saturates	4g
Salt	1.5g
Fiber	8g

Mixed mushroom and bok choy stir-fry

This dish uses cultivated mushrooms that originate from Japan. They are widely available in supermarkets, but cremini mushrooms can be substituted, if necessary.

Dairy free

High fiber

SERVES 4
PREP 10 MINS
COOK 8 MINS

9oz (250g) dried soba or brown udon noodles

6 tbsp tamari or 4 tbsp reduced-salt soy sauce

1 tbsp lemon juice

2 tsp grated fresh ginger

2 garlic cloves, crushed

1 tsp chopped lemongrass (or lemongrass purée)

1 tbsp granulated sugar

¼–½ tsp wasabi paste

8oz (225g) fresh shelled or frozen edamame

3 tbsp sunflower or vegetable oil

1 bunch of scallions, trimmed and sliced

2 celery stalks, cut into matchsticks

3½oz (100g) shiitake mushrooms, sliced

3½oz (100g) oyster mushrooms, sliced

3½oz (100g) enoki mushrooms, trimmed of base and separated

2 heads bok choy (approx. 7oz/200g), coarsely shredded

2 tbsp sesame seeds, to garnish

1 Cook the noodles according to the package directions. Drain and set aside.

2 Whisk the tamari sauce, lemon juice, ginger, garlic, lemongrass, sugar, and wasabi paste in a small bowl with 2 tablespoons water and set aside. Boil the edamame in water for 3 minutes. Drain and set aside.

3 Heat the oil in a large frying pan or wok. Add the scallions and celery and stir-fry for 2 minutes. Add all the mushrooms and stir-fry for 3 minutes. Add the bok choy and edamame and stir-fry for 1 minute.

4 Add the noodles and the bowl of tamari sauce. Toss until everything is heated through and coated. Spoon into bowls and sprinkle with sesame seeds before serving.

NUTRITION PER SERVING	
Energy	460kcals/1925kJ
Carbohydrate	50g
of which sugar	7g
Fat	18g
of which saturates	2.5g
Salt	2g
Fiber	6g

Brown rice stir-fry

Brown rice really comes into its own in this super-healthy stir-fry. It's nutty and deliciously savory.

Low saturated fat

Dairy free

SERVES 4
PREP 10 MINS
COOK 10 MINS

5½oz (150g) sugarsnap peas, cut into ½in (1cm) pieces

2 asparagus spears, cut into ½in (1cm) pieces

salt

2 tbsp sunflower or vegetable oil

5½oz (150g) zucchini, cut into ½in (1cm) cubes

4 scallions, finely sliced

2 garlic cloves, finely chopped

1½in (4cm) piece of fresh ginger, finely chopped

1 green chile pepper, seeded and finely chopped

1¾lb (800g) cooked, cold brown rice

2 tbsp oyster sauce

2 tbsp soy sauce

2 tbsp rice wine or dry sherry

2 tbsp pumpkin seeds

2 tbsp sunflower seeds

NUTRITION PER SERVING	
Energy	441kcals/1856kJ
Carbohydrate	67g
of which sugar	4g
Fat	14g
of which saturates	2g
Salt	2.5g
Fiber	5g

1 Blanch the sugarsnap peas and asparagus in a large pan of boiling salted water for 1 minute, then drain and refresh them under cold water.

2 Heat the oil in a large wok and stir-fry the zucchini over high heat for 2 minutes until they start to color. Add the scallions, garlic, ginger, and chile and cook for another minute.

3 Add the blanched vegetables and cook for a minute, then add the rice with the remaining ingredients. Stir-fry for a minute or two until everything is well combined and the rice is hot.

Sweet potato cakes

Spring onion adds a crunchy texture to these cakes.
Sweet potatoes are a rich source of Vitamin A.

Low saturated fat

Dairy free

Gluten free

Low salt

SERVES 4
PREP 10 MINS
COOK 20 MINS

1lb 2oz (500g) cooked sweet
   potato, mashed

2in (5cm) piece of fresh ginger,
   peeled and grated

bunch of spring onions,
   finely chopped

pinch of freshly grated nutmeg

2 eggs, lightly beaten

salt and freshly ground
   black pepper

flour for dusting

3–4 tbsp polenta

vegetable oil, for shallow frying

lime wedges, to serve

1 Add the sweet potato to a large bowl. Add the ginger,
spring onions, and nutmeg, then add a little of the egg, a
drop at time, reserving plenty for coating, until the mixture
binds together. Season well with salt and black pepper.

2 Scoop up a handful of the mixture, roll into a ball, then
flatten out into a cake. Repeat until all the mixture is used.

3 Dust the cakes in flour, dip in the reserved egg, then lightly
coat with polenta. Heat the oil in a nonstick frying pan and
add the cakes a couple at a time. Cook for 2–3 minutes or
until the underside turns golden, then carefully flip and cook
for another 2–3 minutes or until evenly golden brown. Serve
with lime wedges for squeezing over.

NUTRITION PER SERVING	
Energy	272kcals/1140kJ
Carbohydrate	36g
of which sugar	16g
Fat	12g
of which saturates	2g
Salt	0.2g
Fiber	3.5g

Lentils with leeks and mushrooms

Lentils and mushrooms are both meaty, tasty ingredients that give this quick vegetarian dish depth and flavor. Use dried puy lentils instead of canned, for added texture.

Low saturated fat

Dairy free

Low salt

High fiber

SERVES 4
PREP 5–10 MINS
COOK 25 MINS

1 tbsp olive oil

1 onion, finely chopped

1 bay leaf

salt and freshly ground black pepper

2 garlic cloves, grated or finely chopped

3 leeks, trimmed and sliced

2 tsp Marmite or Vegemite, or a splash of light soy sauce

8oz (225g) cremini mushrooms, halved, or quartered if large

1 x 14oz (400g) can green lentils or puy lentils, drained and rinsed

1¼ cups hot vegetable stock

handful of curly-leaf parsley, leaves picked and finely chopped

NUTRITION PER SERVING	
Energy	146kcals/611kJ
Carbohydrate	14g
of which sugar	5g
Fat	4g
of which saturates	0.5g
Salt	1g
Fiber	8g

1 Heat the oil in a large frying pan over low heat. Add the onion, bay leaf, and a little salt, and cook for 5 minutes until the onion is soft and translucent. Add the garlic and leek and stir in the Marmite, Vegemite, or soy sauce. Cook for another 5 minutes until the leeks begin to soften.

2 Add the mushrooms and cook until they release their juices—you may need to add a little more oil. Season well with salt and pepper, then stir in the lentils and hot stock. Bring to a boil, reduce the heat, and simmer gently for 15 minutes.

3 Remove from the heat and stir in the parsley. Taste and season again if needed. Serve with some roasted tomatoes and fresh crusty bread.

Spicy raw vegetable spaghetti

Raw vegetables provide more enzymes, vitamins, and other essential nutrients than cooked ones, and the combination of ingredients used here has a cleansing effect on the body. The spiralizer turns the vegetables into lovely spaghetti-like strands, which changes their texture—the root vegetables in particular taste surprisingly light and vibrant.

Low carb

Low saturated fat

Dairy free

Gluten free

Low salt

High fiber

SERVES 4
PREP 20 MINS
COOK 5 MINS

a handful of pine nuts

2 tbsp furikake, or 1 tbsp each of black and white sesame seeds

2 carrots, peeled

2 medium beets, peeled

1 zucchini and 1 yellow squash, stalks removed

3 small radishes

a large bunch of fresh cilantro leaves, large stalks removed, and finely chopped

FOR THE DRESSING
juice of 3 celery stalks (about ¼ cup)

1 tbsp hemp oil

2 tbsp pumpkin seed oil

1 tbsp fresh lemon juice

2 tsp tahini

salt and freshly ground black pepper

1 To make the dressing, combine all the ingredients together in a food processor or blender, then set aside.

2 To toast the pine nuts and sesame seeds, heat a small skillet over medium heat, add the pine nuts and seeds, and dry-fry, stirring until lightly golden.

3 Put the carrots, beets, zucchini, yellow squash, and radishes through a vegetable spiralizer to turn them into long, thick spaghetti-like strips. Or, use a vegetable peeler and cut them into long thick ribbons.

4 Place all the vegetable strips, except the beets, in a serving bowl and toss with the chopped cilantro leaves (adding the beets separately stops the whole salad from turning pink). Distribute among four serving plates, add the beets, pour over the dressing, scatter each portion with a few of the pine nuts and furikake or sesame seeds, and serve.

NUTRITION PER SERVING	
Energy	257kcals/1075kJ
Carbohydrate	7g
of which sugar	6g
Fat	22g
of which saturates	3g
Salt	0.1g
Fiber	6g

Roasted chickpeas with spinach

This classic Spanish combination of chickpeas and spinach makes a quick vegetarian supper when heaped on country bread toasted with olive oil.

Low saturated fat

Low salt

High fiber

SERVES 4
PREP 5 MINS
COOK 15–20 MINS

3 tbsp olive oil

1 large mild onion, finely chopped

2–3 garlic cloves, crushed

1 tsp cumin seeds

1 tsp ground cumin

1 tsp smoked pimentón
  (Spanish paprika)

salt and freshly ground black pepper

1lb 2oz (500g) fresh spinach leaves,
  rinsed and drained

1 x 8oz (240g) can chickpeas, rinsed
  and drained

1 tbsp Spanish sherry vinegar, plus
  a little more (optional)

2–4 slices of sourdough bread, halved

1 heaping tbsp finely snipped flat-
  leaf parsley

FOR A GLUTEN-FREE OPTION
use gluten-free bread

1 Heat 2 tablespoons of the oil in a large frying pan over medium heat. Add the onion and cook for 2–3 minutes, until soft. Stir in the garlic and cook gently for 2–3 minutes, then stir in the cumin and paprika and cook until the spices smell fragrant, stirring frequently. Season lightly.

2 Add the spinach and cook for 2–3 minutes. Stir in the chickpeas and vinegar, then add ½ cup cold water and simmer. Reduce the heat. Cover and cook for 5–8 minutes, shaking the pan occasionally.

3 Meanwhile, in a frying pan, heat the remaining oil over medium-high heat. Add the bread and cook until golden all over. Drain on a double layer of paper towels.

4 Remove the lid. Season and stir in a few drops of vinegar, if you like. Stir in the parsley and spoon on the bread to serve.

NUTRITION PER SERVING	
Energy	306kcals/1280kJ
Carbohydrate	32g
of which sugar	5g
Fat	12g
of which saturates	1.5g
Salt	0.8g
Fiber	9g

Snow pea, sweet potato, and cashew red curry

Cooking the green vegetables quickly retains their color and texture. Butternut squash or pumpkin can be substituted for sweet potato and tofu for cashews.

Dairy free
Gluten free
Low salt
High fiber

SERVES 4
PREP 10 MINS
COOK 20 MINS

2 tbsp sunflower or vegetable oil

1 bunch scallions, cut into short lengths

1 sweet potato (approx. 1lb 5oz/600g), peeled and cut into walnut-sized pieces

1 garlic clove, crushed

1 tsp grated fresh ginger or galangal

1 tsp finely chopped lemongrass (or lemongrass purée)

3 tbsp Thai red curry paste

14oz (400ml) can reduced-fat coconut milk

6oz (175g) snow peas, trimmed

2 zucchini, cut into batonettes

12 cherry tomatoes

4oz (115g) raw cashews

1 tbsp chopped cilantro

squeeze of lime juice

jasmine rice, to serve

1 fat red chile, seeded and cut into thin strips, to garnish

1 Heat the oil in a large saucepan or wok. Add the scallions and stir-fry gently for 2 minutes until softened but not colored. Add the sweet potato and cook, stirring, for 1 minute.

2 Stir in the garlic, ginger, lemongrass, curry paste, and coconut milk. Bring to a boil, reduce the heat, cover, and simmer gently for 10 minutes or until the sweet potato is tender.

3 Meanwhile, cook the snow pea and zucchini batonettes in boiling water for 2–3 minutes until just tender. Drain.

4 Stir the snow peas and zucchini into the curry with the tomatoes, nuts, and cilantro. Spike with a squeeze of lime juice and simmer for 2 minutes until the tomatoes are softened slightly but still hold their shape. Spoon the curry over jasmine rice served in bowls and garnish with strips of red chile.

NUTRITION PER SERVING	
Energy	521kcals/2180kJ
Carbohydrate	44g
of which sugar	16g
Fat	30g
of which saturates	10g
Salt	0.6g
Fiber	10g

Tofu and mushroom stroganoff

Tofu is a complete source of protein, containing all eight amino acids. With no cholesterol, it is also a good source of iron and calcium.

Low carb

Low salt

SERVES 4
PREP 10 MINS
COOK 12–15 MINS

2 tbsp sunflower oil

12oz (350g) tofu, diced

1 red onion, sliced

2 garlic cloves, crushed

1 red pepper, sliced

1 orange pepper, sliced

9oz (250g) mixed mushrooms, quartered

2 tsp cornstarch

2 tbsp tomato paste

2 tbsp smooth peanut butter

²⁄₃ cup vegetable stock

7oz (200g) reduced-fat crème fraîche or sour cream

salt and freshly ground black pepper

handful of chives, finely chopped, to garnish

rice, to serve

FOR A GLUTEN-FREE OPTION
use gluten-free stock

NUTRITION PER SERVING	
Energy	276kcals/1155kJ
Carbohydrate	10g
of which sugar	7g
Fat	20g
of which saturates	6g
Salt	0.4g
Fiber	4g

1 Heat 1 tablespoon of the oil in a large saucepan. Add the tofu and stir-fry over high heat until golden. Remove from the heat and set aside.

2 Add the remaining oil to the saucepan, reduce the heat, add the onion and garlic, and fry until softened. Add the peppers and mushrooms, and stir-fry for 5 minutes.

3 In a bowl, mix the cornstarch with a little water to form a paste and set aside.

4 Add the tomato paste, peanut butter, and tofu to the saucepan. Stir in the vegetable stock and cornstarch paste, and cook for 3 minutes. Add the crème fraîche, season to taste, and simmer for 2 minutes. Transfer to a plate, sprinkle with chives, and serve with rice.

Chile tofu stir-fry

This quick and easy dish takes advantage of tofu's ability to take on other flavors.

SERVES 4
PREP 10 MINS
COOK 15 MINS

2 tbsp sunflower oil

¾ cup unsalted cashews

10oz (300g) firm tofu, cut into 1in (2.5cm) cubes

1 red onion, thinly sliced

2 carrots, thinly sliced

1 red bell pepper, seeded and chopped

1 celery stalk, chopped

4 cremini mushrooms, sliced

6oz (175g) bean sprouts

2 tsp Asian chile-garlic sauce

2 tbsp light soy sauce

1 tsp cornstarch

¾ cup vegetable or chicken stock

FOR A GLUTEN-FREE OPTION
use gluten-free tamari to replace soy sauce

1 Heat the oil in a wok over high heat. Add the cashews and stir-fry for about 30 seconds or until lightly browned. Using a slotted spoon, transfer to paper towels.

2 Add the tofu and stir-fry about 2 minutes, or until golden. Transfer to the paper towels. Add the onion and carrots and stir-fry for 2 minutes, until crisp and tender; add the red pepper, celery, and mushrooms and stir-fry for 3 minutes more. Finally, add the bean sprouts and stir-fry for 2 minutes, until hot. Always keep the heat under the wok high so that the vegetables sear quickly without overcooking.

3 Meanwhile, mix the stock, soy sauce, and chili sauce in a small bowl. Add the cornstarch, and stir to dissolve. Return the cashews and tofu to the wok and add the stock mixture. Stir until the sauce is bubbling and slightly thickened. Serve hot.

NUTRITION PER SERVING	
Energy	300kcals/1255kJ
Carbohydrate	14g
of which sugar	8g
Fat	20g
of which saturates	3g
Salt	0.5g
Fiber	5g

Black-eyed pea, spinach, and tomato curry

A delicious and nutritious meal, this curry makes a satisfying weeknight dinner that's quicker and cheaper than ordering in.

Low saturated fat

Low salt

High fiber

SERVES 4
PREP 5 MINS
COOK 15 MINS

3 tbsp sunflower oil

½ tsp mustard seeds

2 garlic cloves, finely chopped

10 curry leaves

1 large onion, chopped

2 green chiles, split lengthwise and seeded

½ tsp chile powder

1 tsp ground coriander

½ tsp ground turmeric

3 tomatoes, chopped

3½oz (100g) spinach, chopped

14oz (400g) can black-eyed peas, rinsed and drained

salt

1¼ cups plain yogurt

naan bread or rice, to serve

1 Heat the oil in a large saucepan and add the mustard seeds. When they start to pop, add the garlic, curry leaves, and onion. Cook over medium heat for 5 minutes, or until the onion is soft.

2 Add the green chiles, chile powder, coriander, and turmeric. Mix well and add the tomato pieces. Stir, then add the spinach. Cook over low heat for 5 minutes.

3 Finally, add the black-eyed peas and salt to taste. Cook for another minute, or until everything is hot. Remove the pan from the heat and slowly add the yogurt, stirring well. Serve warm with naan bread or rice.

NUTRITION PER SERVING	
Energy	228kcals/956kJ
Carbohydrate	22g
of which sugar	12g
Fat	12g
of which saturates	2.6g
Salt	1.2g
Fiber	7g

Vegetable ramen noodle bowl

Miso paste enhances the flavor of this dish, but omit it if preferred and season with more tamari. Use dashi powder to make the vegetable stock, if it is available.

Low saturated fat

Dairy free

High fiber

SERVES 4
PREP 10 MINS, PLUS SOAKING
COOK 10 MINS

2 × 4in (10cm) pieces wakame seaweed

2 heaped tbsp dried shiitake mushrooms

9oz (250g) dried ramen noodles
  (or brown rice noodles)

3½ cups vegetable stock

2 tbsp tamari or light soy sauce

2 tsp light brown sugar

3 tbsp mirin (or dry sherry)

4 scallions, chopped

1 red bell pepper, seeded
  and finely sliced

2 heads of bok choy, cut into thick
  shreds

1 zucchini, cut into matchsticks

4 radishes, sliced

7oz (225g) can bamboo shoots, drained

1 tsp dried chile flakes (optional)

1 tbsp red miso paste

9oz (250g) block firm tofu, cut into
  8 slices

sweet chili sauce, to drizzle

FOR A GLUTEN-FREE OPTION
use gluten-free noodles

1 Soak the wakame and mushrooms in 1¼ cups warm water for 30 minutes. Lift out the wakame and cut out any thick stalk, if necessary. If the wakame is large, cut into pieces before returning to the soaking water with the mushrooms.

2 Cook the noodles according to the package directions. Drain. Put the stock in a large saucepan with the remaining ingredients, except the miso paste and tofu. Add the wakame, mushrooms, and soaking water. Bring to a boil, reduce the heat, and simmer for 3 minutes.

3 Blend a ladleful of the stock with the miso paste until smooth. Pour back into the pan and stir gently. Taste and add more tamari, if necessary. Make sure the soup is very hot but not boiling.

4 Divide the noodles between 4 large open soup bowls. Add 2 slices of tofu to each bowl and ladle the very hot soup over. Serve at once with sweet chili sauce to drizzle over, if using.

NUTRITION PER SERVING	
Energy	381kcals/1596kJ
Carbohydrate	61g
of which sugar	14g
Fat	5g
of which saturates	1g
Salt	4g
Fiber	7g

Braised cauliflower with chile and cilantro

A few spices can turn the humble cauliflower into something far more interesting. This dish can be served simply with some buttery basmati rice or as part of an Indian meal.

Low carb

Dairy free

Gluten free

Low salt

SERVES 4
PREP 10 MINS
COOK 10 MINS

14oz (400g) cauliflower, outer leaves removed, chopped into small florets

2 dried red chiles

1 tsp cumin seeds

2 tbsp sunflower or vegetable oil

1 tsp black mustard seeds

½ tsp turmeric

2 garlic cloves, crushed

pat of butter

sea salt

2 tbsp cilantro leaves, finely chopped

1 Blanch the cauliflower in salted boiling water for 1–2 minutes, drain, and rinse under cold water.

2 Grind together the chiles and cumin seeds in a mortar and pestle until coarsely crushed. Heat the oil in a large, deep frying pan or wok, and add the chile and cumin seeds, mustard seeds, turmeric, and garlic. Cook gently for 1 minute until the mustard seeds start to pop.

3 Add the cauliflower and enough water so that it covers the bottom of the pan (about 6 tbsp). Bring the water to a boil and cover the pan or wok. Turn the heat down and simmer the cauliflower for 3–5 minutes, until almost cooked through.

4 Uncover the pan or wok and turn up the heat. Allow the water to cook off, turning the cauliflower all the time. When all the water has evaporated (about 5–6 minutes), add the butter and mix well until it melts. Season with sea salt and sprinkle with cilantro before serving.

try this....
Cauliflower with tomatoes, chile, cilantro, and lentils

In step 3, add 7oz (200g) **baby cherry tomatoes** along with the cauliflower. While the cauliflower is cooking, drain 2 cans **brown lentils** and gently heat in a separate pan. At the end of step 4, combine the cauliflower and lentils. Serve with **tzatziki dip**.

NUTRITION PER SERVING	
Energy	102kcals/427kJ
Carbohydrate	4g
of which sugar	3g
Fat	8g
of which saturates	1g
Salt	0.1g
Fiber	2g

Mediterranean vegetable medley

This dish features a variety of colored vegetables with antioxidant and anti-inflammatory phytonutrients that help protect the body at a cellular level.

Low saturated fat

Dairy free

Gluten free

Low salt

High fiber

SERVES 4
PREP 5–10 MINS
COOK 25 MINS

1 tbsp olive oil

4 shallots, minced

salt and freshly ground black pepper

a pinch of oregano or marjoram

2 red bell peppers, seeded and chopped

2 yellow bell peppers, seeded and chopped

1 medium eggplant, chopped

1 medium zucchini, chopped

4 tomatoes, skinned (optional), and chopped

2 garlic cloves, crushed

2 tbsp olive oil

¼ cup finely chopped parsley leaves, plus leaves to garnish

brown basmati rice, to serve

1 Heat the olive oil in a large, heavy saucepan over medium to low heat. Add the shallots and a pinch of salt, and stir until the shallots begin to turn translucent. Add a dash of water to bring the temperature down and to add moisture to the pan. After 2–3 minutes add the oregano or marjoram and the peppers. Cook until the peppers have softened.

2 Add the eggplant and the zucchini, and when the liquid in the pan has reduced, add the tomatoes. Let the mixture simmer for 15 minutes over low heat, taking care not to let the vegetables stick to the bottom of the pan and burn.

3 Add the garlic and a little more olive oil for added flavor and cook for another 5 minutes. Stir in the chopped parsley and season with salt and black pepper to taste. Serve on a bed of brown basmati rice with some parsley scattered on top.

try this....
Mediterranean vegetable salad

Follow the above recipe to the end of step 2. Stir in 2 tablespoons **pine nuts**, 2 tablespoons **raisins**, 1 tablespoon **capers**, and ½ can **chickpeas**, rinsed and drained. Chill for at least 30 minutes before serving.

NUTRITION PER SERVING	
Energy	158kcals/661kJ
Carbohydrate	12g
of which sugar	12g
Fat	9g
of which saturates	1.5g
Salt	trace
Fiber	7g

Lemon rice

This is a wonderfully tangy side dish from South India that can be easily rustled up when you are in a hurry.

Low saturated fat

Dairy free

Gluten free

Low salt

SERVES 4
PREP 10 MINS
COOK 5 MINS

3 tbsp vegetable oil

1 tsp yellow mustard seeds

6 green cardamom pods, split

10 fresh or dried curry leaves

2 red chiles, split lengthwise

½ tsp turmeric

½in (1cm) piece of fresh ginger, finely chopped

1 garlic clove, crushed

3 tbsp lemon juice, or to taste

10oz (300g) cooked, cold white basmati rice

2oz (60g) cashews, lightly toasted

2 tbsp chopped cilantro leaves

1 Heat the oil in a large frying pan, add the spices, ginger, and garlic, and cook over medium heat for 2 minutes, or until aromatic, stirring all the time.

2 Add the lemon juice and cook for 1 minute, then add the rice. Stir until the rice is heated through and coated in the spices.

3 Transfer to a serving dish, scatter with the cashews and cilantro, and serve at once.

NUTRITION PER SERVING	
Energy	264kcals/1101kJ
Carbohydrate	24g
of which sugar	1g
Fat	16g
of which saturates	3g
Salt	trace
Fiber	0.7g

Baked tomatoes stuffed with couscous, black olives, and feta

These can be the centerpiece of a meal or can accompany a simple grilled or baked fish dish.

Low saturated fat

SERVES 2
PREP 20 MINS
COOK 15 MINS,
PLUS RESTING

4–8 beefsteak or other large tomatoes, depending on size

⅔ cup couscous

2 tbsp olive oil, plus extra for drizzling

⅔ cup boiling vegetable stock

2 large scallions, finely chopped

8 pitted black olives, finely chopped

finely grated zest of ½ lemon

1¾oz (50g) feta cheese, crumbled

2 tbsp finely chopped mint leaves

1 tbsp finely chopped chives

freshly ground black pepper

1 Preheat the oven to 400°F (200°C). Slice the tops off the tomatoes and carefully scoop out and discard the interior flesh, reserving the tops for later.

2 Put the couscous in a wide, shallow dish and rub in 1 tablespoon of the oil with your fingers (to keep the grains from sticking together). Pour in the stock, stir briefly, and immediately cover tightly with plastic wrap. Leave for 10 minutes, then uncover. The couscous should be soft and the liquid absorbed. Fluff the couscous with a fork and let cool slightly.

3 When the couscous has cooled, add the remaining ingredients, except the tomatoes, with the remaining 1 tablespoon of oil. Season well with pepper (the feta and olives are salty enough), and carefully stuff the tomatoes with the mixture.

4 Place the tomatoes in a small ovenproof dish that fits them tightly, put the reserved tops on, and drizzle with oil. Bake in the hot oven for 15 minutes, until the tomatoes are soft but still hold their shape and the tops are golden. Rest for 5 minutes, then serve.

NUTRITION PER SERVING

Energy	448kcals/1874kJ
Carbohydrate	50g
of which sugar	28g
Fat	20g
of which saturates	6g
Salt	1.4g
Fiber	10g

Chargrilled shrimp and pepper couscous

Omit the shrimp for a flavorful vegetable couscous that can also be served as a side dish.

Low saturated fat	
Low salt	
High fiber	

SERVES 4
PREP 15 MINS
COOK 15 MINS

7oz (200g) couscous

1 cup boiling water

1 tbsp butter, softened

4 red bell peppers

5 tbsp olive oil

salt and freshly ground black pepper

1 leek, white part only, sliced into ¼in (5mm) disks

2 garlic cloves, crushed

6oz (175g) cooked and peeled jumbo shrimp

grated zest and juice of 1 lemon

¼ cup chopped flat-leaf parsley

2 tbsp chopped mint leaves

1 Put the couscous in a large bowl. Add the boiling water and the butter, and stir to combine. Cover the bowl with plastic wrap, and set aside for 5–10 minutes. Using a fork, separate and fluff up the grains. Set aside.

2 Heat the barbecue grill until hot. Cut off and discard the tops of the peppers, then cut the peppers in half lengthwise. Remove all the seeds. Put the peppers in a shallow dish, add 3 tablespoons of the oil, and season with salt and black pepper. Mix until the peppers are well coated in the oil. Grill the peppers over high heat for about 10 minutes until they are charred all over and softened. Allow to cool a little. Peel off the skin and reserve the pepper halves.

3 Heat the remaining olive oil in a frying pan over low heat. Add the leeks, and sweat gently, stirring occasionally, for about 5 minutes. Add in the garlic, and cook for 30 seconds. Remove from the heat.

4 To finish, cut or tear the pepper halves into strips, and put in the bowl with the couscous. Add the shrimp, the leek and garlic mixture, lemon zest and juice, parsley, and mint. Stir through well, and serve.

NUTRITION PER SERVING

Energy	413kcals/1727kJ
Carbohydrate	45g
of which sugar	7.5g
Fat	18g
of which saturates	4g
Salt	0.5g
Fiber	6g

Kale with soba buckwheat noodles

Kale is the ultimate leafy vegetable, full of antioxidants and omega-3 fatty acids that benefit the heart. It is best cooked lightly for a minimal amount of time.

| Low saturated fat |
| Dairy free |
| High fiber |

SERVES 4
PREP 10 MINS
COOK 20 MINS

14oz (400g) soba (buckwheat) noodles

2 tbsp walnut oil, plus extra for sprinkling

pinch of salt (optional)

1 red chile, seeded and minced

2 garlic cloves, crushed

2 tbsp tamari soy sauce

1¼lb (600g) fresh kale, cut into strips with the stalks removed

2 tbsp fresh orange juice

¼ cup walnut pieces, toasted, to garnish

FOR A GLUTEN-FREE OPTION
use gluten-free noodles

1 Cook the soba noodles following package directions. Add a dash of walnut oil and a pinch of salt to the water before you add the noodles, if you like.

2 Meanwhile, place a large, heavy saucepan with a lid over medium heat and add the walnut oil along with 2 tablespoons of water. When the oil has warmed through, add the minced chile and crushed garlic, and stir. Add the tamari soy sauce, followed by the kale, and stir to coat the leaves in the other ingredients.

3 Add the orange juice, cover, and let the kale steam for 2–3 minutes, or until it is just cooked. Stir occasionally while it cooks, to stop it from sticking to the bottom of the pan, and add a dash of water if necessary. Remove from the heat. Arrange the soba noodles on a warmed serving dish, pile the kale on top, and scatter with the toasted walnuts. Sprinkle the dish with a few drops of walnut oil to serve.

NUTRITION PER SERVING

Energy	556kcals/2326kJ
Carbohydrate	71g
of which sugar	8g
Fat	20g
of which saturates	2g
Salt	2.5g
Fiber	7g

Tomato, bean, and zucchini stew

Packed with vitamins, this hearty stew makes a perfect dinner on a chilly winter evening.

| Low saturated fat |
| Dairy free |
| Low salt |
| High fiber |

SERVES 4
PREP 10 MINS
COOK 20 MINS

3 tbsp olive oil

1 large onion, finely chopped

2 zucchini, cut into bite-sized chunks

3 garlic cloves, finely sliced

1 x 14oz (400g) can borlotti beans, drained and rinsed

3 fresh tomatoes, diced

1 tsp paprika

1 tsp dried oregano

sea salt and freshly ground black pepper

hot chili oil, to serve (optional)

crusty bread, to serve

1 Heat the oil in a deep-sided frying pan, add the onion, and cook over medium heat for 3 minutes. Add the zucchini and cook for another 5 minutes, stirring frequently.

2 Add the garlic and beans, cook for 1 minute, then stir in the tomatoes, paprika, and oregano. Cook for 10 minutes, stirring occasionally, then season with salt and pepper. Drizzle with chili oil, if desired, and serve with crusty bread.

NUTRITION PER SERVING	
Energy	168kcals/696kJ
Carbohydrate	15g
of which sugar	5.5g
Fat	9g
of which saturates	1.5g
Salt	0.1g
Fiber	7g

Mixed root tempura

Root vegetables and leeks are given a Japanese treatment in this quick tempura recipe. Serve to your guests with sweet chili sauce for dipping.

Low saturated fat

Dairy free

Low salt

High fiber

SERVES 6
PREP 10 MINS
COOK 20 MINS

1 parsnip, cut into short fingers

1 large carrot, cut into short fingers

½ small celery root, cut into small chunks

½ small rutabaga

1 leek, cut into thick slices

2 tbsp cornstarch

sunflower oil, for deep-frying

FOR THE BATTER

½ cup self-rising flour

½ cup cornstarch

¾ cup sparkling mineral water

2 tsp sunflower oil

½ tsp salt

¾ tsp cumin seeds

1 Bring a large saucepan of water to a boil. Carefully add the vegetables and cook for about 2 minutes until blanched. Remove from the heat and drain using a colander.

2 Transfer the vegetables onto paper towels, pat dry, and transfer to a large bowl. Sprinkle over the cornstarch, toss to coat well, and set aside.

3 For the batter, place all the ingredients in a separate bowl and, using a balloon whisk, mix until well combined.

4 Heat the oil in a large wok over high heat. Dip the vegetables in the batter, a few at a time, to coat lightly, shaking off any excess. Then deep-fry for 2–3 minutes, turning occasionally, until golden.

5 Using a slotted spoon, remove the tempura from the pan. Drain on a double layer of paper towels. Serve immediately.

NUTRITION PER SERVING	
Energy	313vkcals/1310kJ
Carbohydrate	36g
of which sugar	6g
Fat	16g
of which saturates	2g
Salt	0.7g
Fiber	6g

WHOLESOME PASTAS

Spaghetti with garlic, oil, and red chile

This vibrant Sicilian sauce is ready in minutes and often dresses spaghetti, arguably the star of Italian pasta.

Low saturated fat

Low salt

SERVES 4
PREP 10 MINS
COOK 10 MINS

salt and freshly ground
   black pepper

14oz (400g) dried
   spaghetti

⅓ cup olive oil

2 garlic cloves, crushed

1 small red chile, seeded
   and finely chopped

3 tbsp snipped flat-leaf
   parsley

freshly grated ricotta
   salata, pecorino, feta,
   or Parmesan cheese,
   to serve (optional)

1 Bring a large saucepan of lightly salted water to a boil, then add the spaghetti and cook until al dente, or according to the package instructions.

2 Meanwhile, heat 5 tablespoons of the oil in a large sauté pan or nonstick frying pan and cook the garlic and chile over low heat, stirring frequently, until the garlic turns golden. Add ¼ cup of spaghetti water. Remove from the heat, stir, and set aside until the spaghetti is cooked.

3 Drain the spaghetti in a colander. Over high heat, stir the garlic sauce until emulsified and pour in the spaghetti. Stir in the remaining oil and the parsley. Toss until thoroughly coated. Adjust the seasoning. Serve immediately, with grated ricotta salata or other cheese, if you like.

NUTRITION PER SERVING	
Energy	526kcals/2201kJ
Carbohydrate	72g
of which sugar	2g
Fat	19g
of which saturates	3g
Salt	0g
Fiber	5g

Chanterelles and chiles with pasta

Kamut is an ancient grain closely related to modern wheat. It contains gluten, but has been found to be more easily digestible for people with wheat intolerance.

Low salt

High fiber

SERVES 4
PREP 10 MINS
COOK 15–20 MINS

14oz (400g) fresh chanterelle mushrooms, sliced

4 tsp olive oil

2–3 garlic cloves, crushed

1–2 small chiles, seeded and finely chopped

⅓ cup sour cream

salt and freshly ground black pepper

1lb 2oz (500g) pasta, such as tagliatelle or spaghetti, made from kamut wheat

1 tbsp finely chopped flat-leaf parsley leaves, to garnish

1 Place the mushrooms in a medium saucepan and dry-fry them over low heat, shaking the pan gently, until their juices run. Then turn the heat up so the liquid evaporates and the mushrooms are soft, but reasonably dry. Add 3 teaspoons of the olive oil to coat the mushrooms, then add the garlic, chiles, and sour cream. Let the mixture simmer over low heat for 2–6 minutes. Season with salt and black pepper.

2 Meanwhile, cook the pasta following package directions until it is al dente, adding the last teaspoon of olive oil to the cooking water to prevent it from boiling over and to enhance the flavor of the pasta. Drain and transfer to a warmed serving dish. Spoon the sauce over the pasta, garnish with the parsley, toss the ingredients well to combine, and serve with a green salad.

try this....
Mushrooms, scallions, and chiles with pasta

Replace the chanterelles with **oyster mushrooms**. Add 1 bunch of finely chopped **scallions** with the garlic and chile. Once the mushrooms are cooked, stir in 10oz (300g) **white crabmeat** and then continue with step 2.

NUTRITION PER SERVING	
Energy	557kcals/2330kJ
Carbohydrate	90g
of which sugar	3.5g
Fat	11g
of which saturates	4g
Salt	0.3g
Fiber	6g

Farfalle with spinach, avocado, and tomatoes

Slow-roasted tomatoes are sold in vacuum packs. Sun-dried tomatoes, drained of oil, may be used instead.

Dairy free

Low salt

High fiber

SERVES 4
PREP 10 MINS
COOK 16 MINS

14oz (400g) dried farfalle pasta

2 tbsp olive oil

4 scallions, cut into short lengths

1 garlic clove, finely chopped

1 tsp dried chile flakes

12oz (350g) baby spinach leaves

⅔ cup vegetable stock

4 sun-dried tomatoes, chopped

6oz (175g) baby plum tomatoes, halved

1oz (30g) pitted black olives, sliced

1½ tbsp pickled capers

2 avocados, peeled, pitted, and diced

squeeze of lemon juice

salt and freshly ground black pepper

3 tbsp pumpkin seeds

lemon wedges and a few torn basil leaves, to garnish

1 Cook the pasta according to the package directions. Drain. Heat the oil in a deep-sided sauté pan or wok. Add the scallions and garlic and fry, stirring gently, for 1 minute. Stir in the chiles.

2 Add the spinach and stock and simmer, turning over gently for about 2 minutes until beginning to wilt. Gently fold in the pasta and the remaining ingredients. Simmer for 3 minutes until most of the liquid has been absorbed.

3 Pile into warmed, shallow bowls. Garnish with lemon wedges and a few torn basil leaves.

NUTRITION PER SERVING	
Energy	680kcals/2845kJ
Carbohydrate	79g
of which sugar	7g
Fat	29g
of which saturates	6g
Salt	0.5g
Fiber	11g

try this....
Brown rice and shrimp

Replace the farfalle with 10oz (300g) **brown basmati rice**, cooked according to the package instructions. In step 1, add 10oz (300g) cooked, peeled **shrimp**.

Spaghetti with chile flakes, broccoli, and spring onion

This is a simple way to enjoy fresh greens at their best. You can use other pasta instead if you prefer—try the sauce with bucatini or the large, flat pappardelle for a change.

Low saturated fat

Low salt

High fiber

SERVES 4
PREP 10 MINS
COOK 12 MINS

12oz (350g) dried spaghetti

salt and freshly ground black pepper

7oz (200g) sprouting broccoli or broccoli rabe

5 tbsp olive oil

bunch of scallions, trimmed and chopped

1 tsp dried chile flakes

1 tbsp lime juice

Parmesan cheese, grated, to serve

FOR A GLUTEN-FREE OPTION
use gluten-free pasta

1 Cook the spaghetti in boiling salted water according to package instructions. Drain and return to the pan.

2 Meanwhile, trim the broccoli, cut the heads into small florets, and chop the stalks.

3 Heat the oil in a large frying pan or wok. Add the broccoli and spring onions or scallions and stir-fry for about 4 minutes until just tender.

4 Pour the contents of the pan into the spaghetti. Add the flakes, lime juice, and seasoning to taste. Toss gently, pile onto plates, and serve with plenty of Parmesan cheese.

try this....
Spaghetti with broccoli, capers, and smoked salmon

Replace white spaghetti with **whole grain spaghetti**. At the end of step 3, combine the broccoli and spaghetti, then stir in 10oz (300g) coarsely chopped **smoked salmon**, 2 tablespoons **capers**, ½ cup **half-and-half**, and **zest** from 1 **lemon**.

NUTRITION PER SERVING	
Energy	462kcals/1933kJ
Carbohydrate	64g
of which sugar	3g
Fat	16g
of which saturates	2g
Salt	0g
Fiber	6g

Pasta with asparagus and zucchini

This pasta dish is an easy and delicious way to get plenty of green vegetables—and thus plenty of fiber and antioxidants—into your diet.

Low saturated fat

Low salt

High fiber

SERVES 4
PREP 10 MINS
COOK 20 MINS

1 tbsp olive oil

1 onion, finely chopped

pinch of sea salt

4 small zucchini, 2 diced and 2 coarsely grated

3 garlic cloves, finely chopped

1 bunch thin asparagus, trimmed and stalks cut crosswise into thirds

½ cup dry white wine

1–2 tsp capers, rinsed and chopped

finely grated zest of 1 lemon

12oz (350g) dried penne

handful of finely chopped flat-leaf parsley

finely grated Parmesan cheese, for serving

FOR A GLUTEN-FREE OPTION
use gluten-free pasta

NUTRITION PER SERVING	
Energy	392kcals/1661kJ
Carbohydrate	68g
of which sugar	6g
Fat	5g
of which saturates	0.8g
Salt	0.3g
Fiber	7g

1 Heat the oil in a large frying pan, add the onion and a pinch of salt, and cook over low heat for 5 minutes or until soft. Add all the zucchini and cook for 10 minutes, stirring frequently, until they have cooked down and softened. Do not allow them to brown.

2 Stir in the garlic and asparagus. Add the wine, increase the heat, and allow to bubble for 2–3 minutes. Return to a simmer. Cook for 2–3 minutes, until the asparagus is tender, then stir in the capers and lemon zest.

3 Meanwhile, cook the pasta as the package directs. Drain, reserving a small amount of the cooking water. Return the pasta to the pot and toss together with the reserved cooking water. Add the vegetable mixture and parsley, and toss again. Sprinkle with Parmesan and serve.

Pasta with peas and pancetta

This meal is a speedy pasta dish that relies on a handful of pantry essentials to make a satisfying dinner. Replace the pancetta with thinly sliced ham for a leaner cut of pork.

High fiber

SERVES 4
PREP 10 MINS
COOK 15 MINS

10oz (300g) dried shell pasta, such as conchigliette

salt and freshly ground black pepper

7oz (200g) frozen peas or tender young peas

2 tbsp olive oil

3½oz (100g) pancetta, chopped

2 garlic cloves, crushed

1¾oz (50g) finely grated Parmesan

FOR A GLUTEN-FREE OPTION
use gluten-free pasta

1 Cook the pasta in boiling salted water according to the package instructions. A minute or two before the end of cooking, throw the peas in with the pasta to cook through. Drain (reserving a ladleful of the cooking water) and return it to the pan with the reserved water.

2 Meanwhile, heat the oil in a large frying pan. Cook the pancetta for 3–5 minutes over medium heat until crispy. Add the garlic and cook for another minute, then remove from the heat.

3 Toss the garlicky pancetta through the pasta and peas and follow with the Parmesan cheese. Season well to taste and serve with extra Parmesan cheese.

try this....
Pea and shrimp pasta

Omit the pancetta and Parmesan cheese. In step 2, add 10oz (300g) cooked, peeled **shrimp**. In step 3, add the **juice** and **zest** of 1 small **lemon** and season to taste.

NUTRITION PER SERVING	
Energy	507kcals/2121kJ
Carbohydrate	60g
of which sugar	3g
Fat	19g
of which saturates	6.5g
Salt	1.2g
Fiber	6g

Pasta with crab and lemon

Rich in omega-3s, crab is a good source of protein and the minerals chromium and selenium.

SERVES 4
PREP 5 MINS
COOK 10 MINS

1 tbsp olive oil

1 large onion, cut into quarters, then finely sliced

salt and freshly ground black pepper

2 garlic cloves, finely sliced

grated zest and juice of 1 lemon

handful of fresh flat-leaf parsley, finely chopped

7oz (200g) fresh or canned crabmeat, picked over to remove any shell

12oz (350g) linguine or spaghetti

chili oil, to serve (optional)

FOR A GLUTEN-FREE OPTION
use gluten-free pasta

1 Heat the oil in a large frying pan, add the onion and a pinch of salt, and cook over low heat for 5 minutes, until soft. Stir in the garlic and lemon zest and cook for a few seconds more.

2 Stir in the parsley and crabmeat, then season well with salt and lots of pepper. Add lemon juice to taste.

3 Meanwhile, cook the pasta according to package directions, until tender but still firm to the bite. Drain, reserving a small amount of the cooking water. Return the pasta to the pot and toss together with the reserved cooking water. Add the crab sauce, toss again, drizzle with chili oil, and serve.

NUTRITION PER SERVING

Energy	415kcals/1739kJ
Carbohydrate	66g
of which sugar	4g
Fat	6g
of which saturates	1g
Salt	0.4g
Fiber	5g

Trofie with pesto

The original pasta of Genoa, trofie is often dressed with pesto and is particularly good with green beans and, surprisingly, diced potatoes.

> Low saturated fat

> Low salt

> High fiber

SERVES 4–6
PREP 10 MINS
COOK 15–20 MINS

sea salt and freshly ground black pepper

7oz (200g) small green beans, trimmed and cut into 1½in (3cm) segments

2 potatoes, peeled and diced

1lb–1lb 2oz (450g–500g) dried trofie

handful of small basil leaves, to garnish

2 tbsp Parmesan shavings, to garnish

FOR PESTO GENOVESE

3–4 garlic cloves

5–6 tbsp pine nuts

3–4 large handfuls of basil leaves, torn

2 tbsp coarsely grated Parmesan or pecorino cheese

4–6 tbsp fruity olive oil

FOR A GLUTEN-FREE OPTION
use gluten-free pasta

1 For the pesto, crush the garlic using a mortar and pestle. Add the pine nuts and pound well until creamy. Add the basil and a little salt. Pound until you get a rough, fragrant purée. Add the cheese and pound until mixed. Work in the oil, a little at a time, working in the same direction, until you get a thick, bright green sauce. Season and cover with plastic wrap.

2 Bring a large saucepan filled with water to a boil over high heat. Season with salt, add the beans, and boil for 4–6 minutes, until just tender. Remove the beans with a slotted spoon, refresh under cold running water, then drain and set aside.

3 Add the potatoes to the saucepan and return to a boil. Add the trofie and cook, according to the package instructions, until al dente. Meanwhile, put the pesto in a serving bowl and pour in 3 tablespoons of the boiling cooking liquid.

4 Drain the pasta and potatoes. Pour into the bowl with the pesto, add the beans, and toss gently. Adjust the seasoning with pepper and scatter with the basil and Parmesan.

NUTRITION PER SERVING	
Energy	769–512kcals/ 3234–2156kJ
Carbohydrate	100–68g
of which sugar	5–3g
Fat	31–20.5g
of which saturates	6–4g
Salt	0.4–0.2g
Fiber	8–6g

Shrimp and garlic "pasta"

Also known as "zoodles" (zucchini noodles), the spaghetti-like ribbons of zucchini in this quick and enticing dish offer a healthy, carb- and gluten-free alternative to pasta.

Low carb

Low saturated fat

Dairy free

Gluten free

Low salt

SERVES 4
PREP 20 MINS
COOK 5 MINS

6 zucchini

1 tbsp olive oil, plus extra for drizzling

1 garlic clove, crushed

1 red chile, deseeded and chopped

10oz (300g) raw shrimp, peeled and deveined

2 tbsp chopped fresh dill

squeeze of lemon juice

salt and freshly ground black pepper

1 Cut off a thin slice along the length of each zucchini (to keep them from rolling around), and place on a cutting board. Use a julienne peeler to slice the zucchini into thin ribbons, stopping and rotating each zucchini when you reach the seeds.

2 Heat the oil in a large frying pan. Add the garlic, chile, and shrimp and sauté until the shrimp are pink and cooked through. Remove from the heat. Stir in 1 tablespoon dill.

3 While the shrimp is cooking, blanch (briefly boil) the zucchini. Place enough water to cover the zucchini in a large saucepan. Add a pinch of salt and bring to a boil. Then add the zucchini, cook for 1 minute, and remove. Plunge the zucchini into a bowl of ice water to stop the cooking process.

4 Drain the zucchini, drizzle with the lemon juice and a little oil, and season to taste. Toss to mix, top with the shrimp, sprinkle over the remaining dill, and serve.

try this....
Pesto, cherry tomatoes, and garlic zucchini

For a vegetarian option, omit the shrimp, stir through some **pesto sauce**, and top with halved **cherry tomatoes**.

NUTRITION PER SERVING	
Energy	131kcals/548kJ
Carbohydrate	3g
of which sugar	3g
Fat	7g
of which saturates	1g
Salt	0.3g
Fiber	2g

Swordfish in salmoriglio

Swordfish has long been caught off the coasts of Sicily, where it is very popular. Use only sustainable swordfish. Its firm meaty texture makes it perfect for grilling and broiling.

| Low carb |
| Low saturated fat |
| Dairy free |
| Gluten free |
| Low salt |

SERVES 4
PREP 10 MINS,
PLUS MARINATING
COOK 8 MINS

2 swordfish steaks, at least
 1in (2.5cm) thick, about 1½lb
 (700g) total weight

1 tbsp snipped herbs, such
 as parsley, oregano, or mint,
 to finish

FOR THE SALMORIGLIO SAUCE

finely grated zest and juice
 of 1 lemon

1 tbsp snipped flat-leaf parsley

1–2 garlic cloves, crushed

½ tbsp chopped fresh oregano,
 or 1 tsp dried oregano

½ tsp chile powder

salt and freshly ground
 black pepper

6 tbsp olive oil

1 For the sauce, place the lemon zest and juice, parsley, garlic, oregano, and chile powder in a bowl, mix well, and season. Whisk in the oil and 2 tablespoons of cold water and the oil. Brush the steaks with half the sauce and let marinate for 5 minutes.

2 Preheat the broiler to high, or preheat a griddle pan. Broil or grill the steaks for 3–4 minutes only on each side, or until just cooked through but still moist in the center, since swordfish tends to get dry quickly.

3 To serve, cut each steak in half and spoon over the remaining sauce. Season with a little extra pepper, scatter with the snipped herbs, and serve immediately.

NUTRITION PER SERVING

Energy	353kcals/1469kJ
Carbohydrate	0g
of which sugar	0g
Fat	24g
of which saturates	4g
Salt	0.6g
Fiber	0g

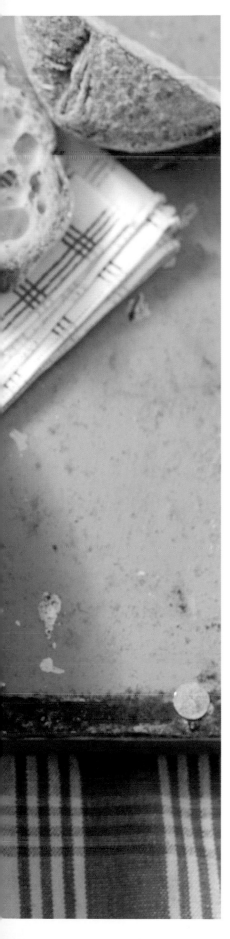

Marinated tuna

Briefly frying or poaching fish, then marinating it to finish the cooking is a favorite Mediterranean cooking method.

SERVES 4–6
PREP 10 MINS,
PLUS CHILLING
COOK 10–15 MINS

⅓ cup olive oil

1lb (450g) fresh boneless tuna or other fish fillet, cut into ½in (1cm) thick slices

1 large mild onion, cut into thin rings, rings halved

salt and freshly ground black pepper

2 garlic cloves, crushed

1 tsp smoked pimentón (Spanish paprika)

1 scant tsp ground cumin or coriander

1 tbsp snipped flat-leaf parsley

a few sprigs of thyme

1 lemon, thinly sliced

3 tbsp white wine vinegar

Low carb

Low saturated fat

Dairy free

Gluten carb

Low salt

1 Heat 1 tablespoon of the oil in a frying pan. Add the tuna slices and sear over medium heat for 2 minutes on each side, until colored and a little stiff. Place the slices in a nonmetallic dish.

2 Add 2 tablespoons of the oil to the pan, stir in the halved onion rings, season, and cook for 3–5 minutes over medium heat. Add the garlic, paprika, and cumin. Fry for another 2 minutes, stirring occasionally. Spoon the contents of the pan over the fish and spread with the back of a spoon to coat evenly. Season again lightly and stir.

3 Scatter over the parsley and thyme. Cover the tuna with the slices of lemon. Mix the remaining oil with the vinegar and pour over the fish. Cover with plastic wrap and refrigerate overnight or for 24 hours. Serve as an appetizer, chilled, or at room temperature.

try this....
Swordfish and orange escabeche
....
Replace the tuna with
4 **swordfish steaks** and replace
the lemon with **orange**.

NUTRITION PER SERVING

Energy	189kcals/791kJ
Carbohydrate	2g
of which sugar	1.5g
Fat	11g
of which saturates	1.7g
Salt	0.1g
Fiber	0.5g

Seared tuna with cucumber and fennel

This tuna is served very rare, so use the freshest possible fish. Avoid bluefin tuna, which is endangered.

Low carb
Low saturated fat
Dairy free
Gluten free
Low salt

SERVES 4
PREP 15 MINS, PLUS COOLING
COOK 6 MINS

6 tbsp olive oil, plus extra
  for brushing

4 x 5½oz (150g) tuna steaks

salt and freshly ground black pepper

1 fennel bulb, sliced

2 shallots, finely chopped

1 cucumber, deseeded, skinned,
  and finely chopped

1oz (30g) mint, parsley, and chervil
  leaves, torn and mixed

juice of 1 lemon

8 anchovy fillets

lemon wedges, to serve

1 Rub 2 tablespoons of oil over the tuna steaks and sprinkle with lots of black pepper. Set aside.

2 Heat 2 tablespoons of olive oil and sauté the fennel for 4–5 minutes, or until just tender. Season with salt and pepper. Tip the fennel into a large bowl and set aside to cool a little.

3 Add the shallots, cucumber, and herbs to the fennel. Stir in the lemon juice and remaining oil.

4 Heat a heavy frying pan or grill pan until smoking. Lightly brush the tuna steaks with oil, then pan-fry for 30 seconds. Brush the top with a little more oil, turn over, and cook for another 30 seconds.

5 Place a tuna steak on each serving plate, with the salad piled on top, and two anchovies draped over. Drizzle with the remaining lemon and oil from the bowl, and serve with a wedge of lemon. This dish is good with a salad of warm parsley-buttered new potatoes.

try this....
Seared tuna with mango salsa

Prepare and cook the tuna as above and serve with a salsa made from 1 diced **mango**, 1 **red bell pepper**, and 1 **red onion**, mixed with a handful of chopped **cilantro leaves**.

NUTRITION PER SERVING

Energy	370kcals/1548kJ
Carbohydrate	2g
of which sugar	2g
Fat	21.5g
of which saturates	3g
Salt	1.2g
Fiber	2.4g

Tuna steaks with cucumber and red onion relish

Tuna is a fabulous fish to cook on the grill; its robust, meaty texture means the steaks hold together well.

Low carb

Low saturated fat

Dairy free

Gluten free

SERVES 4
PREP 10 MINS, PLUS MARINATING
COOK 10 MINS

6in (15cm) piece of cucumber

2 tbsp rice wine or white wine vinegar

1 tsp granulated sugar

pinch of chile flakes

pinch of salt

¼ red onion, finely sliced

4 tuna steaks, approx.
 3½oz (100g) each

1 tbsp olive oil

1 tsp smoked paprika

salt and freshly ground black pepper

lemon or lime wedges, to serve

1 Prepare the grill for cooking. Slice the cucumber in half lengthwise and scoop out the seeds with a spoon. Slice each half again lengthwise to make four long, thin pieces. Slice thinly on a diagonal.

2 In a bowl, whisk together the vinegar, sugar, chile flakes, and salt. Mix in the sliced cucumber and red onion, cover, and leave in the refrigerator to rest for 30 minutes (this helps soften the taste of the raw onion).

3 Rub each tuna steak on both sides with a little oil and smoked paprika and season them well. Cook the tuna on the hot grill for 2–3 minutes on each side for medium, or 3–4 minutes for well done (and less for rare tuna, but only serve it this way if it is very fresh). It is easy to see if the tuna has cooked on one side, because the fish will turn opaque from the bottom upward when looked at from the side. Remember that the fish will continue to cook when removed from the grill.

4 Serve with the cucumber relish and a wedge of lemon or lime to squeeze over.

NUTRITION PER SERVING	
Energy	174kcals/729kJ
Carbohydrate	2g
of which sugar	1.5g
Fat	7.5g
of which saturates	1.5g
Salt	0.4g
Fiber	0.8g

try this....
Tuna steaks with black-eyed peas and avocado salsa

Serve with a salsa made from 14oz (400g) **canned black-eyed peas**, rinsed and drained, 1 diced **avocado**, and 1 finely chopped **onion** mixed with a handful of chopped **cilantro leaves**.

Red snapper in rakı sauce

Once the favorite fish of the Romans, red snapper is one of the most prized fish in the eastern Mediterranean. In this popular Turkish recipe, the fish is doused in rakı, Turkey's national spirit and the preferred drink to accompany mezze and fish.

Low carb
Low saturated fat
Dairy free
Gluten free
Low salt

SERVES 4
PREP 5 MINS
COOK 12 MINS

4 fresh red snapper, gutted
 and cleaned

2–3 tbsp olive oil

salt and freshly ground
 black pepper

about ⅔ cup rakı or ouzo

small bunch of flat-leaf parsley,
 finely chopped

1 lemon, cut into quarters

1 Preheat the broiler. Brush the fish with oil on both sides and season. Line a grill pan with aluminum foil and place the fish on top.

2 Place the grill pan under the broiler and cook the fish for 5–6 minutes on each side, allowing the skin to buckle and brown. Remove from the broiler and place the fish on a serving dish. Splash with the rakı or ouzo, set it alight, and wait until the flames die down before serving.

3 To serve, garnish with a sprinkling of parsley and serve each fish with a drizzle of rakı and a wedge of lemon to squeeze over.

NUTRITION PER SERVING	
Energy	309kcals/1293kJ
Carbohydrate	0g
of which sugar	0g
Fat	13g
of which saturates	0.8g
Salt	0.5g
Fiber	0g

Rockfish with herb crust

This recipe works well with fish that have a slightly earthy taste, such as rockfish. Soaking the rockfish in a little acidulated water before cooking improves its flavor.

SERVES 4
PREP 15 MINS
COOK 12–15 MINS

4 rockfish or gray mullet fillets, about 6oz (175g) each, peeled

1 tbsp olive oil

1 tbsp chopped flat-leaf parsley

juice of ½ lemon

salt and freshly ground black pepper

a few sprigs of sage, to garnish

lemon wedges, to garnish

FOR THE CRUST
8 tbsp fresh bread crumbs

1 tbsp melted butter

1 tbsp chopped sage

1 tbsp snipped chives

grated zest of ½ lemon

1 Preheat the oven to 400°F (200°C). Arrange the fish on a baking sheet. Mix the oil, parsley, and lemon juice, and season with salt and plenty of pepper.

2 To make the crust, mix together the bread crumbs, melted butter, sage, chives, and lemon zest. Season lightly and sprinkle over the fish, pressing to stick to the butter.

3 Roast in the oven for 12–15 minutes, or until the fish is cooked—it will be firm, white, and opaque.

4 Transfer to a warmed serving dish, garnish with the sage and lemon wedges, and serve with green beans.

try this....
A Parmesan, olive, and sun-dried tomato crust

Mix 8 tablespoons fresh bread crumbs with 2 tablespoons grated **Parmesan**, 1 tablespoon chopped, pitted **black olives**, and 4 finely chopped **sun-dried tomatoes**, and continue as above.

NUTRITION PER SERVING

Energy	363kcals/1519kJ
Carbohydrate	22g
of which sugar	1.5g
Fat	13g
of which saturates	4g
Salt	0.7g
Fiber	0.3g

Baked fish with a herb crust

This easy fish recipe looks amazing with its vivid green crust, and is an aromatic crowd-pleaser.

Low carb

Low saturated fat

Dairy free

Low salt

SERVES 4

PREP 5 MINS

COOK 10 MINS

1 cup fresh white bread crumbs

2 tbsp roughly chopped basil leaves

2 tbsp roughly chopped flat-leaf parsley leaves

2 tbsp roughly chopped chives

finely grated zest of ½ lemon

salt and freshly ground black pepper

¼ cup olive oil, plus extra for brushing

4 fillets firm-fleshed, white, sustainable fish, such as cod or haddock, approx. 5½ oz (150g) each

FOR A GLUTEN-FREE OPTION

use gluten-free breadcrumbs

1 Preheat the oven to 425°F (220°C). In a small food processor, pulse the bread crumbs, herbs, lemon zest, and seasoning, until the bread crumbs are bright green.

2 Add the oil in a slow stream, with the food processor running, until it forms a thick, bright green paste.

3 Brush the fish fillets with a little oil on both sides and season them well. Press the herb crust onto the top (or skinless side) of the fillets, packing it down well. Place on a nonstick baking sheet and bake in the top of the oven for 10 minutes, or until cooked through and turning crispy on top.

NUTRITION PER SERVING	
Energy	290kcals/1214kJ
Carbohydrate	9g
of which sugar	0g
Fat	15g
of which saturates	2g
Salt	0.5g
Fiber	0.5g

Whole fish with tomato sauce

Make sure you use flavorful tomatoes, since they make all the difference to the finished dish. You can make the tomato sauce 2–3 days in advance, cover, and refrigerate.

Low carb

Low saturated fat

Dairy free

Gluten free

Low salt

SERVES 4
PREP 10 MINS
COOK 25 MINS

4 small sea bream or black rockfish, about 12oz (350g) in total, scaled, gutted, and trimmed

1 tbsp buckwheat flour

salt and freshly ground black pepper

5 tbsp extra virgin olive oil

1 onion, finely chopped

2 celery stalks, finely sliced

2 garlic cloves, chopped

8 plum tomatoes, coarsely chopped

5 tbsp dry white wine

pinch of sugar

2 tbsp chopped flat-leaf parsley

1 Preheat the oven to 375°F (190°C). Slash the rockfish 3–4 times on each side with a sharp knife. Mix the flour with some salt and pepper and dust it over the fish. Arrange on a baking sheet.

2 Heat the oil in a pan over low heat, add the onion, celery, and garlic, and cook for 2–3 minutes, until the vegetables soften. Add the tomatoes and wine, and cook for 3–4 minutes, until the juices run. Season with salt and pepper and add the sugar.

3 Spoon the tomato sauce over the fish and bake in the oven for 15–20 minutes, or until cooked. The flesh will be white and opaque.

4 Slide the fish onto a large, warmed serving dish, sprinkle with parsley, and serve immediately.

NUTRITION PER SERVING	
Energy	282 kcals/1180kJ
Carbohydrate	11g
of which sugar	8g
Fat	17g
of which saturates	2g
Salt	0.3g
Fiber	3g

Barbecued mackerel with fennel and tomato salad

The strong flavors of mackerel are complemented well by this robust marinade and the bright, zingy salad.

Low carb

Dairy free

Gluten free

Low salt

SERVES 4
PREP 20 MINS,
PLUS MARINATING
COOK 6 MINS

1 hot red chile, seeded
  and finely chopped

1 tbsp small capers, rinsed,
  dried, and chopped

2 tbsp olive oil, plus extra
  for brushing

juice of 1 lemon, plus extra
  lemon wedges to serve

4 large skin-on mackerel fillets

salt and freshly ground
  black pepper

FOR THE SALAD

1 bulb fennel, thinly sliced

9oz (250g) cherry tomatoes,
  halved

2 red chiles, seeded and thinly
  sliced lengthwise

½ bunch chives, snipped into
  1in (2.5cm) lengths

large handful of flat leaf parsley,
  chopped

4 sprigs of dill, chopped

2 tbsp olive oil

juice of ½ lemon

1 garlic clove, crushed

1 Mix together the chile, capers, olive oil, and lemon juice in a wide, shallow bowl. Add the mackerel fillets and season well on both sides. Rub the mixture over the fish, cover, and marinate in the refrigerator for 1 hour.

2 Cook the fish, skin-side down, for 2–3 minutes, or until the skin is golden brown. Turn it gently, brush with the marinade, and cook for another 2–3 minutes. Remove from the heat and divide between four warmed serving plates.

3 Put the salad ingredients in a serving bowl, toss gently, and serve with the fish, with lemon wedges for squeezing.

NUTRITION PER SERVING	
Energy	504kcals/2089kJ
Carbohydrate	3g
of which sugar	2.5g
Fat	40g
of which saturates	7g
Salt	0.6g
Fiber	2.1g

Grilled halibut with green sauce

A fresh-tasting dish that is easy to prepare and cooks in minutes. The high water content of halibut makes it a mild-flavored, low-calorie fish.

Low carb

Low saturated fat

Dairy free

Gluten free

Low salt

SERVES 6
PREP 10 MINS
COOK 4 MINS

FOR THE SAUCE
1 cup packed mixed herbs (parsley, chives, mint, tarragon, and chervil)

½ cup olive oil

1 tbsp tarragon vinegar

2 garlic cloves

salt and freshly ground black pepper

sugar (optional)

FOR THE FISH
6 thick halibut fillets, about 5oz (140g) each

1 tbsp olive oil

salt and freshly ground black pepper

lemon wedges, for serving

1 Process the herbs, oil, tarragon vinegar, and garlic in a blender until smooth. Season with salt and pepper. If it tastes slightly bitter, add sugar to taste. Transfer the sauce to a bowl, cover, and refrigerate until serving.

2 Preheat the broiler or start an outdoor grill. Lightly brush each fillet with oil and season with salt and pepper. Broil or grill, turning once, about 4 minutes, until the fish is barely opaque when pierced with the tip of a sharp knife. Transfer to plates and serve, with the green sauce and the lemon wedges.

try this....
Halibut with a cherry tomato sauce

Prepare and cook the halibut as in step 2. To make the tomato sauce, first slice 2 cartons **cherry tomatoes** in half. Heat 1 tablespoon olive oil in a pan, then add the tomatoes and cook over low heat for 5 minutes. Add 1 teaspoon **balsamic vinegar** and ½ cup **vegetable stock**, and simmer until the liquid starts to thicken.

NUTRITION PER SERVING	
Energy	294kcals/1230kJ
Carbohydrate	0.3g
of which sugar	0.3g
Fat	19g
of which saturates	3g
Salt	0.2g
Fiber	0g

Asian halibut en papillote

Though the flavorings here are Chinese in origin, the method of cooking food in paper parcels is French. Noodles and stir-fried crisp vegetables would make excellent sides.

Low carb

Low saturated fat

Dairy free

SERVES 4
PREP 15–20 MINS
COOK 10–12 MINS

salt

4½oz (125g) snow peas, trimmed

1in (2.5cm) piece fresh ginger, finely chopped

4 garlic cloves, finely chopped

2 tbsp black bean sauce

3 tbsp reduced-salt soy sauce

2 tbsp dry sherry

½ tsp granulated sugar

1 tbsp sesame oil

2 tbsp vegetable oil

1 egg

4 x 6oz (175g) skinned halibut fillets or steaks

4 scallions, thinly sliced

1 Half-fill a saucepan with salted water and bring to a boil. Add the snow peas and simmer for 1–2 minutes. Drain.

2 Combine the garlic, ginger, black bean sauce, soy sauce, sherry, sugar, and sesame oil in a bowl. Stir well to mix, then set aside.

3 Fold a sheet of baking parchment (about 12x15in/30x34.5cm) in half and draw a curve with a pencil to make a heart shape when unfolded. It should be large enough to leave a 3in (7.5cm) border around a fish fillet. Cut out the heart shape with scissors. Repeat to make four paper hearts. Open each out and brush with the oil, leaving a border about 1in (2.5cm) wide at the edges.

4 Put the egg and ½ teaspoon salt in a small bowl and beat together. Brush this egg glaze evenly on the border of each of the paper hearts.

5 Preheat the oven to 400°F (200°C). Rinse the fish fillets and pat dry with paper towels. Arrange a quarter of the snow peas on one side of each paper heart and set a halibut fillet on top. Spoon a quarter of the black bean mixture on top of each fillet and sprinkle with a quarter of the scallions. Fold the paper over the fish and stick the two sides of paper together. Make small pleats to seal the edges.

6 Twist the "tails" of each paper case to secure. Lay the cases on a baking sheet and bake for 10–12 minutes, until puffed and brown. Transfer to warmed plates, allowing each guest to open their own aromatic fish package.

NUTRITION PER SERVING	
Energy	319kcals/1335kJ
Carbohydrate	5g
of which sugar	4g
Fat	13g
of which saturates	2g
Salt	2.4g
Fiber	1.4g

Lemon sole with herbs

One serving of lemon sole will meet almost half of an adult's daily requirement for protein while also being low in calories. It is a good source of B vitamins.

Low carb

Low saturated fat

Dairy free

Gluten free

Low salt

SERVES 4
PREP 10 MINS
COOK 20 MINS

3 tbsp extra virgin olive oil

1 tbsp white wine vinegar

1 tsp Dijon mustard

small handful of fresh mixed herbs, such as parsley, thyme, and dill

sea salt and freshly ground black pepper

4 lemon sole or other sole fillets, or other flat white fish fillets such as plaice, about 6oz (175g) each

1 Preheat the oven to 400°F (200°C). To make the dressing, whisk together the oil and vinegar in a small bowl. Mix in the mustard and herbs to blend. Season well with salt and pepper.

2 Lay out the fish in a roasting pan, then add enough water to cover by about ¼in (5mm). Season well with salt and pepper. Bake in the oven for 10–15 minutes until the fish is cooked through and the water has nearly evaporated.

3 Using a spatula, carefully lift the fish onto a serving dish or individual plates. Spoon some of the herb dressing over each fillet. Serve hot with sautéed potatoes and broccoli.

NUTRITION PER SERVING	
Energy	222kcals/930kJ
Carbohydrate	0g
of which sugar	0g
Fat	11g
of which saturates	1.5g
Salt	0.5g
Fiber	0g

Chinese-style steamed bass

This restaurant-style dish is surprisingly easy to prepare. Sea bass offers high levels of protein but does contain mercury, so eat it only occasionally.

Low carb

Dairy free

SERVES 2
PREP 15 MINS
COOK 10–12 MINS

3 tbsp reduced-salt soy sauce

4 tbsp Chinese rice wine or dry sherry

3 tbsp shredded fresh ginger

2 small sea bass, scaled, gutted, and rinsed

1 tbsp sesame oil

½ tsp salt

2 scallions, trimmed and shredded

2 tbsp sunflower oil

2 garlic cloves, grated or finely chopped

1 small red chile, seeded and shredded

finely grated zest of 1 lime

1 Prepare a steamer, or position a steaming rack above a wok containing water so that the rack does not touch the water. Bring to a boil.

2 Stir together the soy sauce, rice wine, and 2 tablespoons of ginger, and set aside. Using a sharp knife, make slashes in the fish, 1in (2.5cm) apart and not as deep as the bone, on both sides. Rub the fish inside and out with the sesame oil and salt.

3 Scatter half the scallions over a heatproof serving dish that will hold the two fish and fit in the steamer or on the steaming rack. Place the fish on the dish and pour over the sauce.

4 Place the dish in the steamer or on the rack, cover, and steam for 10–12 minutes, or until the fish flakes easily when tested with a knife. Remove the fish, cover, and keep warm.

5 Meanwhile, heat the sunflower oil in a small saucepan over medium-high heat until it shimmers. Scatter the fish with the remaining scallions and ginger, and the garlic, chile, and lime zest. Drizzle the hot oil over the fish and serve.

NUTRITION PER SERVING	
Energy	553kcals/2314kJ
Carbohydrate	5g
of which sugar	2.5g
Fat	36g
of which saturates	6.5g
Salt	3.5g
Fiber	0.7g

Roast hake with remoulade

Remoulade is similar to tartar sauce and both work equally well with deep-fried, pan-fried, or roasted white fish.

Low carb

Low saturated fat

Gluten free

Low salt

SERVES 4
PREP 5–10 MINS
COOK 6–8 MINS

4 hake fillets, about 6oz (175g) each, pinboned and skinned

1 tbsp extra virgin olive oil

salt and freshly ground black pepper

4 small sprigs of thyme

sprigs of watercress, to serve

lemon wedges, to serve

FOR THE REMOULADE

5 tbsp mayonnaise

5 tbsp half-fat crème fraîche

1 tsp Dijon mustard

2 tsp chopped capers

2 tsp chopped gherkins

1 tbsp chopped tarragon

1 tbsp chopped chervil, or flat-leaf parsley

½–1 tsp anchovy paste, to taste

1 Preheat the oven to 400°F (200°C). To make the remoulade, mix all the ingredients in a small bowl and season to taste with anchovy paste and pepper.

2 Brush the hake with the olive oil and season lightly. Arrange on a baking sheet and put the thyme on top. Bake in the oven for 6–8 minutes, or until cooked; it will be opaque and the flesh white and firm. Remove the fish and drain well on paper towels.

3 Transfer the fish onto a warmed serving dish and garnish with the watercress and lemon wedges. Serve the remoulade separately.

NUTRITION PER SERVING	
Energy	347kcals/1452kJ
Carbohydrate	1.5g
of which sugar	1g
Fat	24g
of which saturates	4g
Salt	0.6g
Fiber	0g

Hake in green sauce

Add **extra** vegetables, such as lightly cooked peas or asparagus tips, to the sauce in keeping with its green theme.

Low carb

Low saturated fat

Dairy free

Low salt

SERVES 4
PREP 10 MINS
COOK 14–16 MINS

2 tbsp olive oil

2 garlic cloves, finely chopped

2 tbsp all-purpose flour

²⁄₃ cup dry white wine

¾ cup fish stock

¼ cup chopped flat-leaf parsley leaves

salt and freshly ground black pepper

4 skin-on hake fillets, approx. 5½oz (150g) each

sautéed potatoes and green beans, to serve

1 Heat the oil in a large, nonstick frying pan over medium heat. Gently cook the garlic for 1 minute.

2 Sprinkle the flour into the pan and stir thoroughly with a wooden spoon. Cook for 2 minutes, stirring until smooth. Gradually add the wine, followed by the stock, stirring constantly.

3 Stir in the parsley and simmer very gently over low heat for about 5 minutes.

4 Season the fish and add to the pan, skin-side down. Spoon some sauce over the top and cook for 2–3 minutes. Turn and cook for another 2–3 minutes, or until cooked through.

5 Transfer to warmed plates and serve immediately with sautéed potatoes and green beans.

NUTRITION PER SERVING	
Energy	238kcals/998kJ
Carbohydrate	6g
of which sugar	0.3g
Fat	9g
of which saturates	1.5g
Salt	0.8g
Fiber	0.3g

Keralan fish curry

The flavor and aroma of this curry is beautifully subtle and fragrant, so try it with any firm white fish. Tamarind paste offers a slight sourness.

Low saturated fat

Dairy free

Low salt

SERVES 4
PREP 10 MINS
COOK 15 MINS

1¾lb (800g) skinless haddock fillets, cut into bite-sized pieces

2 tsp ground turmeric

salt and freshly ground black pepper

1 tbsp vegetable oil

1 large onion, finely sliced

1 tsp black mustard seeds

5 curry leaves

1½in (4cm) fresh ginger, finely chopped

2 tbsp tamarind paste

¾ cup coconut milk

⅔ cup fish stock

2 scallions, finely sliced

1 red chile, seeded and finely chopped (optional)

basmati rice and chopped cilantro leaves, to serve

FOR A GLUTEN-FREE OPTION
use gluten-free stock

1 Place the haddock in a bowl, sprinkle with the turmeric, season, and stir to coat. Set aside.

2 Heat the oil in a large, nonstick frying pan over medium heat, and add the onion, black mustard seeds, and curry leaves. Cook gently for 10 minutes, stirring occasionally, until the onion is lightly brown.

3 Add the ginger and cook for 1 or 2 minutes, then add the tamarind paste, coconut milk, and stock, and stir well. Heat the sauce to a low simmer.

4 Add the fish and simmer gently for 3–4 minutes or until it is just cooked. Stir in the scallions and chile (if using).

5 Serve the curry with basmati rice, sprinkled with chopped cilantro leaves.

NUTRITION PER SERVING	
Energy	213kcals/905kJ
Carbohydrate	5.5g
of which sugar	5g
Fat	4.5g
of which saturates	0.5g
Salt	0.8g
Fiber	0.8g

Grilled sardines in harissa

Very fresh sardines have a sweet and delicate flavor.
And they're a rich source of calcium and potassium.

Low carb

Dairy free

Gluten free

Low salt

SERVES 4
PREP 25 MINS
COOK 2–3 MINS

12–16 sardines, scaled, gutted, and trimmed

1–2 tbsp olive oil

salt and freshly ground black pepper

1 tsp ground coriander

FOR THE HARISSA DRESSING

2 tbsp extra virgin olive oil

2 tbsp harissa paste

2 tsp honey, to taste

grated zest and juice of 1 lime

FOR THE SALAD

large handful of cilantro

2 Little Gem lettuces, finely sliced

grated zest and juice of 1 lemon

pinch of sugar

3 tbsp extra virgin olive oil

1 Preheat a grill until the coals are glowing and gray in appearance.

2 Cut three slashes in either side of each sardine. Brush with olive oil and season generously with salt, pepper, and ground coriander. Set aside.

3 To make the dressing, whisk together the oil, harissa, honey, and lime zest and juice, season, and add more honey if necessary to balance the acidity of the lime. Set aside.

4 Prepare the salad: toss the cilantro with the lettuce and pile onto a large, flat serving dish. Whisk together the lemon zest, juice, sugar, and olive oil. Season and drizzle over the salad.

5 Cook the sardines on the grill (or under a preheated broiler) for 2–3 minutes or until the flesh is white and opaque. Brush with the harissa paste and grill the other side for another 30 seconds. Pile onto the cilantro salad and serve immediately.

NUTRITION PER SERVING	
Energy	303kcals/1263kJ
Carbohydrate	3.5g
of which sugar	3.5g
Fat	21.5g
of which saturates	4g
Salt	0.5g
Fiber	0g

Grilled sardines

Make sure you use sustainable sardines for this delightful Mediterranean dish. You don't need to descale or brush the fish with oil. Sardines are one of the best sources of omega-3 fatty acids.

| Low carb |
| Low saturated fat |
| Dairy free |
| Gluten free |

SERVES 4
PREP 15–20 MINS
COOK 4–8 MINS

1lb 2oz (500g) fresh sardines

1 tbsp salt

lemon quarters, to serve

1 Gut the sardines—or have the fishmonger do this for you—leaving the heads and scales in place. Gutting is easily done by pushing your index finger through the soft belly and scooping the innards from the cavity. Sprinkle the flanks with salt.

2 Heat a heavy-bottomed metal pan, broiler, or barbecue grill until it is really hot. Grill or broil the sardines fiercely, turning them once, until the skin blisters and turns black. Cook for 2–4 minutes on each side, depending on the thickness of the fish. Serve with quartered lemons.

NUTRITION PER SERVING

Energy	206kcals/864kJ
Carbohydrate	0g
of which sugar	0g
Fat	11.5g
of which saturates	3.5g
Salt	3.3g
Fiber	0g

Blackened salmon

A spice rub, rather than a marinade, is useful to have in your grilling repertoire, and works for meat and fish. Organic or wild salmon offers optimum nutrition.

Low carb
Low saturated fat
Dairy free
Gluten free
Low salt

SERVES 4
PREP 5 MINS, PLUS
RESTING
COOK 10 MINS

1 tsp cayenne pepper

1 tsp celery salt

2 tsp dried oregano

1½ tbsp light brown sugar

freshly ground black pepper

4 skinless salmon fillets, approx.
   5½oz (150g) each

1 tbsp olive oil

lemon or lime wedges, to serve

1 Prepare the grill for cooking. Grind all the dry ingredients together in a mortar and pestle to a fine consistency.

2 Rub all sides of the salmon fillets with the spice rub, cover, and rest in the refrigerator for 1 hour to let the flavors soak into the fish. Drizzle each piece of fish with a little oil and rub it gently all over.

3 Grill the salmon on the barbecue for 2–3 minutes on each side, until brown and crispy, but still moist. Serve with lemon or lime wedges to squeeze over.

try this....
Salmon baked with maple syrup and mustard

Mix 1 tablespoon **maple syrup** with 2 tablespoons **whole-grain mustard**, then brush over the salmon and proceed as above.

NUTRITION PER SERVING

Energy	316kcals/1316kJ
Carbohydrate	5.5g
of which sugar	5.5g
Fat	19g
of which saturates	3g
Salt	1.2g
Fiber	0g

Cajun-spiced salmon

This simple, Louisiana-inspired rub instantly livens up any fish, and it's particularly good with salmon. You can serve the salmon with a thinly-sliced onion, avocado, and cherry tomato salad for a light, flavorful dinner.

Low carb

Low saturated fat

Dairy free

Gluten free

Low salt

SERVES 4
PREP 10 MINS
COOK 10 MINS

1 tsp smoked paprika

1 tsp cayenne pepper

1 tsp garlic powder

½ tsp dried thyme

1 tsp light brown sugar

½ tsp salt

4 skinless salmon fillets, approx. 5½oz (150g) each

2 tbsp olive oil

thinly sliced onion, avocado, and cherry tomato salad, to serve

1 Combine the spices, thyme, sugar, and salt in a mortar and pestle or a spice grinder. Grind to a fine powder.

2 Rub the mixture over both sides of the fish, cover with plastic wrap, and let rest in the refrigerator while you prepare the broiler.

3 Preheat the broiler to its highest setting and line a grill pan with foil. Brush the fish with a little oil on both sides, being careful not to dislodge the spice rub, and broil for 3–4 minutes on each side, depending on thickness.

4 Once done, serve the grilled salmon on a plate with the onion, avocado, and cherry tomato salad.

try this....
Tandoori salmon

Mix 3 tablespoons **tandoori curry paste** with 7oz (200g) **2% fat Greek yogurt**. Place the fish in the yogurt mixture and continue as above from step 2.

NUTRITION PER SERVING	
Energy	324kcals/1348kJ
Carbohydrate	1g
of which sugar	1g
Fat	22g
of which saturates	3.5g
Salt	0.8g
Fiber	0g

Baked salmon with cucumber dill sauce

Equally good with salmon steaks or fillets, this light dish is quickly prepared.

| Low carb |
| Gluten free |
| Low salt |

SERVES 4
PREP 10 MINS,
PLUS STANDING
COOK 10 MINS

½ cucumber

salt and freshly ground
    black pepper

1 cup plain yogurt

2 tsp Dijon mustard

1 scallion, finely chopped

1 tbsp chopped dill

4 salmon steaks or fillets,
    skinned

2 tsp olive oil

juice of ½ lemon

1 Finely dice the cucumber and place in a sieve over a bowl. Sprinkle with salt and leave to drain for 1 hour. Rinse with cold water and pat dry with paper towels. Stir the drained cucumber into the yogurt and add the mustard, scallion, and dill. Season to taste with salt and pepper. Set aside.

2 Preheat the oven to 400°F (200°C). Arrange the salmon fillets in a shallow baking dish, brush with oil, and season to taste with salt and pepper.

3 Sprinkle the salmon with lemon juice and roast for 8–10 minutes, depending on the thickness, until just cooked through but still moist inside. Remove from the oven and stir the juices from the dish into the cucumber sauce.

4 Serve the salmon hot or cold, with the sauce spooned over it.

try this....
Baked salmon with freekeh, cherry tomatoes, and capers

Prepare the salmon as in steps 2 and 3. While the salmon is cooking, heat 1⅓ cups **ready-to-eat freekeh** according to package instructions. Turn the freekeh into a large bowl and stir in 7oz (200g) halved **cherry tomatoes**, 1 bunch finely chopped **scallions**, 5 tablespoons finely chopped fresh **parsley**, 2 tablespoons coarsely chopped **capers**, and the **zest** and juice of 1 **lemon**.

NUTRITION PER SERVING	
Energy	339kcals/1418kJ
Carbohydrate	5g
of which sugar	5g
Fat	19g
of which saturates	4.5g
Salt	0.3g
Fiber	0.3g

Steamed trout in lettuce

Steaming is a good way to enjoy trout while keeping it low in fat. Cooked lettuce is a slightly bitter revelation.

Low carb

Gluten free

Low salt

SERVES 2
PREP 15 MINS
COOK 10 MINS

8 large Iceberg lettuce leaves

4 trout fillets, pinboned and skinned

salt and freshly ground black pepper

1 tbsp sunflower oil

4 scallions, finely sliced

8 shiitake mushrooms, finely sliced

2 tbsp chopped tarragon

splash of lemon juice

FOR THE DRESSING

⅔ cup Greek yogurt

1 tbsp chopped capers

2 tbsp chopped parsley

1 shallot, finely chopped

1 Blanch the lettuce leaves in boiling water for 20–30 seconds. Rinse under running cold water and pat dry with paper towels. Trim out the thick center veins so it is possible to lay the leaves flat. Overlap two leaves together, arrange a trout fillet on each, and season.

2 Heat the oil in a small saucepan, add the scallions and mushrooms, and fry over brisk heat for 3–4 minutes until cooked. Add the tarragon and lemon juice, then cool.

3 Divide the mushroom mixture over each trout fillet. Fold the lettuce over to encase.

4 Lift the trout onto a large bamboo steamer. Do not allow the parcels to touch. Steam for 5–6 minutes, until the fish flakes to the touch.

5 Meanwhile, mix the yogurt, capers, parsley, and shallot together and season lightly. Lift the fish parcels on to a large serving dish and serve the dressing separately.

NUTRITION PER SERVING	
Energy	429kcals/1795kJ
Carbohydrate	6g
of which sugar	5g
Fat	24g
of which saturates	8g
Salt	0.7g
Fiber	1.5g

Thai red curry with snapper

Homemade curry paste adds a delicious fragrance and warmth to the curry. Snapper is a low-calorie and lean source of protein.

Low carb

Dairy free

SERVES 4
PREP 10 MINS
COOK 20 MINS

2 tbsp sunflower oil

2 tsp shrimp paste

1 large onion, finely chopped

2 garlic cloves, crushed

1 tbsp palm sugar,
   or dark brown sugar

4 tomatoes, seeded and diced

14oz (400g) can reduced-fat
   coconut milk

1¼ cup fish or shellfish stock

1–2 tbsp Thai fish sauce, to taste

juice of ½–1 lime

4 snapper fillets, about 6oz (175g)
   each, scaled, pinboned, and halved

3 tbsp roughly chopped
   cilantro leaves

steamed rice, to serve

FOR THE CURRY PASTE
4 red chiles, seeded and chopped

1 red bell pepper, broiled, skin
   removed

1 tbsp ground coriander

2 stalks lemongrass, roughly
   chopped

2 tbsp grated galangal
   or fresh ginger

1 tbsp Thai fish sauce

1 tsp shrimp paste

1 tsp palm sugar

FOR A GLUTEN-FREE OPTION
use gluten-free stock

1 Place all the ingredients for the curry paste in a food processor and pulse to a paste.

2 Heat the oil in a wok, add the shrimp paste, and stir over low heat for 1–2 minutes. Add the onion and cook for another 2 minutes; add the garlic, palm sugar, tomatoes, and curry paste. Stir for 2 minutes; add the coconut milk and stock. Bring to a boil and simmer for 4–5 minutes; season with fish sauce and lime juice.

3 Add the snapper, return to a boil, then reduce the heat and simmer for 5–6 minutes or until the fish is just cooked; it will be white and beginning to flake. Sprinkle over the cilantro and serve with steamed rice.

NUTRITION PER SERVING	
Energy	357kcals/1494kJ
Carbohydrate	14g
of which sugar	12g
Fat	16g
of which saturates	8g
Salt	2.5g
Fiber	2.8g

Asian-style soy and sesame fish bites

A great way to get children to eat fish, these sweet and sticky fish bites both look and taste delicious.

SERVES 4
PREP 10 MINS, PLUS
COOLING AND
MARINATING
COOK 10 MINS

¼ cup soy sauce

¼ cup rice wine
 or dry sherry

2 tbsp rice vinegar
 or white wine vinegar

1 tbsp light brown sugar

1 tbsp honey

2 tsp sesame oil

1lb 2oz (500g) firm white-
 fleshed fish fillets, cut into
 ¾in (2cm) cubes

2 tbsp sesame seeds

FOR A GLUTEN-FREE OPTION
use gluten-free tamari to
 replace soy sauce

1 Combine the soy sauce, rice wine, vinegar, sugar, honey, and oil in a small, heavy-bottomed saucepan and bring it to a boil.

2 Reduce the heat to a simmer and cook, uncovered, for 5 minutes, until the sauce has reduced. Allow it to cool.

3 Turn the fish in the cooled sauce to coat, cover, and marinate in the refrigerator for 1 hour.

4 Preheat the broiler to its highest setting. Line a baking sheet or broiler pan with foil and spread out the marinated fish in a single layer. Sprinkle half the sesame seeds evenly over the fish.

5 Broil the fish for 3–4 minutes, until it is beginning to turn crispy at the edges, then turn it over carefully, sprinkle with the remaining sesame seeds, and broil for another 3–4 minutes.

NUTRITION PER SERVING	
Energy	210kcals/881kJ
Carbohydrate	8.5g
of which sugar	8.5g
Fat	7g
of which saturates	1g
Salt	2.9g
Fiber	1g

SEAFOOD

Pilpil shrimp

In this specialty of the tapas bars of Andalusia, freshly caught raw shrimp are cooked to order in little earthenware *cazuelas*. They contain more protein than chicken, for fewer calories and less fat.

Low carb

Low saturated fat

Dairy free

Low salt

SERVES 2
PREP 5 MINS
COOK 1–2 MINS

5½oz (150g) raw peeled shrimp

3–4 tbsp olive oil

1–2 garlic cloves, thickly sliced

4–5 small dried chiles, whole but seeded

sea salt

soft-crumbed bread, to serve

FOR A GLUTEN-FREE OPTION
use gluten-free bread

1 Clean the shrimp and devein them, if necessary.

2 Heat the oil in an earthenware *cazuela* or a small frying pan. Add the shrimp, garlic, and chiles, sprinkle with a little salt, and cook for 1–2 minutes, until the shrimp change color and become opaque.

3 Serve immediately with toothpicks or wooden forks and plenty of soft-crumbed bread for soaking up the juices.

NUTRITION PER SERVING	
Energy	259kcals/1072kJ
Carbohydrate	0g
of which sugar	0g
Fat	23g
of which saturates	3.5g
Salt	0.4g
Fiber	0g

Moroccan-style shrimp

Originally from Morocco and also found in Provence, this easy dish tastes as good as it smells. Serve with a salad for a quick lunch, or tapas-style with cocktail sticks.

Low carb

Low saturated fat

Dairy free

Gluten free

Low salt

SERVES 4–6
PREP 5 MINS
COOK 5 MINS

1lb 2oz (500g) uncooked peeled large shrimp (defrosted if frozen)

¼ cup olive oil

½ tsp harissa paste or hot paprika

1 tsp ground ginger

1 tsp ground cumin

½ tsp ground coriander

3 garlic cloves, crushed

1 tbsp snipped flat-leaf parsley

1 tbsp snipped cilantro

1 Drain the shrimp on a double layer of paper towels. Heat the oil in a large frying pan, pour in the spices and garlic, and stir for a minute to release the flavors.

2 Add the shrimp and cook for 1–2 minutes over medium-high heat until they turn a little pink, then turn over. Cook until the shrimp are pink all over, stirring frequently. Stir in the fresh parsley and cilantro and serve hot.

NUTRITION PER SERVING	
Energy	194–130kcals/ 810–540kJ
Carbohydrate	0–0g
of which sugar	0–0g
Fat	12–8g
of which saturates	1.7–1.1g
Salt	0.6–0.4g
Fiber	0–0g

Pan-fried shrimp in garlic butter

The shrimp can be peeled or not; provide finger bowls and plenty of paper napkins If you leave the shell on. Parsley is rich in antioxidants.

SERVES 4
PREP 5 MINS
COOK 10 MINS

scant 1oz (25g) unsalted butter

juice of 1 lemon, plus more to serve

2 garlic cloves, crushed

2 tbsp finely chopped flat-leaf parsley, plus extra sprigs, to serve

salt and freshly ground black pepper

2 tbsp olive oil

16–20 raw shrimp, peeled, deveined, and butterflied

lemon wedges, to serve

1 Mix the butter, lemon juice, garlic, and parsley together, and season to taste with salt and plenty of pepper.

2 Heat the oil in a large frying pan, add half the shrimp, and pan-fry over medium heat for 2 minutes, or until they have lost their translucency and turned pink. Lift onto a large serving platter and keep warm while you cook the remaining shrimp in the same way.

3 Wipe out the frying pan if necessary and add the garlic butter. Heat until hot and foaming and the garlic is soft, but not brown. Add a splash of lemon juice to stop the cooking and immediately pour over the shrimp.

4 Garnish with parsley and lemon wedges and serve at once.

NUTRITION PER SERVING	
Energy	173kcals/724kJ
Carbohydrate	0g
of which sugar	0g
Fat	11g
of which saturates	4g
Salt	0.7g
Fiber	0g

Spinach and coconut shrimp curry

This mild, creamy curry flavored with coconut makes a low-calorie and fragrant supper dish that is easy to prepare.

Low carb

Dairy free

Low salt

High fiber

SERVES 4
PREP 15 MINS
COOK 15–20 MINS

2 tbsp sunflower oil

2 red onions, finely chopped

4 garlic cloves, finely chopped

2in (5cm) piece of fresh ginger, finely grated

¼–½ tsp chili powder

½ tsp turmeric

2 tsp ground cumin

1 tsp ground coriander

4 large tomatoes, peeled and finely chopped

1 x 14fl oz (400ml) can reduced-fat coconut milk

10 fresh or dried curry leaves (optional)

5½oz (150g) spinach, shredded

14oz (400g) raw large shrimp, shelled and deveined

½ tsp granulated sugar

salt

basmati rice, warmed naan bread, and lime wedges, to serve

FOR A GLUTEN-FREE OPTION
use gluten-free naan bread

1 Heat the oil in a large, deep-sided frying pan or wok. Add the onions, garlic, and ginger and cook for 2–3 minutes over low heat until softened, but not browned. Add the spices and cook for another 1 or 2 minutes to release the flavors.

2 Add the tomatoes and continue to cook over low heat for another 2 minutes, until the tomato flesh starts to break down. Add the coconut milk and curry leaves (if using), and bring to a boil. Mix in the spinach and reduce the heat, continuing to cook until the spinach has wilted. Baby spinach will take 1 or 2 minutes, bigger leaves up to 4 minutes.

3 Add the shrimp, sugar, and a pinch of salt, and cook for another 2 minutes over high heat, or until the shrimp turns a bright pink color. Serve with basmati rice, warmed naan bread, and lime wedges on the side.

NUTRITION PER SERVING	
Energy	271kcals/1134kJ
Carbohydrate	12g
of which sugar	9g
Fat	15g
of which saturates	7g
Salt	0.9g
Fiber	4g

Laksa lemak

This Malaysian dish is rich with coconut milk. This is high in fat, although mostly in a form that is converted to energy and not stored in the body.

Dairy free

SERVES 4
PREP 20 MINS
COOK 10–15 MINS

14oz (400g) can reduced-fat coconut milk

1¾ cups low-salt shellfish stock

1 stalk lemongrass

4 kaffir lime leaves

1in (2.5cm) piece galangal or fresh ginger, peeled and finely sliced

1lb (450g) mahi mahi fillets, pinboned, skinned, and cut into large chunks

12 raw jumbo shrimp, peeled and deveined, tails left on

1lb (450g) mussels, prepared

2 squid, gutted, cleaned, and cut into rings

12oz (350g) vermicelli, to serve

lime wedges, to serve

FOR THE CURRY PASTE
2 tsp vegetable oil

splash of sesame oil

2 tsp palm sugar

3 garlic cloves, halved

½ bunch of scallions, roughly chopped

1 tsp shrimp paste

2 red chiles, seeded and chopped

1 large bunch of cilantro (with roots, if possible)

1 tsp cumin

1 tsp turmeric

½ tsp salt

FOR A GLUTEN-FREE OPTION
use gluten-free stock

1 Put all the ingredients for the curry paste in a food processor and pulse. Blend in half the coconut milk to make a smooth paste.

2 Heat a large wok, add the paste, and cook over low heat for 1 minute. Add the remaining coconut milk and the stock, bring to a boil, and add the lemongrass, lime leaves, and galangal; simmer for 5 minutes. Add the fish, shrimp, and mussels, and cook for 3–4 minutes. Add the squid.

3 Meanwhile, cook the vermicelli according to package instructions. Divide between four bowls and ladle laksa on top. Serve with lime wedges.

NUTRITION PER SERVING	
Energy	606kcals/2536kJ
Carbohydrate	66g
of which sugar	6g
Fat	14g
of which saturates	7.5g
Salt	2.6g
Fiber	5g

Simple Italian roast lobster

This Neapolitan dish is easy to prepare and the lobster offers significant amounts of protein and zinc.

Low carb

Low saturated fat

Dairy free

Low salt

SERVES 4
PREP 15 MINS
COOK 15 MINS

2 cooked lobsters, preferably rock lobsters, split and prepared

4 tbsp Italian extra virgin olive oil

4 tbsp finely chopped flat-leaf parsley, plus extra sprigs, to serve

2 garlic cloves, crushed

3–4 tbsp fresh bread crumbs

salt and freshly ground black pepper

lemon wedges, to serve

FOR A GLUTEN-FREE OPTION
use gluten-free bread crumbs

1 Preheat the oven to 375°F (190°C). Place the split lobsters on a large baking sheet or baking dish.

2 Heat the olive oil in a small saucepan, add the parsley and garlic, and sizzle for 30 seconds, then stir in the bread crumbs and season well.

3 Spoon the mixture over the cut lobster flesh. Bake in the oven for 7–10 minutes, or until the lobsters are piping hot. Remove from the oven and arrange on a large, warmed serving dish with lemon wedges.

NUTRITION PER SERVING

Energy	233kcals/975kJ
Carbohydrate	8g
of which sugar	0.5g
Fat	13g
of which saturates	2g
Salt	0.9g
Fiber	0g

Moules marinières

This classic French recipe—mussels in wine, garlic, and herbs—translates as "in the fisherman's style." Offering an important source of vitamins and minerals, mussels are also sustainable and cheap.

Low carb

Gluten free

SERVES 4
PREP 15–20 MINS
COOK 15 MINS

3 tbsp butter

2 onions, finely chopped

8lb (3.6kg) mussels, prepared

2 garlic cloves, crushed

2 cups dry white wine

4 bay leaves

2 sprigs of thyme

salt and freshly ground black pepper

2–4 tbsp chopped flat-leaf parsley

1 Melt the butter in a large, heavy saucepan, add the onions, and fry gently until lightly browned. Add the mussels, garlic, wine, bay leaves, and thyme. Season to taste. Cover, bring to a boil, and cook for 5–6 minutes, or until the mussels have opened, shaking frequently.

2 Remove the mussels with a slotted spoon, discarding any that remain closed. Transfer them to warmed bowls, cover, and keep warm.

3 Strain the liquor into a pan and bring to a boil. Season to taste, add the parsley, pour over the mussels, and serve at once.

NUTRITION PER SERVING	
Energy	415kcals/1736kJ
Carbohydrate	1g
of which sugar	1g
Fat	14g
of which saturates	6g
Salt	2g
Fiber	0g

Spicy stir-fried squid

A traditional Thai recipe, although such recipes are legion in many countries and regions across Asia.

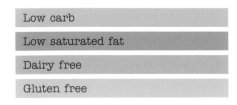

Low carb

Low saturated fat

Dairy free

Gluten free

SERVES 4
PREP 20 MINS
COOK 5–6 MINS

8 small squid, gutted and cleaned

1 tbsp vegetable oil

1 stalk lemongrass, split into 4 lengthwise

2 kaffir lime leaves

1 yellow or orange bell pepper, seeded and diced

handful of basil leaves, preferably Thai, shredded

salt and freshly ground black pepper

FOR THE PASTE

3 garlic cloves, chopped

2 shallots, coarsely chopped

1 tbsp grated fresh ginger

1–2 red chiles, to taste (seeded for a milder result)

1¾oz (50g) chopped cilantro, preferably both leaves and roots

large splash of vegetable oil

1 tbsp palm sugar or dark brown sugar

1 tbsp Thai fish sauce

1 Score the squid tubes and set aside with the tentacles.

2 To make the paste, put the garlic, shallots, ginger, chile, cilantro, vegetable oil, palm sugar, and fish sauce into a food processor. Process to form a finely chopped green paste.

3 Heat the 1 tbsp vegetable oil in a large wok, add the paste, and cook over low to medium heat for 2–3 minutes or until it smells aromatic. Add the squid, lemongrass, lime leaves, and pepper. Stir-fry, tossing over medium-high heat until the squid is opaque and coated in the other ingredients. (Avoid overcooking the squid, because it will become tough.)

4 Stir in the basil and adjust the seasoning, then remove the lemongrass and lime leaves. Serve with rice or noodles and a green salad.

NUTRITION PER SERVING	
Energy	170kcals/711kJ
Carbohydrate	6g
of which sugar	6g
Fat	5.5g
of which saturates	1g
Salt	1.5g
Fiber	1.1g

Scallops with bacon

Bacon, chorizo, and pancetta are all excellent to
serve with pan-fried scallops.

Low carb

Dairy free

Gluten free

Low salt

SERVES 4
PREP 5–10 MINS
COOK 15 MINS

4 bacon strips, diced

12 scallops

1 tbsp chopped flat-leaf
parsley

squeeze of lemon juice

salt and freshly ground
black pepper

handful of arugula,
to serve

1 Heat a frying pan and add the bacon. Cook over
medium heat until the bacon is brown and frazzled.
Lift on to a plate.

2 Remove the roe from the scallops, if present. Fry
the scallops in the bacon fat for 1–2 minutes on each
side or until golden brown. Do not put too many in
the pan at once, because they will not brown. Lift
onto a plate.

3 Reduce the heat in the pan and fry the roes, if using;
these are likely to pop in the hot fat. They are cooked
when they are firm.

4 Return the scallop muscles and bacon to the pan
and add the parsley and the lemon juice. Season,
and serve with arugula leaves.

NUTRITION PER SERVING	
Energy	75kcals/314kJ
Carbohydrate	6.2g
of which sugar	0.5g
Fat	3g
of which saturates	1.5g
Salt	0.9g
Fiber	0.6g

SUSHI AND CEVICHE

Cured mackerel sashimi with salad

In spring and summer, mackerel has quite a soft texture; curing it firms the flesh.

Low carb

Low saturated fat

Low salt

SERVES 4
PREP 30 MINS

2 very fresh mackerel (preferably still with rigor mortis), filleted, cured, and pinboned

FOR THE SALAD

2oz (60g) arugula, washed

2 Baby Gem lettuces, washed and torn into strips

large handful of cress, washed

handful of cherry tomatoes, halved

½ small cucumber, peeled and thinly sliced

1 ripe avocado, diced

2 tbsp chopped pickled sushi ginger

Japanese soy sauce, to serve

wasabi paste, to serve

FOR THE DRESSING

1 tsp honey

1 tbsp mirin

1 tbsp rice wine vinegar

1 tsp sesame oil

2 tbsp sunflower oil

FOR A GLUTEN-FREE OPTION

use gluten-free tamari to replace soy sauce

1 Slice the mackerel very thinly, and set aside.

2 Put the salad ingredients into a big bowl and toss together. Put the dressing ingredients into a bowl, whisk to blend, then add to the salad, and toss together.

3 Pile the salad onto a large platter and arrange the sliced mackerel on top. Serve with the soy sauce and wasabi in small dishes on the side.

NUTRITION PER SERVING	
Energy	281kcals/1166kJ
Carbohydrate	8.5g
of which sugar	8g
Fat	22g
of which saturates	4g
Salt	0.2g
Fiber	3g

Sesame sushi rolls

Colorful and nutty, these little sushi rolls have contrasting textures that make them so appealing to eat.

Low carb

Low saturated fat

Dairy free

MAKES 24
PREP 30 MINS
COOK 3 MINS

3 tbsp sesame seeds, white and black

4oz (115g) medium shrimp

2 sheets of nori, halved

1 quantity sushi rice (see p259)

½ tsp wasabi paste

½ cucumber, seeded and cut into julienne strips

6 tbsp shoyu (Japanese soy sauce), to serve

1 Toast the seeds in a dry saucepan over low heat for 3 minutes, until nutty and golden. Set aside to cool. Cut the shrimp in half lengthwise. Have a small bowl of water ready for moistening your fingers.

2 Cut one sheet of plastic wrap just larger than half of a nori sheet. Place half of a nori, smooth side down, on a sushi mat or a square of heavy-duty foil. Moisten your fingers with water, then spread a quarter of the rice in an even layer on the nori. Cover with the plastic wrap.

3 Pick up the nori, carefully turn it over, and place on the mat, plastic wrap side down. The nori should now be facing up. Spread a thin line of wasabi lengthwise along the center of the nori with your fingers.

4 Arrange a quarter of the shrimp, cucumber, and 1 teaspoon sesame seeds on top, making sure the fillings extend completely to each end. Pick up the mat and plastic wrap and tightly roll rice around the filling, pressing down firmly as you roll. Unroll the mat and plastic wrap.

5 Gently roll the rice roll in half of the remaining sesame seeds. Roll up tightly in plastic wrap, twisting the ends to secure. Repeat with the remaining nori, rice, wasabi, shrimp, cucumber, and sesame seeds.

6 Trim the ends of each roll, then cut each rice roll into six equal-size pieces with a moist knife. Remove plastic wrap from the cut pieces. Serve at room temperature with shoyu for dipping.

NUTRITION PER SERVING	
Energy	62kcals/259kJ
Carbohydrate	10g
of which sugar	0.5g
Fat	1g
of which saturates	0.2g
Salt	0.8g
Fiber	0.3g

Nori maki

You will need a bamboo mat to make these California-style rolls. Crabmeat is a low-calorie source of protein, B vitamins, omega-3 fats, and minerals.

Dairy free

Gluten free

MAKES 16
PREP 5 MINS

splash of rice vinegar

4 sheets nori seaweed, halved

⅓ quantity sushi rice (see p259)

a little wasabi paste

½ avocado, thinly sliced

4oz (115g) white crabmeat, or 4 pieces of surimi (ocean sticks), halved

1 Lay a bamboo mat on a board. Have on hand a bowl of tepid water mixed with the vinegar.

2 Lay a half piece of nori seaweed on the bamboo mat, shiny side down. Using wet hands, take a small handful of rice and spread it on the nori, pressing gently, and leaving a 1in (2.5cm) border at one end. Don't use too much water or the nori will become wet and tough.

3 If using a single ingredient, use a little more rice to fill the rolls. Make an indentation down the center of the rice, spread on a little wasabi paste, the avocado, and crab or surimi.

4 Roll up the sushi, pressing on the bamboo mat to help keep the roll even.

5 To cut the roll, use a very sharp, wet knife and do not saw, but pull the knife toward you. Cut the roll in half, then in half again and stand each upright. Wipe the knife between cuts.

6 Arrange the cut sushi on a large tray to serve. Serve with soy sauce or gluten-free tamari, pickled sushi ginger, pickled daikon, and wasabi paste.

NUTRITION PER SERVING	
Energy	367kcals/1536kJ
Carbohydrate	69g
of which sugar	8g
Fat	4.5g
of which saturates	1g
Salt	0.9g
Fiber	2g

Seafood ceviche

A brief, light pickling of raw fish conserves its freshness and brings out the true flavor. The paprika lends the dish its red color.

Low carb

Dairy free

Gluten free

Low salt

SERVES 4
PREP 20 MINS,
PLUS FREEZING
AND MARINATING

1lb (450g) very fresh, firm-fleshed fish fillets, pinboned and skinned

1 red onion, finely sliced

juice of 2 lemons or limes

1 tbsp olive oil

½ tsp hot paprika

1 chile, finely chopped

salt and freshly ground black pepper

2 tbsp finely chopped flat-leaf parsley

1 Wrap the fish in plastic wrap or foil, and put it in the freezer for 1 hour to firm up the flesh. This will make it easier to slice. With a sharp knife, slice the fish into very thin slivers.

2 Spread the onion evenly in the bottom of a shallow, non-metallic dish. Pour over the lemon juice and olive oil, then sprinkle with the paprika and chile.

3 Place the fish on the onion, gently turning to coat with the marinade. Cover and marinate in the refrigerator for at least 20 minutes, preferably more than 1 hour. Season, sprinkle with parsley, and serve.

try this....
Seafood ceviche with avocado and fennel

Peel and dice 2 ripe **Hass avocados**, finely slice 1 small bulb of **fennel**, and mix them with the fish.

NUTRITION PER SERVING

Energy	125kcals/525kJ
Carbohydrate	2g
of which sugar	1.5g
Fat	3.5g
of which saturates	0.5g
Salt	0.2g
Fiber	0.5g

Chirashi sushi

This type of sushi requires no rolling and is very easy to make. Daikon is low in calories but high in vitamin C. Its enzymes help digest raw fish.

SERVES 4
PREP 20 MINS,
PLUS COOLING
COOK 20 MINS,
PLUS STEAMING

FOR THE SUSHI RICE

1½ cups short-grain sushi rice

1 small strip of kombu (dried seaweed)

4 tbsp Japanese rice vinegar

2 tbsp sugar

½ tsp salt

ANY SELECTION OF THE FOLLOWING

shredded daikon

thinly sliced cucumber

1 fillet sashimi-grade tuna, thinly and evenly sliced

1 fillet sashimi-grade salmon, thinly and evenly sliced

1 fillet sashimi-grade kingfish, thinly and evenly sliced

8–12 prepared and cooked shrimp

1 cured mackerel fillet, thinly sliced

1 thin squid tube, scored and cut into pieces

wasabi, to serve

Japanese dark soy sauce, to serve

FOR A GLUTEN-FREE OPTION

use gluten-free tamari to replace soy sauce

1 In a sieve, rinse the rice until the water runs clear. Put the rice, kombu, and 1¼ cups water in a heavy saucepan, and cover with a lid. Bring to a boil, then simmer for 11–12 minutes. Remove from the heat and leave to steam, with the lid on, for 10 minutes.

2 Put the vinegar, sugar, and salt into a saucepan and heat slowly until the grains have dissolved.

3 Turn the rice onto a shallow dish. Drizzle the vinegar mixture over, then turn to gloss the rice. Leave to cool.

4 Serve the rice on the dish or in four individual bowls, arranging the vegetables and fish on top. Serve with wasabi and dark soy sauce.

NUTRITION PER SERVING	
Energy	449kcals/1879kJ
Carbohydrate	69g
of which sugar	8g
Fat	6g
of which saturates	1g
Salt	0.8g
Fiber	1g

Quinoa salmon cakes

A fresh take on fish cakes, the peppers and quinoa add a whole new dimension to this quick recipe. Serve these easy-to-make cakes with a light tossed salad for a delicious and filling meal.

Low carb

Low saturated fat

Dairy free

Low salt

SERVES 4
PREP 10 MINS,
PLUS CHILLING
COOK 20 MINS

14¾oz (418g) can salmon, drained, flaked, and pinboned

½ cup prepared quinoa

2 eggs, beaten

2 garlic cloves, crushed

grated zest of 1 lemon

1½oz (40g) green bell peppers, seeded and finely chopped

1 tsp freshly ground black pepper

sea salt

2–3 tbsp olive oil

1 lemon, cut into wedges, to serve

1 Place the salmon, quinoa, eggs, garlic, lemon zest, green bell peppers, and black pepper in a large bowl. Season to taste with sea salt and mix well until fully incorporated.

2 Divide the mixture into eight equal-sized portions. Gently form each portion into a patty-shaped cake. Place the cakes on a plate and chill in the refrigerator for about 15 minutes.

3 Heat the oil in a large frying pan over medium heat. Gently place the cakes in the pan and fry for 4 minutes on each side, until golden brown and cooked through. Do this in batches to avoid overcrowding the pan. Remove from the heat and serve hot with lemon wedges and a watercress salad.

NUTRITION PER SERVING	
Energy	171kcals/715kJ
Carbohydrate	8g
of which sugar	0.6g
Fat	13g
of which saturates	2.5g
Salt	1.4g
Fiber	1g

Shrimp and asparagus stir-fry with polenta

In this satisfying dish, shrimp and asparagus are stir-fried in a light white wine sauce and served over creamy, cheesy polenta. Quick and easy, it is perfect for dinner or even impressing your friends!

SERVES 4
PREP 10 MINS
COOK 20 MINS

2 tbsp extra virgin olive oil

3 garlic cloves, crushed

6–8 scallions, white and green parts, finely chopped

1lb (450g) asparagus, ends removed and cut into 1in (2.5cm) pieces

1lb (450g) shrimp, peeled and deveined

¼ cup white wine

salt and freshly ground black pepper

1 cup uncooked polenta

1 cup freshly grated Asiago or Parmesan cheese, plus extra to garnish

1 lemon, sliced, to serve

1 Heat the oil in a large frying pan over medium heat. Add the garlic, scallions, and asparagus. Cook for 5 minutes, stirring occasionally, until the onions have softened. Then add the shrimp and cook for 3 minutes, stirring, until just beginning to turn pink.

2 Pour in the wine and stir to combine. Cook for another 2–3 minutes or until the shrimp are cooked through and pink. Remove from the heat and season to taste if needed.

3 Meanwhile, place 3 cups of water and ¼ teaspoon salt in a large saucepan and bring to a boil. Stir in the polenta and reduce the heat to medium-low. Cook for about 5 minutes, stirring occasionally. Remove from the heat and stir in the cheese.

4 Divide the polenta evenly between four plates and top with one-quarter of the shrimp and asparagus stir-fry. Garnish with cheese and serve hot with lemon slices.

NUTRITION PER SERVING	
Energy	412kcals/1724kJ
Carbohydrate	30g
of which sugar	3g
Fat	15g
of which saturates	6g
Salt	2.2g
Fiber	4g

Cherry and pistachio freekeh pilaf

This tasty freekeh dish is made with warming, aromatic spices and mixed with dried cherries and pistachios, creating a savory and sweet pilaf unlike any you've had before.

Low saturated fat

Dairy free

Low salt

SERVES 4
PREP 5 MINS
COOK 20–25 MINS

1 cup uncooked freekeh

8 cardamom pods

8 whole cloves

1 tbsp oil

1 onion, finely chopped

1 tsp ground cinnamon

pinch of salt

⅔ cup dried cherries, coarsely chopped

¾ cup pistachios, coarsely chopped

FOR THE DRESSING

3 tbsp olive oil

2 tbsp lemon juice

pinch of salt

1 Place the freekeh in a large saucepan, cover with 1 quart of water, and place over medium heat. Add the cardamom and cloves and simmer for 20 minutes or until all the water has been absorbed. Drain any remaining water and remove and discard the cardamom and cloves. Set aside.

2 Meanwhile, heat the oil in a large frying pan over medium heat. Add the onions and cook for 5–10 minutes, stirring occasionally, until softened and translucent. Then add the cinnamon and cook for another 2 minutes.

3 For the dressing, place all the ingredients in a small bowl and mix to combine. Add the freekeh to the onion mixture, season with the salt, and stir to mix. Then add the cherries and pistachios and stir until evenly distributed. Remove from the heat. Serve hot with the dressing drizzled over the dish.

NUTRITION PER SERVING	
Energy	506kcals/2112kJ
Carbohydrate	55g
of which sugar	18g
Fat	24g
of which saturates	3g
Salt	0.6g
Fiber	2.5g

Tabbouleh and cacik

Warmed pita bread makes a fitting and delicious accompaniment to these mezze salads. Mezze are little dishes of vegetables, salads, olives, and suchlike that are standard features of meals all over the Middle East.

Low saturated fat

Low salt

SERVES 4
PREP 30–35 MINS, PLUS
SOAKING AND CHILLING

3½oz (100 g) bulgur wheat

1 small cucumber

salt and freshly ground black pepper

9oz (250g) tomatoes, peeled, seeded, and chopped

2 scallions, trimmed and chopped

small bunch of flat-leaf parsley, leaves chopped

3 tbsp lemon juice

½ cup olive oil

1 bunch of mint, leaves chopped

1 large garlic clove, finely chopped

¼ tsp ground coriander

¼ tsp ground cumin

1 cup natural yogurt

3–4 pita breads

1 Put the bulgur wheat in a large bowl and pour in enough cold water to cover generously. Let it soak for 30 minutes, then drain through a sieve and squeeze out any remaining water with your fist.

2 Trim the ends from the cucumber, cut in half lengthwise, and scoop out the seeds with a teaspoon. Cube the cucumber halves, put in a colander, sprinkle with salt, and stir to mix. Leave for 15–20 minutes, to draw out the bitter juices, then rinse under cold running water and drain.

3 For the tabbouleh, in a large bowl, combine the bulgur, tomatoes, scallions, parsley, lemon juice, oil, two-thirds of the mint, and plenty of salt and pepper. Mix and taste for seasoning, then cover and chill in the refrigerator for at least 2 hours.

4 To make the cacik, put the cucumber in a bowl and add the garlic, remaining mint, ground coriander, ground cumin, and salt and pepper. Pour in the yogurt. Stir to combine and taste for seasoning. Chill in the refrigerator for at least 2 hours, to allow the flavors to blend.

5 Warm the pita breads in a low oven for 3–5 minutes, then remove and cut into strips. Take the salads from the refrigerator and allow to come to room temperature, then arrange them in separate bowls with the warm pita bread fingers alongside.

NUTRITION PER SERVING	
Energy	436kcals/1833kJ
Carbohydrate	63g
of which sugar	10g
Fat	14.5g
of which saturates	3g
Salt	0.9g
Fiber	3g

Beef and edamame stir-fry

In this quick recipe, sirloin steak is stir-fried with a homemade sauce and fresh vegetables. Served over whole-grain freekeh, it makes for a healthy alternative to the traditional beef stir-fry.

Low saturated fat

Dairy free

SERVES 4
PREP 10 MINS
COOK 25 MINS

1¼ cups uncooked freekeh

1 tbsp light olive oil

1lb (450g) beef sirloin steak, cut into strips

8oz (225g) carrots, shredded

8oz (225g) frozen shelled edamame

⅔ cup low-sodium soy sauce

¼ cup beef stock

¼ cup rice vinegar

½ tbsp cornstarch, mixed with a little warm water

1 tsp freshly grated ginger

½ tsp freshly ground black pepper

handful of chopped scallions, to garnish

1 Place the freekeh and 3 cups of water in a large, lidded saucepan over medium heat. Bring to a boil, then reduce the heat to a simmer. Cover and cook for 20–25 minutes, until almost all the water has been absorbed. Remove from the heat, drain any excess water, and set aside.

2 Meanwhile, heat the oil in a large, lidded frying pan over medium heat. Add the beef and cook for about 1 minute, stirring occasionally. Remove with a slotted spoon and set aside. Add the carrots and edamame to the pan, cover, and cook for about 5 minutes, stirring occasionally.

3 Place the soy sauce, beef stock, rice vinegar, cornstarch, ginger, and pepper in a bowl. Whisk until well combined. Pour the liquid mixture into the pan. Then add the beef, stir well to combine, and bring to a boil. Cook, stirring frequently, for another 10–12 minutes or until the sauce thickens slightly. Remove from the heat. Divide the freekeh between four serving bowls and top with the stir-fry. Serve hot, garnished with scallions.

NUTRITION PER SERVING	
Energy	540kcals/2259kJ
Carbohydrate	61g
of which sugar	6g
Fat	13g
of which saturates	3g
Salt	4g
Fiber	4.5g

Spiced bulgur wheat with feta and a fruity salsa

A tasty grain mixed with salty feta and fresh beans. The ingredients for the salsa are all rich sources of Vitamin C, so serve as quickly as possible.

SERVES 4
PREP 15 MINS
COOK 10 MINS

10oz (280g) bulgur wheat

10fl oz (300ml) hot vegetable stock

5½oz (150g) fine green beans, chopped into ½in (1cm) pieces

salt and freshly ground black pepper

4½oz (125g) reduced-fat feta cheese, crumbled

FOR THE SALSA

½ fresh pineapple, diced

1 mango, diced

juice of ½–1 lime

1 red chile, seeded and finely chopped

1 First, make the salsa: mix all the ingredients together in a small bowl and let stand for a while to allow the flavors to develop.

2 Put the bulgur wheat into a large heatproof bowl and pour over the stock; it should just cover it—if not, add a little extra hot water. Let stand for 8–10 minutes then fluff up with a fork, separating the grains.

3 Add the beans to a pan of salted boiling water and cook for 3–5 minutes until they just soften but still have a bite to them. Drain and stir into the bulgur wheat. Season well with salt and pepper, then stir in the feta. Add a spoonful of the fruity salsa on the side and serve. You can enjoy this on its own, with a few salad leaves, or for a more substantial meal you could add a piece of grilled chicken.

NUTRITION PER SERVING	
Energy	370kcals/1547kJ
Carbohydrate	70g
of which sugar	16g
Fat	4g
of which saturates	2g
Salt	0.5g
Fiber	2.5g

Tomato bulgur wheat with capers and olives

This dish gives Middle Eastern bulgur wheat a Mediterranean character.

High fiber

Low salt

SERVES 4
PREP 15 MINS,
PLUS STANDING

2 cups bulgur wheat
salt and freshly ground
  black pepper
⅔–1¼ cups tomato juice
1 tbsp capers, drained

12 black olives, such
  as Kalamata, pitted
  and halved
12 green olives, pitted
  and halved

1 Pour the bulgur wheat into a large heatproof bowl, then pour in just enough boiling water to cover—about 1¼ cups. Let stand for 15 minutes.

2 Season generously with salt and pepper, and stir well with a fork to fluff up the grains. Add the tomato juice, a little at a time, until the bulgur has absorbed all the juice. Let stand for a few minutes between each addition—the bulgur will absorb quite a lot of moisture.

3 Now add the capers and olives, taste, and season again if needed.

NUTRITION PER SERVING	
Energy	360kcals/1506kJ
Carbohydrate	66g
of which sugar	2g
Fat	4g
of which saturates	0.7g
Salt	0.7g
Fiber	7g

try this....
Quinoa salad with mackerel and pomegranate

Replace bulgur with 10oz (300g) **quinoa**, cooked according to the package instructions. Leave out the capers and olives, and replace them with the seeds from 1 large **pomegranate**, 9oz (250g) flaked **smoked mackerel**, and **zest** and **juice** of 1 small **lemon**.

Millet cashew stir-fry with chile and lime sauce

This simple stir-fry is light, yet full of flavor and color. The lime gives it an added zing that pairs well with the sweetness of the toasted cashews and crunchy vegetables.

Dairy free

Low salt

High fiber

SERVES 2
PREP 20 MINS
COOK 20 MINS

½ cup uncooked millet

½ cup cashew nuts

2 tbsp light olive oil

3¾oz (110g) carrot,
   coarsely chopped

3¾oz (110g) cabbage,
   coarsely chopped

3½oz (100g) bean sprouts

3oz (80g) red onion, thinly sliced

FOR THE SAUCE

juice of 1 lime and grated zest
   of ½ lime

2 tbsp soy sauce

2 tbsp honey

1 red chile, seeded
   and finely chopped

FOR A GLUTEN-FREE OPTION

use gluten-free tamari to replace
   soy sauce

1 Place the millet in a large saucepan. Cover with ½ cup of water and simmer for about 10 minutes or until all the water has been absorbed. Then remove from the heat and set aside.

2 Heat a large wok or frying pan over high heat. Add the cashew nuts and toast until lightly colored. Remove from the heat and coarsely chop. Add the oil to the pan. Then add the carrots, cabbage, bean sprouts, and onions. Cook, stirring frequently, for about 5 minutes or until lightly cooked.

3 Meanwhile, for the sauce, place all the ingredients in a bowl and mix to combine. Add the millet to the vegetables and mix well. Pour over the chile and lime sauce, mix well, and cook for 1–2 minutes. Remove from the heat and serve hot.

NUTRITION PER SERVING	
Energy	544kcals/2268kJ
Carbohydrate	66g
of which sugar	25g
Fat	25g
of which saturates	4g
Salt	2.8g
Fiber	6g

Polenta with tomato, mozzarella, prosciutto, and pesto

Polenta is the perfect foundation for this light dish. The salty prosciutto is complemented by the creamy mozzarella, with the pesto adding a hint of warm Italian summers.

SERVES 4
PREP 15 MINS,
COOK 10 MINS

1 tbsp light olive oil

8 x ½in (1cm) thick slices of baked polenta or precooked, store-bought polenta, about 10oz (300g) in total

2 tomatoes, cut into 8 slices

8 x ½in (1cm) thick slices of mozzarella cheese, about 10oz (300g) in total

8 slices of prosciutto

3oz (85g) store-bought basil pesto

1 Heat the oil in a large frying pan set over medium heat. Add the polenta and fry for about 5 minutes on each side, until golden brown. Remove from the pan.

2 Divide the polenta slices between four plates. Top each one with a slice of tomato and mozzarella. Place a slice of prosciutto on each stack and drizzle evenly with the pesto. Serve immediately.

NUTRITION PER SERVING

Energy	432kcals/1799kJ	
Carbohydrate		3g
of which sugar		1.5g
Fat		32g
of which saturates		12g
Salt		1.5g
Fiber		0.7g

SIDES

DIPS

Taramasalata

The commercial version of this creamy fish dip—a familiar sight in many Mediterranean refrigerators—is a pale shadow of the real thing. In Greece, the basis is *tarama*—the salted, pressed roe of the sole.

SERVES 4
PREP 10 MINS

4 slices of dry country bread (not sliced white)

3½oz (100g) tarama paste or salted cod roe, skinned

2 garlic cloves, crushed

¾ cup olive oil, plus extra for drizzling

juice of 1 lemon

salt

1 Roughly chop the bread and process or liquidize into crumbs. Alternatively, if the bread is very hard and stale, soak it in water and squeeze dry. Reserve.

2 Process the roe with 2 tablespoons of the reserved bread crumbs. Add the garlic, purée to blend, and trickle in the oil, alternating with bread crumbs and the lemon juice diluted with its own volume of water, until the mixture is light and fluffy—it should not become grainy. Taste and add more lemon juice and salt, if needed.

3 Serve swirled onto a shallow plate, topped with a single black olive and maybe an extra drizzle of oil, with pita bread or raw vegetables and Romaine lettuce leaves for scooping.

NUTRITION PER SERVING

Energy	456kcals/1910kJ
Carbohydrate	19g
of which sugar	1g
Fat	38g
of which saturates	5g
Salt	1g
Fiber	1.3g

Tapenade

Tapenade, which takes its name from the Provençal word for capers, *tapeno*, is the quintessential tapas of Provence. The most traditional one is made with black olives.

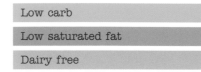

Low carb

Low saturated fat

Dairy free

SERVES 6–8
PREP 5 MINS

5½oz (150g) black olives, pitted and chopped

1 garlic clove, crushed

1 tbsp capers, drained

2 tbsp lemon juice

1 tsp lemon zest

¼ cup olive oil

freshly ground black pepper

1 Place the olives, garlic, capers, lemon juice, and zest in a mortar or the small bowl of a food processor. Add 1 tablespoon oil and pound or purée, gradually adding more oil until you have a thick paste.

2 Taste, season with pepper, and serve immediately. Tapenade can be refrigerated, covered with plastic wrap, for up to 4 days.

NUTRITION PER SERVING	
Energy	87kcals/364kJ
Carbohydrate	0.2g
of which sugar	0.1g
Fat	9g
of which saturates	1.5g
Salt	0.5g
Fiber	0.6g

Artichoke and fennel dip

Artichokes and fennels both contain heart-friendly levels of potassium.

Low carb

Dairy free

SERVES 8
PREP 15 MINS

1 x 14oz (400g) can artichoke hearts, drained

1 x 14oz (400g) fennel bulb, trimmed and chopped

2 tbsp tahini

juice of 1 lemon

1 garlic clove, chopped

1 tbsp olive oil

sea salt and freshly ground black pepper

1 Combine the artichokes, fennel, tahini, lemon juice, garlic, and oil in a food processor. Process until smooth and creamy. Season with salt and pepper to taste.

2 Serve with grilled Turkish flat bread, pita bread, or over a fresh tomato and parsley salad.

NUTRITION PER SERVING	
Energy	57kcals/209kJ
Carbohydrate	2.5g
of which sugar	2.5g
Fat	4g
of which saturates	0.5g
Salt	0.1g
Fiber	3g

Smoked salmon pâté

Smoked salmon can be expensive, but cheaper packages of salmon trimmings work well for this recipe.

SERVES 4
PREP 10 MINS,
PLUS CHILLING

7oz (200g) low-fat cream
   cheese, at room
   temperature

7oz (200g) smoked salmon
   trimmings, very finely
   chopped

finely grated zest and juice
   of ½ lemon

2 tbsp chopped chives

freshly ground black pepper

crackers and cucumber
   sticks, to serve

FOR A GLUTEN-FREE OPTION
use gluten-free crackers

1 Place the cream cheese in a mixing bowl and break it up with a fork until smooth. Stir in the salmon, lemon zest and juice, chives, and plenty of pepper.

2 Transfer to a serving dish, cover with plastic wrap, and chill until ready to serve.

3 Spread the pâté on crackers and serve with cucumber sticks.

NUTRITION PER SERVING	
Energy	149kcals/623kJ
Carbohydrate	2g
of which sugar	2g
Fat	8g
of which saturates	4g
Salt	2.3g
Fiber	0g

Labna

This fresh cheese made from strained yogurt is served as a mezze dish in the Middle East. It is good sprinkled with herbs or spices and served with toasted flatbreads.

Low carb

Gluten free

Low salt

SERVES 8
PREP 10 MINS,
PLUS DRAINING

2 cups plain Greek-style yogurt

½ tsp salt

1 Stir the yogurt and salt together until evenly combined. Spoon onto a large square of cheesecloth, then gather together the 4 corners and tie the top of the bundle with string, to make a bag.

2 Suspend the bag over a bowl and leave for at least 12 hours for the whey to drip through.

3 Remove the strained yogurt from the cheesecloth, shape into a ball, and serve.

NUTRITION PER SERVING	
Energy	100kcals/418kJ
Carbohydrate	3.5g
of which sugar	3.5g
Fat	7.5g
of which saturates	5g
Salt	0.45g
Fiber	0g

Anchoïade

There are many versions of this powerful, versatile anchovy paste. Typically French, it has an addictive salty taste, but use sparingly because it goes a long way.

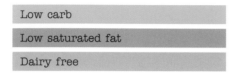

Low carb

Low saturated fat

Dairy free

SERVES 6–8
PREP 5 MINS

12 anchovy fillets in oil or brine

2 garlic cloves, crushed

1 scallion, white part only, chopped

⅓ cup olive oil

juice and grated zest of ½ small unwaxed lemon

freshly ground black pepper

1 Drain the anchovies. If using anchovies in oil, pat dry between layers of paper towels, and if in brine, rinse in cold water before patting dry.

2 Chop the anchovies. Place in the bowl of a food processor, add the garlic, scallion, and a little oil, and purée to make a coarse paste. If you prefer, use a mortar and pestle.

3 Trickle in the rest of the oil, a little at a time, with the motor running. Add the lemon juice and zest and purée until you have a coarse, thick purée.

4 Adjust the seasoning with a little pepper and serve immediately. Any leftovers can be kept in the refrigerator for up to 5 days.

NUTRITION PER SERVING	
Energy	84kcals/351kJ
Carbohydrate	0.3g
of which sugar	0.2g
Fat	9g
of which saturates	1.5g
Salt	0.7g
Fiber	0.1g

Roasted red pepper, almond, and chile pesto

As well as stirring it through pasta, try spreading this zingy pesto on bruschetta and topping it with tomatoes and basil. It also works well on pizza bases.

Low carb

Low saturated fat

MAKES 1 SMALL JAR (ABOUT 6OZ/175G)
PREP 10 MINS

1 red bell pepper, roasted, seeded, and roughly chopped

4 sun-dried tomatoes in oil, drained

1–2 fat red chiles, seeded and roughly chopped

2 garlic cloves, lightly crushed

1oz (30g) ground almonds

1oz (30g) grated Parmesan cheese

2 tbsp tomato oil from the jar

salt and freshly ground black pepper

¼ cup extra virgin olive oil

1 Place the red pepper in a food processor with the sun-dried tomatoes, chiles, garlic, almonds, cheese, tomato oil, and a generous sprinkling of salt and pepper. Run the machine until well blended, stopping and scraping down the sides as necessary. With the machine running, trickle in 2 tbsp olive oil until you have a glistening paste.

2 Alternatively, put the red pepper, tomatoes, chiles, and garlic in a mortar and pound with a pestle. Gradually add the almonds and salt and pepper. Work in a little of the cheese, then add a little each of the tomato oil and olive oil. Continue until the cheese, tomato oil, and 2 tbsp olive oil are used up and you have a glistening paste.

3 Spoon into a clean, sterilized jar, top with the remaining olive oil to prevent air from getting in, screw the lid on, and store in the refrigerator. Use within 2 weeks.

NUTRITION PER SERVING

Energy	83kcals/347kJ
Carbohydrate	0.8g
of which sugar	0.7g
Fat	8g
of which saturates	1.5g
Salt	trace
Fiber	0.3g

Hummus

This chickpea and tahini dip is one of the most widely recognized of all Middle Eastern dishes. It tastes great with warm pita bread and sticks of carrot, cucumber, celery, and bell pepper.

Low saturated fat

Dairy free

Gluten free

SERVES 4
PREP 10 MINS

1 x 14oz (400g) can chickpeas

3 tbsp tahini

juice of 3 lemons

3 garlic cloves, chopped

½ tsp salt

pimentón (Spanish paprika), for sprinkling

olive oil, to drizzle

1 Drain and rinse the chickpeas, reserving 6 tablespoons of the liquid from the can. Put the chickpeas in a blender with 3 tablespoons of the reserved liquid.

2 Add the tahini, lemon juice, and garlic, then blend until smooth and creamy. Add more of the liquid from the can, if required.

3 Season with salt. Transfer hummus to a bowl, sprinkle with paprika, and drizzle with oil. Serve.

NUTRITION PER SERVING

Energy	152kcals/636kJ
Carbohydrate	10g
of which sugar	0.3g
Fat	8g
of which saturates	1g
Salt	0.6g
Fiber	4.5g

try this....
Red pepper hummus
....
Add 3 skinned, roasted **red peppers** with the other ingredients in step 2.

Roasted asparagus with aïoli sauce

Celebrate the first of the new season's asparagus with this easy appetizer. You can use only green asparagus, or include white and purple spears.

Low carb

Dairy free

Gluten free

Low salt

High fiber

SERVES 4
PREP 10 MINS
COOK 20 MINS

24 asparagus spears, including at least 12 green spears

salt and freshly ground black pepper

3 tbsp olive oil

about 6 tbsp aïoli

1 tbsp finely snipped basil

1 tbsp finely snipped dill

1 tomato, blanched, peeled, seeded, and finely chopped

1 Trim the asparagus. In a large frying pan, add water to a depth of 2in (5cm) and bring to a boil. Reduce the heat to medium-high and add a little salt. Blanch the asparagus, starting with the white and purple spears, if using, for 7 minutes. Then add the green spears and cook for another 3 minutes. Drain and refresh under cold running water.

2 Dry the pan and add the oil. Cook the asparagus in a single layer, in batches, for 5 minutes, until a little charred. Remove from the pan and arrange them on plates.

3 Place a generous tablespoon of aïoli on each plate and scatter with the basil, dill, and tomato. Season with a little pepper and serve immediately.

NUTRITION PER SERVING

Energy	268kcals/1121kJ
Carbohydrate	3.5g
of which sugar	3.5g
Fat	26g
of which saturates	2.6g
Salt	0.1g
Fiber	3g

Spring vegetable stew

Serve this with simple grilled chicken or fish.
The stew brings a lovely garlic flavor of its own.

Low carb

Gluten free

Salt free

High fiber

SERVES 4
PREP 10 MINS
COOK 5 MINS

salt and freshly ground
   black pepper

8–10 asparagus stalks, woody
   ends broken off, chopped
   into ¾in (2cm) lengths, tips
   and stalks kept separate

3½oz (100g) frozen young
   sweet peas

1 tbsp butter

1 tbsp olive oil

2 small zucchini, quartered
   lengthwise, cut into ½in
   (1cm) cubes

4 large scallions, white part
   only, cut into ½in (1cm)
   pieces

1 garlic clove, finely chopped

3–4 tbsp white wine

½ cup half-and-half

1 tbsp finely chopped
   mint leaves

1 In a large pan of boiling salted water, blanch the asparagus stalks together with the peas for 1 minute. Add the asparagus tips and cook for another 1 minute. Drain the vegetables and refresh immediately in a large bowl of cold water, then drain again.

2 In the same pan, melt the butter with the oil. Add the zucchini and scallions and cook for 2–3 minutes until they start to brown at the edges. Add the garlic and cook for another minute. Add the wine (it will bubble up and almost evaporate), then the cream, and season well.

3 Add the blanched vegetables to the pan and cook for another minute or two over high heat until the sauce has reduced and thickened. Stir in the mint to serve.

NUTRITION PER SERVING	
Energy	163kcals/672kJ
Carbohydrate	6g
of which sugar	4g
Fat	11.5g
of which saturates	5.5g
Salt	trace
Fiber	4g

Steamed broccoli with bagna càuda

In Italy, this warm, garlicky dip is traditionally served with raw vegetables, such as baby carrots and radishes, but it is also good with simply steamed, sprouting broccoli.

Low carb

Gluten free

High fiber

**SERVES 4, MAKES
ABOUT 5FL OZ (150ML)
DIPPING SAUCE
PREP 10 MINS
COOK 10 MINS**

1lb 2oz (500g) purple or young green broccoli spears, trimmed

4 oil-packed anchovies, drained and chopped

2 garlic cloves, crushed

½ cup extra virgin olive oil

2 tbsp cold butter, cut into small pieces

1 tsp fresh lemon juice

sea salt and freshly ground black pepper

1 Steam the broccoli for no more than 5 minutes, until it is al dente.

2 Put the anchovies into a mortar and pestle, and grind them to a paste. Put them in a small saucepan along with the garlic and oil, and heat gently for 2 minutes until the garlic is lightly colored, but not brown.

3 Remove the pan from the heat and use a wire whisk to add the cold butter in small pieces, beating well between each addition.

4 Add the lemon juice and continue to whisk until the mixture emulsifies slightly. Check the seasoning and add freshly ground black pepper, and a little salt, if necessary. Serve the dipping sauce warm with the broccoli.

NUTRITION PER SERVING

Energy	270kcals/1130kJ
Carbohydrate	4g
of which sugar	2.5g
Fat	24g
of which saturates	6g
Salt	0.6g
Fiber	5g

Roasted asparagus and prosciutto bundles

This easy but elegant dish makes a great appetizer, and each bundle is one perfect serving.

Low carb

Low saturated fat

Dairy free

Gluten free

Low salt

SERVES 4
PREP 10 MINS
COOK 15 MINS

24 thin asparagus spears

2 tbsp olive oil

salt and freshly ground
  black pepper

4 prosciutto slices

1 Preheat the oven to 450°F (230°C). Trim the asparagus spears of their woody ends, put them on a plate, and rub with 1 tbsp of olive oil. Season well.

2 Lay a slice of the prosciutto on a board and put one-quarter of the asparagus spears in the middle. Carefully wrap the prosciutto around the asparagus to make a neat parcel, leaving the tips exposed. Lay it on a baking sheet with the seam of the meat facing down. Repeat to make 4 parcels. Brush the prosciutto with the remaining olive oil.

3 Bake at the top of the hot oven for 15 minutes, until the prosciutto is crispy and the asparagus cooked through. Serve as is, or with a Hollandaise sauce or a poached egg.

NUTRITION PER SERVING	
Energy	119kcals/492kJ
Carbohydrate	2g
of which sugar	2g
Fat	9g
of which saturates	3g
Salt	0.2g
Fiber	2.5g

Green beans with parsley

Very fine green beans are best for this recipe, but the robust parsley dressing can also work its magic on larger beans. The cooking time varies depending on the size of the beans.

Low carb

Low saturated fat

Dairy free

Gluten free

Low salt

SERVES 4
PREP 10 MINS
COOK 15 MINS

1lb 2oz (500g) fine green beans, ends trimmed

sea salt and freshly ground black pepper

FOR THE PERSILLADE

2 tbsp chopped flat-leaf parsley

1 garlic clove, crushed

2½ tbsp extra virgin olive oil

1 In a large saucepan of lightly salted boiling water, add the beans and cook for 8–10 minutes, or until tender but not soft. Drain well and refresh under cold running water. Keep warm.

2 Meanwhile, combine the parsley, garlic, and oil in a small bowl. Season well.

3 Pour the beans into a serving bowl, stir to coat with the persillade, and serve warm.

NUTRITION PER SERVING	
Energy	100kcals/418kJ
Carbohydrate	4g
of which sugar	2.5g
Fat	7.5g
of which saturates	1g
Salt	0g
Fiber	4g

Grilled corn on the cob with lime and chile butter

This butter is an easy way to flavor grilled meat, fish, or vegetables. It freezes well for up to 6 months.

Gluten free

Low salt

SERVES 4
PREP 10 MINS
COOK 10 MINS

3 tbsp unsalted butter, softened

finely grated zest of 1 lime

½ tsp chile powder or cayenne pepper

½ tsp sea salt

freshly ground black pepper

4 corn cobs

a little olive oil

1 Prepare the grill for cooking. In a small bowl, mash the butter with the lime zest, chile powder, sea salt, and black pepper.

2 Cut a square of wax paper, about 6in (15cm) square. Put the butter in the middle of one edge of the paper and shape it like a sausage. Roll the butter sausage up in the paper, then twist the ends so the butter forms a tight shape. Leave in the freezer for at least 30 minutes before use (or freeze until needed).

3 Cook the corn cobs in a large pan of boiling water for up to 5 minutes until the corn is tender (this will depend on the size and age of the cobs). Drain well, rub them in a little oil, and grill for 6 minutes over a hot barbecue, turning them frequently, until they are lightly charred on all sides.

4 Serve the corn with a ½in- (1cm-) thick disk of the chilled butter on top to melt.

NUTRITION PER SERVING	
Energy	139kcals/582kJ
Carbohydrate	8g
of which sugar	2g
Fat	10g
of which saturates	5g
Salt	0.2g
Fiber	2g

Grilled eggplant with garlicky yogurt

These Middle Eastern–inspired eggplant slices are a good vegetarian option at a barbecue.

Low carb

Low saturated fat

Gluten free

Low salt

SERVES 3–4
PREP 10 MINS
COOK 15 MINS

¼ cup olive oil

1 tbsp chopped cilantro

½ tsp ground cumin

2 garlic cloves, crushed

3 tbsp chopped mint leaves

salt and freshly ground black pepper

2 large eggplants, cut into ¾in (2cm) slices

¾ cup Greek yogurt

1 Prepare the grill for cooking. In a small bowl, mix together the oil, cilantro, cumin, one of the crushed garlic cloves, and 1 tablespoon of the mint, and season well.

2 Brush the slices of eggplant with the herby oil and grill them over a hot barbecue for 3–5 minutes on each side until soft and charred in places.

3 Meanwhile, make the sauce by mixing together the Greek yogurt, remaining crushed garlic clove, and remaining 2 tablespoons of mint. Season well and serve in a bowl alongside the eggplant slices.

NUTRITION PER SERVING	
Energy	164kcals/677kJ
Carbohydrate	4g
of which sugar	3.5g
Fat	15g
of which saturates	4g
Salt	0.1g
Fiber	3g

Savoy cabbage with onions and garlic

This delicious cabbage is the perfect accompaniment to mashed potatoes and a warming winter stew.

Low carb

Low saturated fat

Gluten free

Low salt

SERVES 4
PREP 5 MINS
COOK 20 MINS

2 tbsp olive oil

1 tbsp butter

1 onion, finely sliced

1 garlic clove, crushed

14oz (400g) Savoy cabbage, shredded

salt and freshly ground black pepper

1 Heat the oil and butter in a large Dutch oven or heavy-bottomed saucepan with a lid. Add the onion, cover, and cook over medium heat, stirring frequently, for 10 minutes, until it is well softened, but not brown. Add the garlic and cook for another minute.

2 Add the cabbage, seasoning, and ¼ cup of water. The water will practically sizzle away. Mix it all together and cover. Cook over low heat for 10 minutes, stirring occasionally, until the cabbage is cooked through.

NUTRITION PER SERVING	
Energy	237kcals/998kJ
Carbohydrate	7g
of which sugar	1.5g
Fat	6g
of which saturates	0.8g
Salt	trace
Fiber	4.5g

Peas with lettuce

This traditional French dish is often made with canned peas when fresh tender baby peas are not available.

Low salt

High fiber

SERVES 6
PREP 10 MINS
COOK 10 MINS

9oz (250g) pearl onions

2 tbsp butter, softened

1lb 2oz (500g) shelled peas or frozen young peas

½ cup ham stock or water

1 tsp sugar

salt and freshly ground black pepper

1 tbsp all-purpose flour

2 tbsp finely chopped mint or flat-leaf parsley

2 lettuce hearts, such as Little Gem, trimmed and finely shredded

FOR A GLUTEN-FREE OPTION
use water instead of ham stock
use gluten-free flour

1 Put the onions in a bowl and cover with boiling water. Drain, and remove the skins, keeping the roots intact.

2 Melt 1 tbsp of the butter in a large saucepan and add the onions. Cook over medium heat for 2 minutes.

3 Add the peas and stock and bring to a boil. Skim off any sediment, then add the sugar and season to taste with salt and pepper. Lower the heat and simmer for 5–8 minutes.

4 Mix the remaining butter to a smooth paste with the flour. Gradually add this mixture to the peas, stirring to thicken the sauce. Stir continuously until it has been completely incorporated and there are no lumps.

5 Stir in the mint or parsley and the shredded lettuce hearts, transfer to a serving dish, and serve immediately.

NUTRITION PER SERVING	
Energy	145kcals/607kJ
Carbohydrate	15g
of which sugar	5.5g
Fat	5g
of which saturates	2.7g
Salt	0.1g
Fiber	6g

Glazed carrots with nutmeg

A favorite accompaniment to roast chicken, the nutmeg and sugar make these carrots extra special.

Low carb

Low saturated fat

Gluten free

Low salt

1 Cook the carrots in plenty of boiling salted water for about 7 minutes until they are really soft. Drain well.

2 Put the butter in the pan in which you cooked the carrots and allow it to melt over low heat. Stir in the sugar and nutmeg and cook gently until the sugar dissolves. Return the carrots, season well, and turn them in the butter until well glazed.

try this....
Glazed carrots with garlic and ginger

Sauté the cooked carrots with 1 teaspoon grated fresh **ginger** and 1 crushed **garlic clove** in a little **sesame oil** instead of butter. Sprinkle over 1 teaspoon **black sesame seeds** before serving.

SERVES 4
PREP 5 MINS
COOK 10 MINS

10oz (300g) thin, young carrots, peeled weight, cut into ½in (1cm) rounds

salt and freshly ground black pepper

1 tbsp butter

½ tsp granulated sugar

pinch of nutmeg

NUTRITION PER SERVING	
Energy	56kcals/233kJ
Carbohydrate	6g
of which sugar	6g
Fat	3.5g
of which saturates	2g
Salt	0.1g
Fiber	2.5g

Zucchini with garlic and mint

Zucchini, when eaten small, are sweet and juicy. The secret to cooking them well is in this recipe.

Gluten free

Low salt

SERVES 4

PREP 5 MINS

COOK 5 MINS

2 tbsp olive oil

1 tbsp butter

10oz (300g) small zucchini, sliced into ½in (1cm) rounds

1 garlic clove, crushed

1 tbsp finely chopped mint

salt and freshly ground black pepper

1 Melt the oil and butter in a large Dutch oven or heavy-bottomed saucepan with a lid, ideally one that will fit the zucchini in a single layer.

2 Add the zucchini and stir them around so that as many as possible are touching the bottom of the pan. Cover and cook over medium-high heat for 3 minutes.

3 Remove the lid, stir in the garlic and mint, and season well. Cover again and cook for another 2 minutes, shaking occasionally, until the zucchini are just cooked and golden brown in places.

NUTRITION PER SERVING	
Energy	91kcals/373kJ
Carbohydrate	1.5g
of which sugar	1g
Fat	9g
of which saturates	3g
Salt	trace
Fiber	1g

try this....
Zucchini with gnocchi, shrimp, and cherry tomatoes

To make this into a main course dish, cook 1lb 5oz (600g) **gnocchi** according to package instructions. Prepare the zucchini as above, but in step 2 add 10oz (300g) cooked, peeled **shrimp**. Combine the cooked zucchini with the gnocchi and 7oz (200g) halved **cherry tomatoes**.

Treviso-style radicchio

Radicchio has a pleasing, slightly bitter flavor and is refreshing in salads. In this Italian recipe, it is cooked and gently caramelized until richly bitter-sweet.

Low carb

Low saturated fat

Dairy free

Gluten free

Low salt

SERVES 4
PREP 5 MINS
COOK 20 MINS

3 tbsp olive oil

white part of 1 large scallion, chopped

1 garlic clove, crushed

4 heads of radicchio, trimmed at the bottom and quartered

salt and freshly ground black pepper

1 tbsp balsamic vinegar

1–2 tsp superfine sugar

1 In a frying pan, heat the olive oil, add the scallion and garlic, and cook over medium heat until softened and golden.

2 Spread the radicchio in the pan. Cook for 3 minutes, then turn it over using tongs and cook for another 3 minutes. Season. Add about 3–4 tablespoons of cold water, cover, and simmer for 10 minutes.

3 Remove the lid, increase the heat, then add the balsamic vinegar and sugar. Cook for 2–3 minutes, turn the radicchio over, and cook for another 2 minutes. Serve hot.

NUTRITION PER SERVING	
Energy	107kcals/448kJ
Carbohydrate	5.5g
of which sugar	3.3g
Fat	9g
of which saturates	1.5g
Salt	trace
Fiber	1.5g

Sweet potato salad

In Morocco and Tunisia, sweet potatoes are often cooked in tagines, combined with herbs and spices, and served as a side dish or salad. The combination of green olives and preserved lemon is typically Moroccan.

Low carb

Low saturated fat

Dairy free

Gluten free

Low salt

SERVES 4
PREP 15 MINS
COOK 20 MINS

3–4 tbsp olive oil

1 onion, coarsely chopped

1 tsp cumin seeds

scant 1oz (25g) fresh ginger, peeled and finely chopped

1lb 2oz (500g) sweet potatoes, peeled and cut into bite-sized cubes

½ tsp pimentón (Spanish paprika)

salt and freshly ground black pepper

8–10 pitted green olives

peel of 1 preserved lemon, finely chopped

juice of ½ lemon

small bunch of flat-leaf parsley, finely chopped

small bunch of cilantro, finely chopped

1 Heat the oil in a tagine pot or heavy-bottomed pan. Stir in the onion and cook for 1–2 minutes, until it begins to color. Add the cumin and ginger and cook until fragrant.

2 Toss in the sweet potatoes along with the paprika and pour in enough cold water to just cover the bottom of the pot. Cover and cook gently for 10–12 minutes, until tender but firm and the liquid has reduced.

3 Season to taste and add the olives, lemon, and lemon juice. Cover and cook for another 5 minutes to let the flavors combine.

4 Stir in half the herbs and transfer the mixture to a serving dish. Garnish with the rest of the herbs and serve warm or at room temperature.

NUTRITION PER SERVING	
Energy	227kcals/950kJ
Carbohydrate	28g
of which sugar	9g
Fat	11g
of which saturates	1.5g
Salt	0.3g
Fiber	5g

Almond and apricot energy balls

Peanut butter and almonds are both high in monounsaturated fat, and they also offer good amounts of protein and fiber as well as Vitamin E.

Low saturated fat

Dairy free

MAKES 20
PREP 5 MINS

7oz (200g) skin-on almonds

9½oz (280g) ready-to-eat dried apricots

4 tbsp rolled oats

8 tbsp smooth peanut butter

2 tbsp sweetened, shredded coconut or cocoa power, to decorate

FOR A GLUTEN-FREE OPTION
use gluten-free oats

1 Place the almonds, apricots, oats, and peanut butter in a blender and process until combined.

2 Put the mixture onto a clean work surface. With damp hands, shape the mixture into walnut-sized balls.

3 Roll the balls in either shredded coconut or cocoa powder. Store for up to 3 days in an airtight container.

try this....
Ginger, almond, and apricot energy balls

If you like ginger, add 1¾oz (50g) **crystallized ginger** to the mixture in step 1, and continue as above from step 2.

NUTRITION PER SERVING	
Energy	156kcals/653kJ
Carbohydrate	8g
of which sugar	6g
Fat	11g
of which saturates	3g
Salt	0.1g
Fiber	2.5g

Zucchini and saffron bruschetta

These gorgeous little bruschettas have a herbaceous flavor. Adding lemon juice and zest brings out the tastes of summer, and may cut down the need for salt.

MAKES 20
PREP 10 MINS
COOK 10–15 MINS

1 small baguette

1 tsp olive oil, plus extra to drizzle

2 garlic cloves, peeled

2 zucchinis

pinch of saffron threads

1 tbsp lemon juice, or to taste

salt and freshly ground black pepper

TO GARNISH
grated lemon zest
handful of basil or mint leaves

1 Preheat broiler. Slice the baguette thinly on an angle, drizzle with olive oil, and grill until crisp on both sides.

2 Use one garlic clove to rub gently over the crisp bread.

3 Dice the zucchinis and chop the other garlic clove finely. Heat a little oil in a pan and sauté zucchini and garlic for 5 minutes.

4 Add a pinch of saffron and cook until vegetables start to turn golden. Add 1 tablespoon lemon juice or more to taste, then season and use to top crisp bruschetta. Garnish with lemon zest and basil or mint leaves scattered over.

NUTRITION PER SERVING	
Energy	52kcals/220kJ
Carbohydrate	8g
of which sugar	0.6g
Fat	1.5g
of which saturates	0.2g
Salt	0.2g
Fiber	0.7g

Crostini napolitana

A classic Italian appetizer, these crostini are best prepared using fresh mozzarella, slightly squishy ripe tomatoes, and Gaeta olives. They are easy to make at home and are traditionally enjoyed with soup.

MAKES 4
PREP 15 MINS
COOK 4–5 MINS

2 large, very ripe tomatoes

6oz (175g) fresh buffalo mozzarella

4 thick slices of focaccia or ciabatta

4 anchovy fillets, drained and patted dry

freshly ground black pepper

2–3 tbsp fruity olive oil, plus extra for greasing

6 pitted black olives, to finish

leaves from a few sprigs of fresh oregano

1 Blanch the tomatoes in a pan of boiling water for 1–2 minutes, then drain and refresh in cold water. Peel the skins, then quarter, remove the seeds, and finely chop.

2 Preheat the oven to 450°F (230°C) or the broiler to high. Cut the mozzarella and arrange evenly on each slice of bread and cover with a layer of tomato. Place the anchovies between 2 layers of paper towels or plastic wrap and flatten lengthwise with a rolling pin. Cut each fillet crosswise. Place 2 halved fillets on each slice of bread. Season generously with pepper.

3 Lightly grease a baking sheet. Place the slices of bread on the sheet and drizzle with oil. Bake for 7–8 minutes, or broil for 2–3 minutes, until the mozzarella is melting and bubbling. The crostini should be crisp outside but soft inside. Place 3 olive halves on top, scatter with the oregano, and let cool for 5 minutes before serving.

NUTRITION PER SERVING	
Energy	292kcals/1222kJ
Carbohydrate	71g
of which sugar	3g
Fat	17g
of which saturates	7g
Salt	1.5g
Fiber	2.3g

Fennel-marinated feta and olive skewers

Tasting fresh and clean, this recipe is a delicious vegetarian option. Fennel seeds, which range from yellow to greenish-brown, help with digestion.

Low carb

Gluten free

MAKES 20
PREP 10 MINS,
PLUS CHILLING
COOK 5 MINS

2 tbsp sesame seeds

1 tbsp fennel seeds

8oz (225g) feta cheese

grated zest of 1 lemon

1 tbsp lemon juice

2 tbsp olive oil

1½ tsp cracked black pepper

¼ cup finely chopped
  mint leaves

20 mint leaves

½ cucumber, peeled
  and seeded

10 pitted black olives, halved

1 Toast the seeds in a dry pan over low heat until nutty and golden, about 3 minutes. Cool.

2 Gently rinse the feta in cold water. Drain on paper towels.

3 Cut feta into ¾-inch (2-cm) cubes. Toss feta together with the toasted sesame and fennel seeds, lemon juice, oil, and pepper to coat each cube well. Cover and refrigerate for 4 hours to allow the flavors to combine.

4 Sprinkle the feta with chopped mint and toss to coat each cube well.

5 Cut the cucumber into 20 cubes (½in/1cm).

6 Thread one mint leaf, one olive half, one cucumber cube, and one feta cube onto each skewer. Serve chilled or at room temperature.

NUTRITION PER SERVING	
Energy	51kcals/211kJ
Carbohydrate	0.3g
of which sugar	0.3g
Fat	5g
of which saturates	1.8g
Salt	0.4g
Fiber	0.3g

Baked Parmesan and rosemary crisps

The addition of Parmesan and rosemary transforms a simple wrap into a gourmet snack in mere minutes. Parmesan is aged for an average of two years.

Low salt

SERVES 4
PREP 5 MINS
COOK 5–7 MINS

4 large wraps

2 tbsp olive oil

2 tsp rosemary leaves, finely chopped

¼ cup finely grated Parmesan cheese

freshly ground black pepper

hummus or baba ghanoush, to serve

1 Preheat the oven to 400°F (200°C). Lay the wraps on a work surface and brush all over on both sides with the olive oil.

2 Scatter them with the rosemary and Parmesan and season well with pepper. Place on a baking sheet.

3 Bake them at the top of the oven for 5–7 minutes until golden brown, puffed up, and crispy. Watch them carefully for the last minute, since they burn easily.

4 Remove them from the oven, then transfer to a wire rack to cool. When they are cool, break them into jagged, irregular pieces and serve with hummus or baba ghanoush.

NUTRITION PER SERVING	
Energy	295kcals/1242kJ
Carbohydrate	39g
of which sugar	1g
Fat	10.5g
of which saturates	4g
Salt	0.8g
Fiber	2.2g

Multi-seed crackers

These can be adapted using a mixture of the seeds you like.
Be sure to use the larger seeds for decorating.

Low carb

Low saturated fat

Low salt

MAKES 45–50
PREP 20 MINS
COOK 12–15 MINS

1 cup whole wheat flour

½ cup all-purpose flour,
plus extra for dusting

4 tbsp butter, in pieces,
softened

½ tsp fine salt

2 tbsp sesame seeds

2 tbsp flaxseeds

2 tbsp pumpkin seeds,
plus extra for
decorating

2 tbsp sunflower
seeds, plus extra
for decorating

1 tbsp honey

1 large egg white

1 Preheat the oven to 400°F (200°C). In a large bowl with your fingertips, or in a food processor using the pulse-blend setting, blend the flours, butter, and salt until the mixture resembles fine crumbs. Mix in all the seeds.

2 Dissolve the honey in ½ cup of warm water. Make a well in the flour and mix in the water to form a soft dough.

3 Turn the dough onto a floured surface and knead it briefly. Roll out as thinly as possible—aim for ¼–¹⁄₁₂in (1–2mm) thick.

4 Cut the dough into 1½ x 2½in (4 x 6cm) crackers. Leave on the work surface.

5 Whisk the egg white with ½ tbsp of water and brush the crackers. Scatter with the additional pumpkin and sunflower seeds and gently press in.

6 Transfer to 2 baking sheets using a metal spatula, and bake for 12–15 minutes, turning carefully halfway, or until both sides are crisp and golden brown. Let cool on their pans. Store in an airtight container for up to 2 weeks.

NUTRITION PER SERVING	
Energy	38kcals/157kJ
Carbohydrate	3g
of which sugar	0.4g
Fat	2g
of which saturates	0.8g
Salt	trace
Fiber	0.7g

Veggie burgers

These delicious burgers are a great alternative to meat, and contain protein and lots of vitamins and iron.

Low carb

Dairy free

Low salt

MAKES 8
PREP 15 MINS,
PLUS CHILLING
COOK 12–15 MINS

2 tbsp olive oil

1 onion, finely chopped

½ celery stalk, finely chopped

1 small carrot, grated

½ small zucchini, grated, excess moisture squeezed out

1 garlic clove, crushed

1 x 14oz (400g) can of mixed beans, drained and rinsed

½ cup fresh bread crumbs

1 tsp dried mixed herbs

2 tbsp sunflower

FOR A GLUTEN-FREE OPTION
use gluten-free breadcrumbs

1 Heat the oil in a heavy-bottomed saucepan. Cook the onion, celery, carrot, and zucchini for 5 minutes over medium heat until softened. Add the garlic and cook for another minute. Cool.

2 Put the beans in a bowl and mash with a potato masher to the texture you desire. Add the vegetables, bread crumbs, and herbs, and mix.

3 Use damp hands to form eight 2½in (6cm) patties, pressing them lightly between your palms. Cover and chill for 30 minutes.

4 Heat the oil in a frying pan and cook the burgers for 3–4 minutes on each side, turning carefully, until browned and crispy. Serve warm with ketchup.

try this....
Edamame burgers

In step 2, replace the canned beans with 9oz (250g) **edamame**. Place the edamame in a pan of boiling water for 5 minutes, drain well, and then mash or purée. Add the vegetables, bread crumbs, and some fresh **mint** to replace the mixed herbs, and mix well. Continue with steps 3–4 as above. Serve with **sweet chili dipping sauce** (see p320).

NUTRITION PER SERVING	
Energy	112kcals/468kJ
Carbohydrate	12g
of which sugar	2.5g
Fat	6g
of which saturates	0.8g
Salt	0.5g
Fiber	3.4g

Salt and pepper squid

Squid is an economical source of low-fat protein. It is also high in selenium (an antioxidant), copper (vital for forming red blood cells), and B vitamins.

Low saturated fat

Dairy free

SERVES 4
PREP 10 MINS
COOK 6–8 MINS

1 tbsp sea salt flakes

1 tbsp black peppercorns

¼ cup all-purpose flour

¼ cup cornstarch

¼–½ tsp chile flakes (optional)

4 squid tubes, cleaned, approx. 10oz (300g) in total

1¼ cups vegetable oil, for frying

lemon wedges, to serve

1 Using a mortar and pestle, crush the sea salt and peppercorns until fine. Place the flour and cornstarch in a bowl and stir in the sea salt, pepper, and chile flakes (if using).

2 Make a slit down one edge of each squid tube and open it out flat. Using a sharp knife, score a diamond pattern on the inside of each tube. Cut each into eight pieces. Dust the pieces in the seasoned flour.

3 Heat the vegetable oil to 350°F (180°C) in a medium, heavy-bottomed pan. To check the temperature of the oil without a thermometer, carefully lower a cube of bread into the oil. The oil is hot enough when a piece of bread, dropped in, sizzles and starts to turn golden brown after 1 minute.

4 Cook the squid, in four batches, for 1½–2 minutes, or until golden brown, returning the oil to 350°F (180°C) between batches. Transfer to a plate lined with paper towels to drain, then place in a warm oven to keep warm. Repeat, working quickly, to cook all the squid. Serve piping hot, with lemon wedges.

NUTRITION PER SERVING	
Energy	264kcals/1108kJ
Carbohydrate	24.5g
of which sugar	0.5g
Fat	12.5g
of which saturates	2g
Salt	3.9g
Fiber	0.5g

Shrimp and guacamole tortilla stacks

These tasty Mexican-style canapés are simple to make. Assemble the stacks just before serving to keep them fresh.

Low carb

Low saturated fat

Dairy free

Low salt

MAKES 50
PREP 15 MINS,
PLUS MARINATING
COOK 10–15 MINS

5 wheat or corn tortillas

3½ cups sunflower oil

2 ripe avocados,
    pitted and peeled

juice of 1 lime

Tabasco sauce

4 tbsp cilantro, finely chopped,
    plus extra as a garnish

4 spring onions or scallions,
    trimmed and finely chopped

salt and freshly ground
    black pepper

50 large cooked, peeled shrimp

FOR A GLUTEN FREE OPTION
use gluten-free tortillas

1 Cut at least 100 disks out of the tortillas with a 1¼in (3cm) pastry cutter. Heat the oil in a medium-sized saucepan. Drop the tortillas into the oil, a handful at a time, and deep-fry until golden. Do not overcrowd the pan, or the tortillas will not crisp up properly. Remove them with a slotted spoon, drain on paper towels, put aside, and allow to cool.

2 In a bowl, mash the avocados with half the lime juice, a dash of Tabasco, 3 tbsp of the chopped cilantro, the chopped onions, and salt and pepper to taste.

3 When there are about 30 minutes left before serving, marinate the shrimp with the remaining lime juice and the remaining 1 tablespoon chopped cilantro in a small bowl.

4 To serve, pipe a little guacamole onto a tortilla using a piping bag with a small plain nozzle, top it with another tortilla, pipe more guacamole on top, and finish with a shrimp and a little of the remaining cilantro as a garnish.

try this....
Minted pea and shrimp tortilla stacks

In step 2, replace the guacamole with **minted pea purée**. Cook 14oz (400g) frozen **peas** for 4–5 minutes, then drain and place in a blender with 2 tablespoons **mint sauce** and 5½oz (150g) **reduced-fat sour cream**. Purée until smooth.

NUTRITION PER SERVING	
Energy	47kcals/197kJ
Carbohydrate	4g
of which sugar	0.2g
Fat	2.5g
of which saturates	0.5g
Salt	0.2g
Fiber	0.5g

Lemongrass-marinated shrimp skewers

Lemongrass gets its distinctive lemony fragrance from citral, which has antifungal and antimicrobial properties.

| Low carb |
| Low saturated fat |
| Dairy free |

SERVES 4
PREP 15 MINS,
PLUS MARINATING
COOK 10 MINS

2 garlic cloves, roughly chopped

½ red chile, seeded and roughly chopped

2 lemongrass stalks, bottom (thickest) one-third only, peeled of hard layers and roughly chopped

1in (3cm) fresh ginger, finely chopped

1 tbsp chopped cilantro roots or stalks

2 tbsp fish sauce

2 tsp light brown sugar

1 tbsp lime juice, plus lime wedges, to serve

40 raw, shelled, and deveined large shrimp

1 Prepare the grill for cooking. To make the marinade, simply put all the ingredients, except the shrimp, in a blender or food processor and pulse to a fine paste.

2 Toss the shrimp in the marinade, cover, and leave in the refrigerator to marinate for 1 hour. Meanwhile, soak eight bamboo skewers in water, to help to keep them from burning on the grill.

3 Thread five shrimp onto each skewer, threading through the top and bottom of the shrimp to make a curved "C"-shape. Grill the shrimp on the grill for 2–3 minutes on each side, until pink and charred in places. Serve with a squeeze of lime.

NUTRITION PER SERVING	
Energy	128kcals/541kJ
Carbohydrate	3g
of which sugar	3g
Fat	1g
of which saturates	0.1g
Salt	2g
Fiber	0g

Crispy cornmeal fish sticks with easy tartar sauce

Homemade fish sticks are fun and healthy, and a light cornmeal coating gives them a nice crunchy finish.

SERVES 4
PREP 10 MINS,
PLUS CHILLING
COOK 5 MINS

14oz (400g) skinless firm-fleshed white fish fillets, such as catfish

2 tbsp all-purpose flour

1 large egg, lightly beaten

¾ cup fine cornmeal

salt and freshly ground black pepper

sunflower or vegetable oil, for frying

FOR THE TARTAR SAUCE

2 cornichons, coarsely grated

6 heaping tbsp good-quality mayonnaise, preferably homemade mayonnaise

1 tbsp white wine vinegar

1 tbsp capers, very finely chopped

finely grated zest of ½ lemon

1 heaping tbsp finely chopped dill

NUTRITION PER SERVING	
Energy	478kcals/1988kJ
Carbohydrate	23g
of which sugar	0.5g
Fat	32g
of which saturates	4.5g
Salt	0.8g
Fiber	1g

1 Cut the fish into ¾in- (2cm-) thick strips. Pat it dry with paper towels. Lay the flour, egg, and cornmeal out in three shallow bowls. Season the flour well.

2 Coat the fish sticks by first dusting them with the flour, then dipping them in the egg, then rolling them in the cornmeal, until they are well covered. Put them on a plate, cover with plastic wrap, and chill for 30 minutes. This helps the coating stick.

3 Meanwhile, make the tartar sauce. First, put the grated cornichons on a cutting board and chop again, finely, with a sharp knife. Mix the cornichons, mayonnaise, vinegar, capers, lemon zest, and dill, and season well. Cover and chill until needed.

4 Heat a large, deep-sided frying pan and add enough oil to cover the bottom. Fry the fish sticks for 2 minutes on each side, turning carefully, until golden and crisp all over. Set them on a plate lined with paper towels while you cook the rest. Serve with homemade chunky oven fries or Cajun-spiced potato wedges and the tartar sauce.

Shrimp kebabs

A popular way to enjoy the large shrimp caught off the coast of North Africa is to thread them onto skewers and grill them quickly over charcoal.

| Low carb |
| Low saturated fat |
| Dairy free |
| Gluten free |

SERVES 4
PREP 10 MINS,
PLUS MARINATING
COOK 6 MINS

16 large shrimp

juice of 2 lemons, plus 1 lemon extra, cut into wedges, to serve

4 garlic cloves, crushed

1 tsp ground cumin

1 tsp pimentón (Spanish paprika)

sea salt

8–12 cherry tomatoes

1 green bell pepper, cut into bite-sized squares

oil, for greasing

1 Peel the shrimp down to the tail, leaving a little bit of shell at the end. Remove the veins and discard. Mix together the lemon juice, garlic, cumin, paprika, and a little salt and rub over the shrimp. Let the shrimp marinate for 30 minutes.

2 Meanwhile, prepare the charcoal grill. Thread the shrimp onto metal skewers, alternating with the tomatoes and green pepper pieces, until all the ingredients are used up.

3 Place the kebabs on an oiled rack over the glowing coals and cook for 2–3 minutes on each side, basting with any of the leftover marinade, until the shrimp are tender and the tomatoes and peppers are lightly browned. Serve immediately with lemon wedges.

NUTRITION PER SERVING	
Energy	106kcals/444kJ
Carbohydrate	2.5g
of which sugar	2.5g
Fat	4g
of which saturates	0.6g
Salt	0.4g
Fiber	1.5g

Chinese shrimp toasts

These fabulous snacks are always far better when homemade, and are a real children's favorite.

Low saturated fat

Dairy free

SERVES 4
PREP 10 MINS
COOK 10 MINS

6oz (175g) raw large shrimp, shelled, deveined, and roughly chopped

1 tsp cornstarch

2 scallions, finely chopped

½ tsp finely grated fresh ginger

1 tsp soy sauce

1 tsp sesame oil

1 large egg white

4 large slices of day-old white bread, crusts removed

sunflower or vegetable oil, for frying

1oz (30g) white sesame seeds

1 Put the shrimp, cornstarch, scallions, ginger, soy sauce, sesame oil, and egg white into a food processor, and process to a fairly smooth paste.

2 Cut each piece of bread into quarters and spread with a little of the shrimp paste, being sure to go right up to the edges and mounding it up slightly so that all the paste is used up.

3 Heat a 2in (5cm) depth of oil in a large, heavy-bottomed frying pan or deep fryer. It is ready when a crust of spare bread, dropped in, sizzles and starts to turn golden brown. Spread the sesame seeds out on a plate. Press each piece of bread, shrimp-side down, into the sesame seeds, so each is topped with a thin layer.

4 Fry the shrimp toasts in small batches, sesame seed side down, for 1–2 minutes, until becoming golden brown, then carefully turn them over and fry for another minute. Drain the cooked toasts on a plate lined with paper towels while you fry the remaining pieces. Serve hot.

try this....
Chia and sesame shrimp toasts with chili sauce

Replace the white bread with **brown** and half the sesame seeds with **chia seeds**. To make a sweet chili dipping sauce, mix 6 tablespoons **sweet chili sauce** with 2 tablespoons **rice wine vinegar**.

NUTRITION PER SERVING	
Energy	287kcals/1200kJ
Carbohydrate	20g
of which sugar	1.5g
Fat	17g
of which saturates	2.5g
Salt	1g
Fiber	1.5g

Oysters with shallot and vinegar dressing

Take great care when shucking an oyster since the knife can slip all too easily. For safety's sake, wrap your knife-free hand in a thick kitchen towel to protect it.

Low carb

Low saturated fat

Dairy free

Gluten free

SERVES 4–6
PREP 15 MINS

24 oysters in their shells

crushed ice

¼ cup red wine vinegar

1 large or 2 small shallots, very finely chopped

1 To prepare the oysters, discard any that have opened and do not close immediately when tapped on the work surface. Use an oyster knife, and hold the oysters over a bowl as you open them. Carefully shuck the oysters one by one, catching any liquid in the bowl and transferring the opened oysters in their shells and their liquid to the refrigerator as you go.

2 Arrange the oysters on an oyster plate with ice, or pack 4 serving dishes with lots of crushed ice and place the oysters on top.

3 Mix the vinegar and shallots together and put into a small dish. Place in the center of the oysters—or the middle of the table—and serve.

NUTRITION PER SERVING

Energy	125–84kcals/ 530–353kJ
Carbohydrate	0.9–0.6g
of which sugar	0.9–0.6g
Fat	2.4–1.6g
of which saturates	0.4–0.2g
Salt	2.3–1.5g
Fiber	0.5–0.3g

Grapefruit scallop ceviche skewers

The scallops need at least three hours to marinate, which gives you plenty of time to get ahead.

Low carb

Low saturated fat

Gluten free

Low salt

MAKES 20
PREP 20 MINS,
PLUS MARINATING

40 queen scallops or
  20 king scallops

grated zest and juice of
  1 grapefruit

juice of 2 limes

4 tbsp olive oil

1 fresh red chile or
  jalapeño chile, seeded
  and finely chopped

½ red onion, finely
  chopped

½ tsp salt

1 tbsp finely
  chopped cilantro

1 scallion, finely sliced

1 If using king scallops, slice in half crosswise.

2 Combine scallops, zest and juice of grapefruit, juice of lime, oil, chile, onion, and salt in a nonmetallic bowl. Cover and refrigerate for 3 hours, stirring occasionally.

3 Remove scallops with a slotted spoon. Toss to coat with cilantro and scallion. Thread two queen scallops or two king scallop halves onto each of the 20 wooden skewers or toothpicks (3in/7.5cm). Serve chilled with herbed yogurt dip.

NUTRITION PER SERVING	
Energy	48kcals/200kJ
Carbohydrate	1g
of which sugar	1g
Fat	2.5g
of which saturates	0.4g
Salt	0.2g
Fiber	0.1g

Spinach and garlic pizza

This Valencian version of the Neapolitan pizza is given a juicy topping of greens finished with a Middle Eastern sprinkling of pine nuts, raisins, and olive oil.

| Low saturated fat |
| Dairy free |
| Low salt |
| High fiber |

SERVES 2
PREP 10 MINS, PLUS
RISING AND PROOFING
COOK 20 MINS

¾ cup bread flour

salt

scant 1oz (25g) fresh yeast
  or 1 tsp dried yeast

1 tbsp olive oil, plus extra
  for greasing

FOR THE TOPPING

about 1lb 2oz (500g)
  spinach leaves, rinsed

1–2 garlic cloves, slivered

1 tbsp pine nuts, toasted

1 tbsp raisins
  or golden raisins

olive oil, for drizzling

1 Sift the flour with a little salt into a warm bowl. Dissolve the yeast in ¼ cup warm water, sprinkle with a little flour, and leave for about 15 minutes to froth.

2 Make a well in the flour, then pour in the oil and the yeast mixture. Draw the flour into the liquid and knead the dough into a smooth ball. Place the dough in a bowl, cover with plastic wrap or wipe with an oiled palm, and leave in a warm place for 1–2 hours, until doubled in size.

3 Preheat the oven to 425°F (220°C). Wash the spinach, drain all but a little water, and cook it sprinkled with a little salt in a lidded pan. As soon as the leaves start to wilt, remove from the heat, squeeze dry, and chop roughly. Set aside.

4 Knead the dough well to distribute the air bubbles and cut in half, then pat or roll each piece into a round about ½in (1cm) thick. Transfer to a lightly oiled baking sheet, top with the spinach, sprinkle with garlic, pine nuts, and raisins, drizzle with a little olive oil, and leave for 10 minutes to proof.

5 Bake for 15–20 minutes, until the crust is puffy and blistered at the edges.

NUTRITION PER SERVING

Energy	360kcals/1506kJ
Carbohydrate	47g
of which sugar	9g
Fat	13g
of which saturates	1.5g
Salt	0.9g
Fiber	9g

try this....
Spinach and ricotta pizza

At the end of step 3, roughly mix the spinach with 7oz (200g) **ricotta cheese** and 3 tablespoons **Parmesan cheese**. Continue with steps 4 and 5 as above.

Four-fruit power bar

Cherries bring a sharp, lively flavor to these power bars. Add a combination of other dried fruits or nuts, if you like. These bars are best eaten the day you make them.

Low saturated fat

Dairy free

Low salt

MAKES 16
PREP 30 MINS, PLUS
SOAKING AND DRYING

5½oz (150g) wheat grains

1 cup dried apricots

⅓ cup raisins

⅓ cup black currants

⅓ cup sour cherries

⅓ cup walnuts, soaked for 4 hours, dried, and lightly pan-toasted

⅓ cup sesame seeds, pan-toasted

1 To sprout the wheat grains, soak for 12 hours or overnight. Rinse the grains thoroughly and put in a large glass jar (grains expand to two to three times their initial volume). Cover the opening and neck of the jar with cheesecloth and attach it with string or a strong rubber band. Place at a 45° angle in a well-lit spot but not in direct sunlight. Rinse the grains each morning and evening by pouring water through the cheesecloth and emptying it out.

2 The sprouts are ready when seedlings approximately ¼in (0.5–1cm) in length appear. Rinse the seedlings thoroughly in clean water, strain, and spread on a clean cloth to dry. The sprouted grains are ready to use when they are dry to the touch. Place the apricots and raisins in a blender and blend to a paste. Add half of the sprouted grains and black currants and blend until crushed (but not blended to a purée).

3 Transfer to a mixing bowl and add the rest of the grains, berries, and the cherries. Mix well with a wooden spoon. Chop the walnuts into small chunks and add them to the mix. Sprinkle the sesame seeds on a flat surface. Roll out the mixture, or press it with clean hands, over the seeds into a rectangle ½in (1cm) thick. Use a sharp knife to cut the mixture into small rectangular bars. Place the bars on a rack and leave to dry out for a few hours.

NUTRITION PER SERVING	
Energy	111kcals/464kJ
Carbohydrate	16g
of which sugar	8g
Fat	4g
of which saturates	0.6g
Salt	trace
Fiber	2g

Cranberry, orange, and chocolate quinoa bars

The perfect breakfast on the go or handy snack, these sweet, chewy, and wholesome bars feel like a treat, but pack a big nutritional punch and will keep you full all morning.

Dairy free

Gluten free

Low salt

MAKES 12
PREP 20 MINS,
PLUS COOLING
COOK 5 MINS

1 cup almonds, coarsely chopped

3 cups quinoa flakes

¾ cup sunflower seeds

¾ cup chia seeds

⅔ cup dried cranberries

6 cups puffed rice cereal

1¾oz (50g) dark chocolate chips

grated zest of 2 large oranges

⅓ cup coconut oil

½ cup honey

¼ cup brown sugar

1 Place the almonds, quinoa flakes, sunflower seeds, chia seeds, dried cranberries, puffed rice cereal, chocolate chips, and orange zest in a bowl. Mix well with a wooden spoon and set aside. Grease and line an 8 x 10in (20 x 25cm) baking pan with parchment paper.

2 Heat the oil, honey, and sugar in a saucepan over medium heat. Cook, stirring occasionally, for about 5 minutes or until the sugar has melted and the mixture is bubbling. Set aside to cool for about 2 minutes.

3 Pour the cooled honey mixture into the dry ingredients. Mix using a wooden spoon until well incorporated, making sure the chocolate chips have melted and are evenly combined. Spoon the mixture into the prepared baking pan. Press down firmly with the back of a wooden spoon to make a roughly even layer.

4 Place the baking pan in the refrigerator for at least 4 hours to allow the mixture to cool and harden. Remove from the refrigerator, turn out on to a cutting board, and cut into bars. These can be stored in an airtight container in the refrigerator for up to 5 days.

NUTRITION PER SERVING

Energy	292kcals/1222kJ
Carbohydrate	34g
of which sugar	20g
Fat	15g
of which saturates	6g
Salt	0g
Fiber	3g

Avocado and banana smoothie

Almond milk is dairy free, and contains calcium and vitamins that are added by the manufacturer. No lactose means that it is easy to digest.

Low saturated fat

Dairy free

Gluten free

SERVES 2
PREP 5 MINS

1 small ripe Hass avocado, peeled and pitted

1 ripe banana, peeled and sliced

10fl oz (300ml) almond milk

2 tsp maple syrup or honey (optional)

finely grated zest and juice of 1 lime

1 Place all the ingredients, apart from the lime zest, in a blender and process until smooth.

2 Pour the mixture into two glasses, add a couple of ice cubes, sprinkle over the lime zest, and enjoy.

NUTRITION PER SERVING

Energy	227kcals/913kJ
Carbohydrate	15g
of which sugar	13g
Fat	16g
of which saturates	3g
Salt	0.2g
Fiber	4g

Matcha latte

There isn't a hint of bitterness in this blissfully creamy tea. The powdery matcha makes a bubbly froth when whipped and imparts a pale green tinge to this easy-to-make choco-rich latte.

Gluten free

SERVES 2
PREP 5 MINS
COOK 10 MINS

1½ cups plain sweetened
  almond milk

½oz (15g) white chocolate

2 tsp matcha powder, plus
  extra to garnish

½ cup water heated to
  175°F (80°C)

1 Heat the milk and chocolate in a saucepan over medium heat, stirring constantly, until the mixture simmers and becomes creamy. Remove from the heat and set aside.

2 Whisk the matcha powder and hot water in a bowl to form a thin paste. Add the hot milk and chocolate mixture and whisk briskly until foamy. Pour into cups. Garnish with a pinch of matcha powder and serve hot.

NUTRITION PER SERVING	
Energy	82kcals/343kJ
Carbohydrate	9g
of which sugar	9g
Fat	4g
of which saturates	1.5g
Salt	0g
Fiber	0g

Coconut matcha

Naturally sweet and creamy, this smoothie is a great afternoon pick-me-up. The coconut cream brings healthy fatty acids to the mix, while the avocados provide a good dose of potassium and vitamins K and C.

Gluten free

SERVES 2
PREP 5 MINS
COOK 5 MINS

2 tbsp coconut flakes

½ avocado

1 tsp matcha powder

½ cup coconut-flavored yogurt

1 cup chilled coconut water

1 Preheat the oven to 350°F (180°C). Place the coconut flakes on a baking tray and toast for 4½ minutes, or until golden brown.

2 Place the flakes in the blender along with the remaining ingredients and blend until creamy. Serve in chilled glasses with a straw.

NUTRITION PER SERVING	
Energy	307kcals/1284kJ
Carbohydrate	16g
of which sugar	15g
Fat	24g
of which saturates	15g
Salt	0.5g
Fiber	4.4g

Roasted chicory mocha

Cacao nibs are slightly bitter in their raw form, but full of antioxidants, while roasted chicory, long used as a coffee substitute, helps remove toxins from the body and aids digestion. Their combined goodness makes for a potent drink.

Dairy free

Gluten free

SERVES 4
PREP 5 MINS
COOK 5–7 MINS

2 tbsp coarsely ground roasted chicory root

12 raw cacao nibs, crushed

1 quart boiling water

honey or sugar, to taste

1 Place the roasted chicory and cacao nibs (including husks) in a teapot.

2 Add the boiling water and leave to infuse for 4 minutes.

3 Strain the infusion into cups or mugs and sweeten with honey or sugar to taste. Serve at once.

NUTRITION PER SERVING	
Energy	70kcals/293kJ
Carbohydrate	8g
of which sugar	6g
Fat	4.5g
of which saturates	2.5g
Salt	0g
Fiber	1g

Raspberry lemon verbena tea

The raspberries create a beautiful shade of coral, while the verbena is calming, soothing, and a natural tonic that aids digestion. The lemon flavor is tangy but not acidic.

| Low carb |
| Low saturated fat |
| Dairy free |
| Gluten free |
| Low salt |

SERVES 4
PREP 5 MINS
COOK 6–8 MINS

10 large raspberries, fresh or frozen, plus 4 extra, to garnish

3 tbsp dried lemon verbena leaves

1½ pints (900ml) boiling water

1 Place the raspberries in a teapot and muddle them using a muddler or pestle.

2 Add the lemon verbena leaves and pour in the boiling water. Infuse for 4 minutes. Strain into cups or mugs, and garnish each with a raspberry.

NUTRITION PER SERVING	
Energy	3kcals/13kJ
Carbohydrate	0.5g
of which sugar	0.5g
Fat	0g
of which saturates	0g
Salt	0g
Fiber	0.4g

Figs on the terrace

Aromatic sage has a powerful flavor that combines with sweet figs in this Italian summer tea.

Low saturated fat

Dairy free

Gluten free

Low salt

SERVES 2
PREP 10 MINS
COOK 10 MINS

2 fresh or dried figs, quartered

2 fresh sage leaves, or ¼ tsp dried whole sage leaves

½ cup boiling water, plus 1⅔ cups water heated to 185°F (85°C)

2 tbsp Longevity White tea leaves (Shou Mei)

ice cubes

1 Divide the figs and sage between two tumblers. Muddle with a muddler or pestle, then add the boiling water. Leave to cool.

2 Place the tea leaves in a teapot, add the heated water, and infuse for 2 minutes. Then strain into the tumblers and stir to mix with the fig and sage. Leave to cool. Stir and add the ice cubes before serving.

NUTRITION PER SERVING	
Energy	24kcals/100kJ
Carbohydrate	4.5g
of which sugar	4.5g
Fat	0g
of which saturates	0g
Salt	0g
Fiber	1g

Kiwi and pear juice

Kiwis are nutrient-dense, offering good nutrition for few calories. Pears are also very low in calories, and a good source of minerals.

Low saturated fat

Dairy free

Gluten free

SERVES 1
PREP 5 MINS

2 kiwi fruit, peeled

1 large ripe Conference pear

¼ cucumber

large handful of baby spinach

1 Chop the fruits into large chunks. Feed all the ingredients into a juicer and blend until smooth.

2 Pour the juice into a glass, add an ice cube, and serve immediately.

NUTRITION PER SERVING	
Energy	154kcals/581kJ
Carbohydrate	29g
of which sugar	29g
Fat	0g
of which saturates	0g
Salt	0g
Fiber	5g

Blackberry lemonade

Blackberries have antioxidant, kidney-toning, and detoxifying properties while an infusion made from their leaves enhances the anti-inflammatory effects. Serve with ice, or as a warm drink for a sore throat.

Low saturated fat

Dairy free

Gluten free

Low salt

SERVES 2
PREP 10 MINS
COOK 13–15 MINS

4 tsp dried blackberry leaves, or 12 fresh leaves

2 cups blackberries, rinsed

2 lemons, juiced, plus a few thin slices for decoration (optional)

3 tbsp maple syrup

1 To make an infusion with the leaves, boil 1¼ cups water, pour over the leaves, and let it infuse for 10 minutes. Strain the mixture, reserving the liquid to use in the lemonade. Discard the leaves.

2 Place the blackberries in a food processor or blender and purée to a pulp. If you don't like the gritty texture of the seeds in your drink, strain the pulp through a fine mesh strainer and collect the smooth juice.

3 Pour the lemon juice, blackberry juice, and 1 cup of the blackberry leaf infusion into a pitcher, add the maple syrup, and stir well. Pour into large glasses, decorate each with a slice of lemon, and serve.

NUTRITION PER SERVING	
Energy	118kcals/494kJ
Carbohydrate	27g
of which sugar	25g
Fat	0g
of which saturates	0g
Salt	0g
Fiber	6g

Lemon balm and honey purée

This purée requires young leaves, so is best prepared in late spring. Add 1–2 teaspoons to boiling or chilled water.

Low saturated fat

Dairy free

Gluten free

Low salt

MAKES 4½OZ (125G)
PREP 5 MINS

¾oz (20g) fresh lemon balm leaves

⅓ cup honey

juice of ½ lemon

1 Place the leaves in a blender or food processor, add the honey and lemon juice, and blend until you get a smooth green purée.

2 Dilute with water and drink. The purée will last for a week or two, if kept refrigerated.

NUTRITION PER SERVING	
Energy	12kcals/50kJ
Carbohydrate	3g
of which sugar	3g
Fat	0g
of which saturates	0g
Salt	0g
Fiber	0g

Health boost juice

This is a beneficial tonic, especially in the winter. Red kuri squash supplies anti-inflammatory and antioxidant properties, while ginger can improve digestion. Grapefruit helps ward off colds and celery helps detoxify the body.

| Low saturated fat |
| Dairy free |
| Gluten free |

SERVES 2
PREP 15 MINS

3½oz (100g) red kuri squash

1 small piece fresh ginger, skin on

1 large grapefruit, peeled and pith removed

2 celery stalks and leaves, roughly chopped

1 Cut the squash in half, scoop out all the seeds, and discard or reserve them to roast later and use as an ingredient in other recipes, or as a topping for salads and soups. Leave the skin on the squash to benefit from its nutrients and chop the flesh if necessary, so it fits through the hopper of your juicer.

2 Juice all the ingredients and combine in a pitcher. Strain through a sieve to remove the grapefruit seeds and serve immediately in tall glasses.

NUTRITION PER SERVING	
Energy	53kcals/222kJ
Carbohydrate	11g
of which sugar	7g
Fat	0g
of which saturates	0g
Salt	0g
Fiber	4g

Chilled pea and avocado soup shot

Vibrant green and silky, this quick-to-make recipe celebrates the flavors of summer. Homemade stock is a good source of protein and niacin, a B vitamin that helps our nerves to function.

Low carb

Low saturated fat

MAKES 20
PREP 5 MINS
COOK 5 MINS

5oz (140g) frozen peas

2 ripe avocados, halved, peeled, and pitted

4 scallions, trimmed

¼ cup lemon juice

¼oz (10g) cilantro

chili powder to taste

2 cups chicken stock, chilled

1 tbsp sour cream

salt and freshly ground black pepper

TO GARNISH

¼ cup sour cream

2 tbsp finely chopped cilantro

1 Blanch the peas in boiling water for 2 minutes and drain.

2 Purée all the ingredients together in a food processor until smooth; taste to check the seasoning.

3 Garnish with the sour cream and finely chopped cilantro.

NUTRITION PER SERVING	
Energy	43kcals/179kJ
Carbohydrate	1g
of which sugar	0.6g
Fat	4g
of which saturates	1g
Salt	0.2g
Fiber	1g

try this....
Edamame, kale, and avocado soup shots

Replace the peas with **edamame**, then add 2 large handfuls of **baby spinach**, and replace cilantro with 1 tablespoon **fennel**.

Grape, apple, and melon juice

Grapes and melons have a high water content, so they provide few calories but significant nutrients.

Low saturated fat	
Dairy free	
Gluten free	

SERVES 2
PREP 5–10 MINS

½ Ogen or Galia melon

5½oz (150g) seedless green grapes

juice of 1 Granny Smith apple, about ½ cup

1 Remove the skin from the melon and cut the flesh into large chunks.

2 Feed all the ingredients into a juicer and blend until smooth. Pour the juice into two glasses, add an ice cube to each, and serve immediately.

NUTRITION PER SERVING

Energy	113kcals/458kJ
Carbohydrate	24g
of which sugar	24g
Fat	0g
of which saturates	0g
Salt	0g
Fiber	2g

Icy ginger yerba mate

Traditionally, South American yerba mate is served in a gourd cup, sipped through a bombilla straw, and passed from guest to guest. Here is an easy iced version with a little zing from ginger and honey.

Low saturated fat

Dairy free

Gluten free

SERVES 2
PREP 5 MINS
COOK 5–7 MINS,
PLUS CHILLING

2 tbsp yerba mate leaves

½ tsp grated ginger

2 cups water heated to
    195°F (90°C)

1 tsp honey

ice cubes

1 Place the leaves and ginger in a teapot. Add the hot water and steep for 5 minutes.

2 Strain into a glass pitcher. Add the honey and stir. Leave to cool, then chill in the refrigerator. Pour into two tumblers and add the ice cubes.

NUTRITION PER SERVING	
Energy	12kcals/50kJ
Carbohydrate	3g
of which sugar	3g
Fat	0g
of which saturates	0g
Salt	0g
Fiber	0g

Valentine's special

This is a feel-good drink: nutritious, healthy, and life-enhancing. It contains antioxidant-rich fruits and coconut water. Add yogurt instead of coconut water to make a smoothie.

Low saturated fat

Dairy free

Gluten free

SERVES 2
PREP 5 MINS

1 cup raspberries, washed

scant 1 cup blueberries, washed

a dash of rose syrup

¼ tsp cardamom seeds, crushed (no more than 10 pods)

2 tbsp pistachio nuts, shelled

1 cup coconut water

1 Put all the ingredients in a powerful food processor or blender and blend to a smooth consistency. If serving immediately, pour into tall glasses and serve. Otherwise, the drink will last for up to 2 days if stored in a tightly sealed bottle and refrigerated.

NUTRITION PER SERVING	
Energy	146kcals/ 611kJ
Carbohydrate	12g
of which sugar	12g
Fat	7.5g
of which saturates	1g
Salt	0.3g
Fiber	2.5g

Strawberry and macadamia smoothie

This healthy twist on strawberries and cream uses a cream made from coconut water and macadamia nuts. The nuts are a rich source of monounsaturated fatty acids, which are reputed to lower cholesterol.

Gluten free

SERVES 4
PREP 5 MINS

⅓ cup raw macadamia nuts

1¾ cups fresh strawberries

1⅓ cups fat–free Greek yogurt

1 cup coconut water

1 Place all the ingredients in a blender or food processor and pulse to give a smooth, silky texture.

2 Pour into four glasses and serve.

NUTRITION PER SERVING	
Energy	171kcals/715kJ
Carbohydrate	9g
of which sugar	9g
Fat	10g
of which saturates	1.5g
Salt	0.2g
Fiber	3g

Banana and berry smoothie bowl

Pistachios are high in fat, which helps the body absorb the vitamins provided by the fruit. A, E, and K.

Low saturated fat

High fiber

SERVES 1
PREP 25 MINS

1 ripe banana, peeled, sliced, and frozen

scant 1oz (25g) frozen raspberries

2 heaped tbsp fat-free Greek yogurt

¼–½ cup cow's, almond, or oat milk

FOR THE TOPPING

3 strawberries, sliced

5 blackberries, halved

10 blueberries

1 tbsp sugar-free muesli

4 shelled pistachio nuts, roughly chopped

FOR A GLUTEN-FREE OPTION

use gluten-free muesli

1 Remove the banana from the freezer and leave for about 20 minutes, or until the banana is just beginning to soften to the touch but the center is still frozen. Transfer to a blender with the raspberries and yogurt, then purée until smooth, adding enough milk to get a thick, creamy consistency.

2 Transfer the mixture to a bowl and arrange the fruit and muesli on top.

NUTRITION PER SERVING	
Energy	278kcals/1145kJ
Carbohydrate	39g
of which sugar	28g
Fat	8g
of which saturates	2g
Salt	0.1g
Fiber	6g

DESSERTS

FRUITS

Fruit salad with minted sugar syrup

A fruit salad is a refreshing and light dessert option. This minted sugar syrup helps bring out the flavor of the ingredients.

| Low saturated fat |
| Dairy free |
| Gluten free |
| Low salt |

SERVES 4
PREP 15 MINS
COOK 5 MINS, PLUS
COOLING AND CHILLING

1 ripe mango, peeled and cut into ½in (1cm) cubes

2 ripe kiwis, peeled and cut into ½in (1cm) cubes

3½oz (100g) ripe papaya, peeled and cut into ½in (1cm) cubes

3½oz (100g) pineapple, cut into ½in (1cm) cubes

seeds from 1 ripe pomegranate

FOR THE SYRUP

¼ cup granulated sugar

1 tbsp lemon juice

10 large mint leaves

1 For the syrup, place the ingredients in a small heavy-bottomed saucepan. Pour in ¼ cup cold water.

2 Bring to a boil, stirring frequently until the sugar dissolves. Remove from the heat, pour into a heatproof bowl, and let cool. Chill until needed.

3 Combine all the fruit in a large serving bowl, reserving one-quarter of the pomegranate seeds. Strain the syrup into a pitcher. Discard the mint.

4 Pour the syrup over the fruit and toss well to coat. Scatter with the reserved pomegranate seeds and serve. It is best served within 4 hours of preparation.

NUTRITION PER SERVING	
Energy	120kcals/502kJ
Carbohydrate	26g
of which sugar	26g
Fat	0g
of which saturates	0g
Salt	0g
Fiber	4g

Moroccan orange salad

Slices of fresh orange are made more exotic and flavorsome with rose water, pomegranate seeds, and pistachio nuts.

Low saturated fat

Dairy free

Gluten free

Low salt

SERVES 4
PREP 15 MINS

4 oranges

1–2 tbsp honey

2 tbsp rose water

good pinch of ground cinnamon

seeds from 1 pomegranate

small handful of chopped pistachios (optional)

handful of mint leaves, to decorate

1 Slice off the top and bottom from each orange and place on a cutting board. Carefully slice off the skin and pith, leaving as much flesh as possible, and following the sides of the orange so you keep the shape of the fruit. Slice the oranges horizontally into thin strips, discarding any seeds as you come across them. Arrange the orange slices on a serving platter. Pour any remaining juice over the oranges.

2 Drizzle with the honey and rose water, and sprinkle with the cinnamon. Scatter with the pomegranate seeds and pistachios, if using, then decorate with the mint leaves and serve.

NUTRITION PER SERVING

Energy	111kcals/464kJ
Carbohydrate	17g
of which sugar	17g
Fat	3g
of which saturates	0.5g
Salt	0g
Fiber	2.4g

Sweet spiced freekeh with fresh figs

Inspired by the cuisine of the Middle East, the high-fiber freekeh in this dish is cooked with sweet spices and served with honey, pistachios, and figs.

Low saturated fat

Low salt

SERVES 4
PREP 5 MINS
COOK 25 MINS

½ cup cracked freekeh

1 star anise

4 cardamom pods

1 tsp ground cinnamon

½ tsp grated fresh ginger

¼ tsp grated nutmeg

¼ tsp salt

8 fresh figs, stems removed

¼ cup honey, plus extra
   to serve

⅓ cup pistachios,
   coarsely chopped

2 tbsp chopped mint leaves

¼ cup Greek yogurt,
   to serve

1 Place the freekeh, star anise, cardamom, cinnamon, ginger, and nutmeg in a large saucepan. Add the salt and cover with 2 cups of water. Place the pan over medium heat and bring to a boil. Then reduce the heat to a simmer and cook for about 15 minutes or until all the liquid has been absorbed.

2 Meanwhile, preheat the broiler to its medium setting. Grease and line a baking sheet with parchment paper. Cut a cross in the top of each fig, cutting almost to the bottom so they open up like a flower. Place on the baking sheet and drizzle with 2 tablespoons of honey. Place the sheet under the broiler and cook for 10 minutes or until the figs are lightly broiled.

3 Remove and discard the star anise and cardamom pods. Add the remaining honey to the cooked freekeh and mix well. Divide the freekeh mixture between four plates. Top each plate with two figs and a quarter of the pistachios. Garnish with mint and drizzle with honey, if you wish. Serve with Greek yogurt.

NUTRITION PER SERVING	
Energy	253kcals/1065kJ
Carbohydrate	42g
of which sugar	23g
Fat	6g
of which saturates	1g
Salt	0g
Fiber	1g

Chocolate-dipped strawberries

Dip strawberries in rich, dark chocolate for a treat that may help lower the risk of heart disease and stroke, and also prevent memory loss.

Gluten free

Low salt

SERVES 8
PREP 15 MINS
COOK 5 MINS

14oz (400g) strawberries, not too ripe

3½oz (100g) good-quality dark chocolate, more than 60 percent cocoa solids, broken into pieces

1 Wash and dry the strawberries well. Try to leave the hulls in, since this makes the finished fruit easier to pick up.

2 Put the chocolate in a small heatproof bowl and place over a saucepan of simmering water, making sure the bowl does not touch the water. Stir frequently and remove it as soon as it melts.

3 Line a large baking sheet with wax paper. Hold each strawberry by its leaves and dip the end in the chocolate, so half of the fruit is covered in chocolate. Allow any excess chocolate to drip off back into the bowl, then place the strawberries on the baking sheet, making sure they do not touch each other.

4 Put in a cool place to set. These should be served the same day, since the chocolate will soften if the strawberries are overripe, or if they are kept in the refrigerator for too long.

NUTRITION PER SERVING	
Energy	77kcals/324kJ
Carbohydrate	10g
of which sugar	10g
Fat	3.5g
of which saturates	2g
Salt	0g
Fiber	1g

Red fruit medley

This German compôte, *Rote Grütze*, translates as "red grits." Its red berries are anti-inflammatory.

Low saturated fat

Dairy free

Gluten free

Low salt

SERVES 4
PREP 10 MINS
COOK 5 MINS

8oz (240g) Bing cherries, pitted

6oz (175g) raspberries

6oz (175g) red currants, stemmed

6oz (175g) blackberries

6oz (175g) strawberries, quartered if large

stevia, to taste

2 tbsp cornstarch

1 Place all the fruit in a saucepan with ⅔ cup water and bring slowly to a boil.

2 Combine the stevia and cornstarch with 3 tbsp cold water to form a smooth paste. Gradually stir into the fruit. Cook gently, stirring, until the juices begins to thicken.

3 Transfer to a bowl. Spoon the mixture into individual dishes.

NUTRITION PER SERVING	
Energy	122kcals/510kJ
Carbohydrate	24g
of which sugar	13g
Fat	0g
of which saturates	0g
Salt	0g
Fiber	5g

Warm fruit compôte

This dish is ideal for fall and winter, when supplies of fresh fruit are limited. Serve with yogurt on the side and honey drizzled over, if you like.

Low carb

Low saturated fat

Gluten free

Low salt

MAKES 10
PREP 10 MINS
COOK 10 MINS

2 tbsp butter

6 dried prunes, chopped

6 dried apricots, chopped

2 large apples, peeled, cored, and chopped

1 firm pear, peeled, cored, and chopped

1 cinnamon stick

2 tsp sugar

2 tsp lemon juice

yogurt and honey, to serve

1 Melt the butter in a heavy saucepan over medium heat. Add the fruit and cinnamon stick. Cook gently, stirring often, until the fruit has completely softened.

2 Stir in the sugar and heat for another couple of minutes, or until the sugar has dissolved.

3 Remove the pan from the heat, sprinkle with lemon juice, and serve warm with a spoonful of yogurt and a drizzle of honey.

NUTRITION PER SERVING

Energy	68kcals/288kJ
Carbohydrate	9g
of which sugar	9g
Fat	3g
of which saturates	2g
Salt	trace
Fiber	2g

Grilled peaches with ice cream and granola

Grilled peaches are one of summer's tastiest treats. Paired here with a healthy amaranth and millet granola, they are easy to prepare and can also be stored overnight for a filling whole grain breakfast.

High fiber

SERVES 4
PREP 10 MINS
COOK 20 MINS

4 peaches, pitted and halved

2 tbsp canola oil

4 scoops of vanilla ice cream

FOR THE GRANOLA

⅔ cup oats

¼ cup uncooked amaranth

¼ cup uncooked millet

¾ cup almonds, chopped

⅓ cup pumpkin seeds

1 tbsp virgin coconut oil

2 tbsp maple syrup

½ tsp vanilla extract

½ tsp ground cinnamon

½ tsp sea salt

FOR A GLUTEN-FREE OPTION
use gluten-free oats

1 Preheat the oven to 350°F (180°C). For the granola, place all the ingredients in a large bowl and toss to combine. Spread the mixture evenly in a baking tray and place in the oven. Bake the granola for 10–15 minutes or until the oats and nuts are lightly browned. Remove from the heat and leave to cool.

2 Meanwhile, set the broiler at its medium setting. Brush the peach skins with the oil and place under the broiler for 2–3 minutes, on each side, until tender. Remove from the heat. Place the grilled peaches in serving dishes, then top with a scoop of vanilla ice cream, and some of the granola. Serve immediately.

NUTRITION PER SERVING	
Energy	630kcals/2636kJ
Carbohydrate	60g
of which sugar	26g
Fat	35g
of which saturates	10g
Salt	0.4g
Fiber	6g

Pineapple flambé

Rings of fresh pineapple flambéd in rum or brandy make a stylish restaurant-style dessert. Pineapple contains bromelain, which has anti-inflammatory properties.

Low saturated fat

Gluten free

Low salt

SERVES 4
PREP 10 MINS
COOK 10 MINS

1 ripe pineapple
¼ cup dark rum or brandy
2 tbsp fresh lime juice
2 tbsp butter
¼ cup light brown sugar
quark or Greek yogurt, to serve
ground cinnamon, for dusting

1 Peel the pineapple and remove the "eyes." Slice into rounds about ½in (⅓mm) thick, reserving any pineapple juice. Cut out the core using a small round cookie cutter or the tip of a sharp knife.

2 Place the pineapple and its juices, rum, and lime juice in a large frying pan and cook over medium-low heat about 1 minute, just until the liquid is warm. Carefully ignite the pan juices with a long-handled match. Cook until the flames die down.

3 Dot the pineapple with the butter and sprinkle with the brown sugar. Cook while gently shaking the pan until the butter and sugar combine into a glaze. Serve with quark or Greek yogurt and a dusting of cinnamon.

NUTRITION PER SERVING	
Energy	185kcals/774kJ
Carbohydrate	24g
of which sugar	24g
Fat	5g
of which saturates	3g
Salt	0g
Fiber	2g

Summer fruit fool

Traditionally, fruit fools contained only stewed fruit and custard. Modern fools feature fresh fruit puree to create a brighter flavor and fluffier texture—they have become a classic in their own right.

MAKES 4
PREP 10 MINS,
PLUS CHILLING

14oz (400g) mixed hulled strawberries, raspberries, and blueberries

2 tbsp granulated sugar, plus 1 tbsp extra

¾ cup quark

⅔ cup full-fat Greek yogurt

½ tsp vanilla extract

1 Slice the strawberries so they are about the same size as the other fruit. Combine all the fruit with 1 tablespoon of sugar in a large bowl. Then pulse two-thirds of the mixture in a food processor to form a purée.

2 Beat the quark in a bowl until smooth. Add the yogurt, vanilla extract, and remaining sugar. Fold the mixture gently, so that you lose as little air as possible.

3 Gently fold the fruit puree into the quark mixture until no streaks remain.

4 Fold the reserved fruit into the mixture. Divide the mixture between four 3½fl oz (100ml) glass jars or glasses, cover, and chill for 2 hours before serving. You can cover and store them in the refrigerator for up to 1 day.

try this....
Apricot and passion fruit fool

Drain 2 cans of **apricots in natural juice**, then purée the flesh. Mix 7oz (200g) quark with 5½oz (150g) full-fat Greek yogurt and then stir in the apricot purée. Add **honey** or a **calorie-free sweetener**, like **stevia**, to taste. Spoon into jars or glasses, top each one with seeds from 1 **passion fruit**, then serve.

NUTRITION PER SERVING

Energy	151kcals/632kJ
Carbohydrate	16g
of which sugar	16g
Fat	4g
of which saturates	2.5g
Salt	0.1g
Fiber	3.5g

Vanilla pudding with raspberries

This simple pudding is nothing more than a smooth and silky chilled vanilla custard. Serve it with raspberries, rich in antioxidants, for a sweet–sharp flavor contrast.

Gluten free

Low salt

SERVES 4
PREP 10 MINS
COOK 10 MINS,
PLUS CHILLING

½ cup granulated sugar

3 tbsp cornstarch

3 large egg yolks

½ tsp salt

2 cups reduced-fat milk

1 tbsp unsalted butter

3 tsp vanilla extract

30–40 raspberries, to serve

1 Place the sugar, cornstarch, egg yolks, and salt in a large bowl. Pour in half the milk and whisk until well combined and smooth.

2 Heat the remaining milk in a saucepan over medium–low heat, until steaming. Pour half the hot milk into the yolk mixture, in a steady stream, whisking constantly to combine. Then pour the yolk and milk mixture back into the pan and mix well to combine.

3 Increase the heat to medium and bring to a boil, stirring constantly. Reduce the heat to a simmer and cook for another 1 minute, stirring, until the mixture has thickened. Remove and pour through a strainer into a large bowl.

4 Stir in the butter and vanilla extract until evenly combined. Cover with plastic wrap, making sure it touches the top of the pudding. Chill for at least 3–4 hours. Serve it with raspberries. You can store the pudding in an airtight container in the refrigerator for 2–3 days.

NUTRITION PER SERVING	
Energy	288kcals/1205kJ
Carbohydrate	43g
of which sugar	33g
Fat	9.5g
of which saturates	4.5g
Salt	0.8g
Fiber	2g

Eton mess

Using yogurt gives this crowd-pleasing dessert a healthy twist. It is also particularly quick if you use ready-made meringue.

Gluten free

SERVES 6
PREP 10 MINS,
PLUS CHILLING

7fl oz (200ml) heavy cream

1¼ cup 2% fat Greek yogurt

1 tsp vanilla extract

5½oz (150g) ready-made meringues

10oz (300g) strawberries, chopped quite small

5½oz (150g) raspberries

1 Whisk the cream until it is very stiff, then carefully fold in the yogurt and extract.

2 Place the meringues in a freezer bag and beat with a rolling pin to break into uneven pebble-sized pieces. It's nice to have a mixture of large pieces and smaller crumbs, for the best texture.

3 Fold together the cream mixture, the meringues, and the fruit. Cover and chill for at least 1 hour before serving.

NUTRITION PER SERVING	
Energy	288kcals/1205kJ
Carbohydrate	29g
of which sugar	29g
Fat	15g
of which saturates	9g
Salt	0.1g
Fiber	2.7g

Strawberry mousse

This speedy dessert is bound to be a favorite with the kids. Strawberries are high in fiber, which helps to regulate blood sugar, and their bright red color comes from anthocyanidin, a powerful antioxidant.

SERVES 4
PREP 20 MINS,
PLUS CHILLING

1lb (450g) ripe strawberries

¾ cup evaporated milk, well chilled

2 tbsp superfine sugar

1 cup thick, Greek-style yogurt, plus more to serve

1 Slice the strawberries and set a few aside. Divide half the strawberries among four dessert glasses. Purée the remaining strawberries in a food processor or blender. Strain through a sieve to remove the seeds.

2 Beat the chilled evaporated milk with an electric mixer on high speed about 7 minutes, or until doubled in volume. Beat in the sugar. Stir in the strawberry purée and yogurt until well combined. Spoon into the glasses and refrigerate for 15-20 minutes, until lightly set.

3 Serve decorated with a little extra yogurt and the reserved strawberry slices.

NUTRITION PER SERVING	
Energy	211kcals/ 883kJ
Carbohydrate	22g
of which sugar	22g
Fat	10g
of which saturates	6g
Salt	0.3g
Fiber	4g

Apricots with amaretti cookies and mascarpone

Apricots are delicate and should be handled with care. They are rich in vitamin A and carotenes, both essential for good vision.

Low salt

High fiber

SERVES 4
PREP 15 MINS

8 amaretti cookies

7oz (200g) reduced-fat mascarpone cheese

16 ripe apricots, halved and pitted

handful of blanched almonds, halved

1 Lightly crush the amaretti with a rolling pin, then divide among four individual glass dishes. Lightly whip the mascarpone with a wooden spoon until smooth and thick.

2 Layer the apricots and mascarpone on top of the amaretti, finishing with a layer of mascarpone. Sprinkle with the almonds and serve.

try this....
Apricots with ginger and quark

For a lower-fat version, replace the mascarpone with **vanilla quark**, and replace the amaretti biscuits with 8 **ginger snaps**.

NUTRITION PER SERVING	
Energy	436kcals/1824kJ
Carbohydrate	36g
of which sugar	35g
Fat	24g
of which saturates	8g
Salt	0.1g
Fiber	7g

Mango, orange, and passion fruit fool

This creamy, golden fruit fool is rich in vitamin C and fiber, and can be whipped up in minutes.

Gluten free

Low salt

SERVES 4
PREP 10 MINS,
PLUS CHILLING

3 large, ripe mangoes, stoned and flesh roughly chopped

zest of 1 large orange

4 tbsp orange juice

14oz (400g) Greek yogurt

sugar-free sweetener, to taste

4 passion fruit, seeds extracted

1 Place the mango and orange zest and juice in a food processor or blender. Process until smooth. Stir in the Greek yogurt and add sweetener to taste.

2 Divide the mixture among 4 glasses or bowls, and chill for at least 30 minutes.

3 Spoon the seeds from the passion fruit on top of the fool and serve.

NUTRITION PER SERVING	
Energy	229kcals/962kJ
Carbohydrate	28g
of which sugar	26g
Fat	10g
of which saturates	7g
Salt	0.2g
Fiber	4.5g

Traffic-light gelatins

Fresh, sugar-free fruit juices make a healthier gelatin. These take most of the day to set, but only minutes to make.

| Low saturated fat |
| Dairy free |
| Gluten free |
| Low salt |

MAKES 10
PREP 15 MINS,
PLUS SETTING
COOK 5 MINS

3 tsp unflavored gelatin powder

2 cups of 3 different fresh fruit juice, such as pineapple, cranberry, kiwi, and apple (try to get different colors)

1 Place ¼ cup of one of the fruit juices in a small bowl. Sprinkle 1 teaspoon of gelatin over the top and allow it to soften for 5-10 minutes.

2 Heat the remaining 1¾ cups of the juice gently over low heat in a small saucepan. Take the pan off the heat. Add the gelatin and juice mixture, whisking to dissolve. Cool, then divide equally between 10 small plastic glasses. Chill to set.

3 Repeat the process with the second gelatin, making sure you choose a contrasting color to the first. Make sure the second fruit juice mixture is cold before pouring it carefully on top of the set gelatin.

4 Repeat the process with the final fruit juice and return to the refrigerator to set before serving.

NUTRITION PER SERVING	
Energy	61kcals/260kJ
Carbohydrate	12g
of which sugar	12g
Fat	0g
of which saturates	0g
Salt	trace
Fiber	0.2g

Elderflower and grape gelatins

Look for delicate and fragrant elderflower liqueur or syrup—it gives a lovely flavor to this dessert.

SERVES 4
PREP 15 MINS,
PLUS SETTING
COOK 5 MINS

3 tsp unflavored gelatin powder

½ cup elderflower liqueur

4 tbsp whipped cream, to serve

8 seedless green grapes, to serve

1 Sprinkle the gelatin over ½ cup water in a small bowl. Let stand about 5 minutes, or until the mixture is spongy. Place the bowl in a small frying pan of simmering water. Stir the gelatin mixture constantly until melted. Remove from the frying pan.

2 Stir 2 cups tepid water, the liqueur, and the dissolved gelatin together in a large measuring cup until combined. Divide among four 8oz (240ml) dessert glasses. Refrigerate at least 3 hours, until set. Top each with whipped cream and some grapes, and serve chilled.

NUTRITION PER SERVING	
Energy	132kcals/552kJ
Carbohydrate	14g
of which sugar	14g
Fat	6g
of which saturates	4g
Salt	0g
Fiber	0.2g

Quick banana ice cream

This is the quickest and easiest "ice cream" you will ever make! This dessert is a great way to use up any ripening bananas in your fruit bowl.

| Low saturated fat |
| Dairy free |
| Gluten free |
| Low salt |

SERVES 4
PREP 5 MINS,
PLUS FREEZING

4 ripe bananas
1 tsp vanilla extract

1 Simply peel the bananas, chop them into ¾in (2cm) chunks, and place them in a freezer container. Seal and put in the freezer until frozen.

2 When the bananas are frozen solid, process them in a food processor with the vanilla extract, until you have a smooth, thick ice cream. You may need to scrape down the sides a couple of times during the process.

3 Either eat the softened banana ice cream immediately, or freeze for a few minutes to firm it up once more before serving.

try this....
Quick banana and peanut ice cream

In step 2, add 3½oz (100g) **crunchy peanut butter** and continue as above.

NUTRITION PER SERVING
Energy	86kcals/360kJ
Carbohydrate	19g
of which sugar	17g
Fat	0g
of which saturates	0g
Salt	0g
Fiber	1.4g

Banana and cranberry ice cream

Ice cream without any cream—ideal for those who are allergic to cow milk. Ripe bananas can help lower blood pressure, while cranberries have antibacterial properties.

| Low saturated fat |
| Dairy free |
| Gluten free |
| Low salt |

SERVES 4
PREP 10 MINS,
PLUS FREEZING
COOK 10 MINS

4 ripe bananas, sliced

2 cups cranberries

1 tbsp superfine sugar

1 tsp vanilla extract

scant ½ cup pistachio
  nuts, shelled and chopped

1 Put the bananas and cranberries in the freezer and remove when semifrozen. If they are completely frozen, allow to thaw slightly for about an hour. Place them in a blender or food processor and pulse until the fruits are coarsely combined and still have some texture. Divide among 4 freezerproof serving bowls (such as enamel bowls) and place in the freezer for 3 hours. Alternatively, freeze the ice cream in a clean plastic container.

2 Meanwhile, place the sugar in a small saucepan over low heat and add just enough water to wet the sugar. When the sugar has dissolved completely, add the vanilla extract and stir in the pistachios, then remove from the heat and allow to cool.

3 Remove the bowls, or container, from the freezer, let sit at room temperature for a short while, then use an ice-cream scoop to divide the ice cream among 4 serving bowls. Drizzle the sugar solution and nuts over each portion to serve.

NUTRITION PER SERVING	
Energy	212kcals/898kJ
Carbohydrate	34g
of which sugar	28g
Fat	6g
of which saturates	0.8g
Salt	trace
Fiber	3.5g

Mango sorbet

Freezing any food will diminish its flavor, so be sure the fruit is at its peak of ripeness. The citrus juices in this recipe heighten the taste and balance the mango's sweetness.

| Low saturated fat |
| Dairy free |
| Gluten free |
| Low salt |
| High fiber |

SERVES 6
PREP 25–30 MINS,
PLUS FREEZING
COOK 2–3 MINS

½ cup sugar, plus more
  if needed

3 mangoes, total weight
  2¾–3lb (1.25–1.4kg)

juice of 1 lemon

juice of 1 orange

lime zest, to serve

1 Combine the sugar and ½ cup water in a small saucepan. Heat until the sugar has dissolved, then boil the syrup for 2–3 minutes, until it is clear. Set aside to cool.

2 Peel the mangoes. Cut each mango lengthwise into two pieces, slightly off-center to just miss the pit. Cut the fruit away from the other side of the pit. Cut away the remaining flesh. Cut all the mango into cubes. Purée it in batches, in a food processor, until smooth.

4 With the blade turning, pour in the cooled syrup and citrus juices. Taste, adding more sugar if it is tart, remembering that the flavors will be dulled by freezing.

5 Pour the sorbet mixture into an ice-cream maker and freeze until firm, following the manufacturer's directions. Meanwhile, chill a bowl in the freezer.

6 Transfer the sorbet to the chilled bowl. Cover it and freeze for at least 4 hours to allow the flavor to mellow. If necessary, transfer the sorbet to the refrigerator to soften slightly. Scoop the sorbet into chilled glasses and serve immediately, sprinkled with lime zest.

NUTRITION PER SERVING	
Energy	202kcals/845kJ
Carbohydrate	44g
of which sugar	44g
Fat	0g
of which saturates	0g
Salt	0g
Fiber	7g

Espresso granita

This coffee-flavored granita is simple to prepare. Make sure the texture is crystallized, like shaved ice.

Low saturated fat
Dairy free
Gluten free
Low salt

SERVES 4
PREP 5 MINS, PLUS
COOLING AND FREEZING
COOK 5 MINS

½ cup granulated sugar

½ tsp pure vanilla extract

1¼ cup very strong
  espresso coffee, chilled

1 Set the freezer to its coldest setting and place four freezerproof serving bowls or glasses in the freezer. In a small saucepan, dissolve the sugar in 1¼ cup cold water over medium heat. Increase the heat and bring to a boil, then boil for 5 minutes to make a light syrup.

2 Pour the syrup into a shallow, freezerproof dish. Stir in the vanilla extract and coffee, then set aside to cool completely.

3 Transfer to the freezer. Use a fork to break up the frozen chunks every 30 minutes or so. Continue to do this for 4 hours, or until the mixture has the texture of shaved ice, then leave the granita in the freezer until ready to serve.

NUTRITION PER SERVING	
Energy	101kcals/423kJ
Carbohydrate	25g
of which sugar	25g
Fat	0g
of which saturates	0g
Salt	0g
Fiber	0g

Pink grapefruit and rose water sherbet

A sherbet is a cross between an ice cream and a sorbet. It is simple to prepare, and does not require an ice cream maker.

SERVES 6
PREP 15 MINS, PLUS
CHILLING AND FREEZING

1¼ cups granulated sugar, plus extra for sprinkling

grated zest of 1 large pink grapefruit

2 cups pink grapefruit juice

1 tbsp rose water

1½ cups whole milk

1 large egg white

12–16 large edible rose petals, washed and dried

1 Place the granulated sugar, grapefruit zest and juice, and rose water in a blender. Pulse for 2 minutes, until it is well combined and the sugar has dissolved.

2 Transfer the mixture to a bowl and chill for 1 hour. Then transfer to a blender, add the milk, and pulse until well combined. Pour the liquid into a 1½ quart (1.5 liter) shallow freezerproof container.

3 Transfer to the freezer, scraping the frozen edges into the center of the container with a fork every 45 minutes, breaking up any larger ice crystals with the back of the fork. Repeat this process for 3 hours, or until the mixture is well frozen, but not solid, then freeze until needed.

4 Whisk the egg white in a bowl and use to brush the rose petals. Sprinkle the petals evenly with granulated sugar, shake off any excess, and let dry. Serve the sherbet decorated with the rose petals. You can store the sherbet in the container in the freezer for up to 1 month.

NUTRITION PER SERVING	
Energy	233kcals/975kJ
Carbohydrate	50g
of which sugar	50g
Fat	2.5g
of which saturates	1.5g
Salt	0.1g
Fiber	0g

Yogurt, honey, and pistachio semifreddo

Because eggs are omitted from this recipe, this modern take on semifreddo has a firm texture—this also means that it keeps for much longer in the freezer.

SERVES 8
PREP 20 MINS,
PLUS FREEZING

1¾ cups full-fat Greek yogurt

6 tbsp honey, plus extra to serve (optional)

grated zest of 1 large orange

¾ cup heavy cream

¼ cup unsalted and skinned pistachios, finely chopped

1 Line a 1lb (450g) loaf tin with plastic wrap. Beat the yogurt, honey, and orange zest in a large bowl until smooth and well combined. In a separate bowl, beat the cream to form soft peaks and carefully fold into the yogurt mixture. Fold in three-quarters of the pistachios.

2 Pour the mixture into the prepared pan, cover with plastic wrap, and freeze for at least 6 hours. Then remove from the freezer, take off the plastic wrap, and invert the pan over a large serving plate. Shake the pan lightly, if needed, to release the semifreddo.

3 Peel off the plastic wrap. Sprinkle with the reserved pistachios and a drizzle of honey, if desired, and serve immediately. You can store the semifreddo, covered in the freezer, for up to 3 months.

NUTRITION PER SERVING

Energy	205kcals/858kJ
Carbohydrate	14g
of which sugar	13g
Fat	15g
of which saturates	9g
Salt	0g
Fiber	0g

try this....
Mixed dried fruit and rum semifreddo

Soak 10oz (300g) **mixed dried fruits** in ¼ cup **rum**. Mix the dried fruits with the yogurt, and omit the honey and orange zest. Continue with the recipe as directed above.

Avocado and lime cheesecake

Like any cheesecake, this is high in fat, but the avocados contribute a significant amount of omega-3 fats, which help keep the heart healthy.

Low salt

SERVES 6–8
PREP 30 MINS,
PLUS CHILLING
COOK 20 MINS

2 ripe Hass avocados

9oz (250g) ricotta cheese

3 tbsp confectioners' sugar

zest and juice of 5 limes

1 level tbsp gelatin or
    vegetarian equivalent

toasted sliced almonds,
    to decorate

FOR THE BASE

7 tbsp unsalted butter

⅔ cup rolled oats

⅔ cup ground almonds

½ cup whole-wheat flour

3 tbsp brown sugar

1 Melt the butter in a saucepan, add the oats, almonds, flour, and sugar, and mix well. Press the mixture into a 7in (18cm) loose-bottomed cake pan and bake at 375°F (190°C) for 20 minutes. Allow to cool.

2 Slice the avocado in half. Remove the pit, then scoop out the flesh, and mash until the mixture is lump-free. Add the ricotta cheese, sugar, lime zest and juice, and beat well.

3 Place 3 tablespoons of water in a small heatproof bowl, sprinkle over the gelatin, and leave to soak for 5 minutes. Place the bowl over a pan of simmering water and stir until the gelatin melts. Allow to cool slightly, then stir into the avocado mixture. Pour the mixture over the base and transfer to the refrigerator for 2 hours.

4 Carefully remove the cheesecake from the pan, decorate with sliced almonds, and serve.

NUTRITION PER SERVING	
Energy	424kcals/1725kJ
Carbohydrate	27g
of which sugar	15g
Fat	30g
of which saturates	11g
Salt	0.1g
Fiber	3.5g

Simple tuiles

Tuiles are easy to make, but the art lies in timing the bake and shaping them properly. Serve with yogurt and fruit, or use to decorate desserts such as mousses and sorbets.

Low saturated fat

Low salt

MAKES 16
PREP 15 MINS
COOK 6–7 MINS,
PLUS COOLING

4 tbsp unsalted butter, softened

⅓ cup confectioners' sugar, sifted

1 egg, beaten

¼ cup all-purpose flour, sifted

vegetable oil, for greasing

Greek yogurt, to serve (optional)

raspberries, to serve (optional)

1 Preheat the oven to 400°F (200°C). Place the butter and sugar in a large bowl and beat together until light and fluffy. Add the egg and mix well to combine, then fold in the flour.

2 Draw four 3¼in (8cm) wide circles on four sheets of parchment paper, turn them over, and place on baking sheets. Spoon the batter into the traced circles, using the back of a wet spoon to smooth it out to a thin layer. Bake on the top rack of the oven for 5–7 minutes, until the edges are golden brown.

3 Remove from the oven and use a palette knife to lift and drape the tuiles over a greased rolling pin. You have only seconds to shape them before they harden. Bake for another minute to soften them, if needed.

4 Once cooled, gently transfer the tuiles to a wire rack to cool and dry completely. Serve them with Greek yogurt and raspberries, if desired. You can store the tuiles in an airtight container for up to 5 days.

NUTRITION PER SERVING	
Energy	52kcals/218kJ
Carbohydrate	6g
of which sugar	3g
Fat	3g
of which saturates	2g
Salt	0g
Fiber	0g

try this....
Tuile cups with mango and pomegranate

To make tuile cups, draw four 5in (12cm) circles in step 2. Then, in step 3, shape the tuile over an orange. Allow the tuile to cool, and then fill with mixture of diced **mango** and **pomegranate seeds**. Serve with a scoop of **frozen yogurt**. Makes 10.

Chocolate brownies

There is no point pretending that brownies are a nutritional powerhouse. They're not. But using fruit helps reduce the amount of refined sugar. And let's face it, we all want a treat from time to time.

Low saturated fat

Dairy free

Low salt

MAKES 9
PREP 10–15 MINS
COOK 25–30 MINS

1 cup of prunes in syrup, drained and pitted

4½oz (125g) dark chocolate

2 egg whites

⅔ cup all-purpose flour, sifted

1 cup granulated sugar

pinch of salt

½ tsp vanilla extract

1¾oz (50g) pecans, chopped

confectioners' sugar, for dusting

1 Preheat the oven to 400°F (200°C). Grease and line the base of a 7in (18cm) square shallow cake pan with nonstick baking parchment.

2 Place the prunes in a food processor and blend to make a smooth purée. Transfer to a large mixing bowl.

3 Break the chocolate into a heatproof bowl and place over a saucepan of simmering water. Stir occasionally until melted. Remove from the heat and allow to cool slightly.

4 Beat the egg whites until stiff, then beat the melted chocolate, flour, sugar, salt, and vanilla extract into the prune purée and mix well. Stir in the nuts. Fold in the egg whites.

5 Transfer the mixture into the prepared pan and bake for about 25–30 minutes, or until firm to the touch. Leave in the pan to cool for 5 minutes, then transfer to a wire rack to cool completely.

6 Cut into nine squares and dust with confectioners' sugar.

NUTRITION PER SERVING	
Energy	176kcals/715kJ
Carbohydrate	20g
of which sugar	14g
Fat	8g
of which saturates	2.5g
Salt	0.2g
Fiber	2g

Vanilla tapioca pudding

Some associate tapioca pudding with bland flavor and unappealing texture. This version is rich and creamy with a pleasing textural contrast from the tapioca pearls.

Low saturated fat

Gluten free

Low salt

SERVES 6–8
PREP 10 MINS,
PLUS SOAKING
COOK 20 MINS

3 cups reduced-fat milk

⅓ cup small pearl tapioca

2 large egg yolks

¼ tsp salt

¼ cup dark brown sugar

¼ cup granulated sugar

1 vanilla bean

30 blackberries, to serve

half-and-half, to serve

1 Pour ¾ cup milk into a heavy-bottomed saucepan. Add the tapioca pearls and stir to mix. Let the mixture soak for about 45 minutes.

2 Stir in the remaining milk. Add the egg yolks, salt, and both types of sugar and whisk well to combine. Split the vanilla bean with a sharp knife, add to the pan, and stir well to mix.

3 Bring the mixture to a boil over medium heat, stirring constantly. Reduce the heat to a simmer and cook for 15 minutes, stirring occasionally, until the tapioca pearls are soft and the pudding has thickened slightly.

4 Remove from the heat and discard the vanilla bean. Serve warm with blackberries and a swirl of cream; or serve chilled for a thicker texture. You can keep it in an airtight container in the rcfrigcrator for 2–3 days.

NUTRITION PER SERVING	
Energy	190kcals/795kJ
Carbohydrate	33g
of which sugar	23g
Fat	4g
of which saturates	2g
Salt	0.3g
Fiber	0.4g

Index

Entries in **bold** indicate ingredients or types of dish.

Shrimp and asparagus
stir-fry with polenta

Quinoa and
fennel salad

Pea, mint, and avocado
soup with quinoa

Moroccan orange salad

Swordfish in salmoriglio

Polenta with tomato, mozzarella, prosciutto, and pesto

Taramasalata

**Banana and berry
smoothie bowl**

Penguin Random House

DK UK
Project Editor Caroline Curtis
Senior Art Editor Sara Robin
Senior Jacket Creative Nicola Powling
Pre-Production Producer Rebecca Fallowfield
Senior Producer Stephanie McConnell
Managing Editor Stephanie Farrow
Managing Art Editor Christine Keilty

DK INDIA
Project Editor Arani Sinha
Senior Art Editor Ira Sharma
Editors Sugandh Juneja, Shreya Sengupta
Art Editor Bhavika Mathur
Assistant Art Editor Anjali Stella Gari
Deputy Managing Editor Bushra Ahmed
Managing Art Editor Navidita Thapa
Pre-Production Manager Sunil Sharma
DTP Designers Satish Gaur, Anurag Trivedi, Manish Upreti

First American Edition, 2016

Published in the United States by DK Publishing
345 Hudson Street, New York, New York 10014

Copyright © 2016 Dorling Kindersley Limited
DK, a Division of Penguin Random House LLC
16 17 18 19 20 10 9 8 7 6 5 4 3 2 1
001–288449–April/2016

Published in Great Britain by Dorling Kindersley Limited.

A catalog record for this book is available from the Library of Congress.

ISBN 978-1-4654-4484-4

DK books are available at special discounts when purchased in bulk for sales promotions, premiums, fund-raising, or educational use. For details, contact: DK Publishing Special Markets, 345 Hudson Street, New York, New York 10014 SpecialSales@dk.com

Color reproduction by Alta Image
Printed and bound in China

All images © Dorling Kindersley Limited
For further information see: www.dkimages.com

A WORLD OF IDEAS:
SEE ALL THERE IS TO KNOW
www.dk.com

Acknowledgments

DK would like to thank the following:
Recipe testing: Jane Lawrie. **Proofreading:** Claire Cross, Cincy Jose, Seetha Natesh. **Design assistance:** Juhi Sheth. **Indexing:** Vanessa Bird. **Cover illustration:** Amy Holliday.

All photography © Dorling Kindersley